D1560816

Bargain Hunter's Guide to Investing in Real Estate

Bargain Hunter's Guide to Investing in Real Estate

Stuart Paltrowitz
Donna Paltrowitz

LIBERTY HALL
PRESS™

LIBERTY HALL PRESS books are published by LIBERTY HALL PRESS, an imprint of TAB BOOKS. Its trademark, consisting of the words "LIBERTY HALL PRESS" and the portrayal of Benjamin Franklin, is registered in the United States Patent and Trademark Office.

FIRST EDITION
FIRST PRINTING

© 1991 by LIBERTY HALL PRESS, an imprint of TAB BOOKS.
TAB BOOKS is a division of McGraw-Hill, Inc.

Printed in the United States of America. All rights reserved.
The publisher takes no responsibility for the use of any of the materials or methods described in this book, nor for the products thereof.

Library of Congress Cataloging-in-Publication Data

Paltrowitz productions
Paltrowitz, Stuart.
    Bargain hunter's guide to investing in real estate / by Stuart and Donna Paltrowitz.
        p.   cm.
    Includes index.
    ISBN 0-8306-8154-X
    1. Real estate investment. I. Paltrowitz, Donna. II. Title.
HD1382.5.P35   1990
332.63′24—dc20   90-6311
                                                                CIP

TAB BOOKS offers software for sale.
For information and a catalog, please contact:

TAB Software Department
Blue Ridge Summit, PA 17294-0850

Questions regarding the content of this book
should be addressed to:

Reader Inquiry Branch
TAB BOOKS
Blue Ridge Summit, PA 17294-0850

Vice President & Editorial Director: David Conti
Book Editor: Susan L. Rockwell
Production: Katherine G. Brown
Cover Photography: Susan Riley, Harrisonburg, VA

Contents

Acknowledgments

THIS BOOK HAS TAKEN US NINETEEN YEARS TO COMPLETE AS WE RECEIVED A thorough education of the ins and outs of investing in real estate, eighteen years to gain the experience and one year to record it. Along the way we received invaluable inspiration, advice and guidance. For all those who helped make our success possible we thank:

Anne and David Steele
George and Geneva Munkenbeck
Blanche Kulawitz
Barbara Hirsch Realty
Gail and Lester Orlick
N.J.L. Associates
Bill Bresnan
Sonny Bloch
David Conti, our outstanding editor at Liberty Hall Press

And the many attorneys, contractors, tenants and repair people who taught us to look both ways before we cross . . . the t's and dot the i's.

Introduction

THE BARGAIN HUNTER'S GUIDE TO INVESTING IN REAL ESTATE SHOWS HOW you and any other persons with a good job, satisfactory credit rating, and the desire to become independently wealthy can achieve financial success investing in real estate. Late night real estate gurus broadcast from a tropical paradise and promise that buying real estate will bring immediate riches. Increasingly, it is becoming evident that those get-rich-quick schemes are filled with holes. The gurus are not earning their fortunes from real estate, but rather from their costly seminars and tapes.

Purchasing a house without any money from your own pocket sounds enticing. But remember that money will have to be put back in someone's pocket. How are you going to meet the monthly payments? What happens when you pyramid one property atop another and then have vacancies or nonpayers, with no money coming in? Real estate gurus never bring up that subject.

A slower, more reasonable approach to wealth-building makes more sense—if you like sleeping nights. As investors who have made it in real estate in an urban market, we will demonstrate how buying properties below market value is the true key to independent wealth. Money isn't made on the sale but on the purchase. Buy the right property at the right price on the right terms. Just as shopping for bargains in clothing or furniture saves hundreds, shopping for bargains in real estate with the correct techniques saves thousands. With *The Bargain Hunter's Guide to Investing in Real Estate*, you will learn the street-smart bargain techniques for selecting properties, negotiating the best terms, flipping properties, landing major tenants and long-term leases on commercial properties, inspecting property, shopping for attorneys, understanding insurance and mortgages, as well as the ABC's of buying rehab properties. Our methods have worked in the tough major urban and suburban areas and will continue to work, regardless of what happens to the stock market or local economies.

Owning co-ops, condos, single-family homes, as well as multiple-dwellings and mixed-use properties, we have faced and overcome every obstacle from procrastinating attorneys, late payers, and crash pads to two-below-zero oil burner repairs. We do not offer a rags-to-riches story as many real estate experts do today. We did not borrow our last twenty-five dollars for a seminar that changed our lives. As college graduates in civil service, we wanted something more to rely on for our futures than our stagnant jobs. And as far as our assets, we did not want to rely on a fickle stock market where events beyond our control could cause our assets to decline by twenty percent in one day. We needed something that we could control. And that something was real estate. A stock market meltdown of five hundred points will not change the value of your office building. The tenants carry on business as usual and pay the rent on the first or fifteenth of the month.

Looking at our colleagues, we saw people locked into their dead-end jobs with no place to turn after twenty or thirty years. Their family responsibilities prevented them from changing careers. We wanted to avoid that abyss. We uncovered a way to independent wealth without the need to give up the full-time job. We found the good-buy approach to buying real estate—where we did not have to work full-time to get started, and did not need large sums of money or connections to the right people.

Like millions of people, if you remain locked into a job you hate or at best tolerate, with little chance of a rich uncle leaving you a million dollars or winning the lottery, you have to make things happen for yourself. There are two choices available. You can stay in the job you hate, watch the clock, and resent everyone and everything about the job, or you can do something about it. If you are willing to change and invest your time in real estate education, you can change your life.

Investing in real estate is not the easy way to riches, but it is the only way for the working person to still become independently wealthy. You have to find the mission before you can find the energy. It is your asset base and not your salary that determines your standard of living. By building up your asset base through real estate over a period of time, you will be able to become financially independent to choose your future. Though real estate prices have risen sharply in the last ten years and are not likely to appreciate at the same pace, there is still a tremendous opportunity for the motivated person with limited means to invest in real estate.

We are not alone. Hundreds of thousands, perhaps millions, of college-educated people have tired of their jobs and have nowhere to turn. Obviously you are not going to walk into the boss tomorrow and tell him to fold your time card seven ways and file it. Though you would like to quit, you still have to earn a living. What you can do is prepare to quit your job. Just as a toddler starts walking by taking small steps, you as a real estate investor will have to start the same way. If you stumble while taking too large a step, you might be reluctant to walk again.

Frequently you will read about a wealthy individual who was duped in a fraudulent scheme or mismanaged money, and therefore is filing for bankruptcy. Holding on to your money is one of the most difficult skills to master. Those who have invested in real estate have managed to become and remain financially independent. Whether you're a motion picture mogul or a foreman at the electric utility, you have the opportunity to invest and prosper in real estate. You will learn the bargain hunting techniques we and other successful investors have used and continue to use to build our fortunes. Unlike other real estate books, we employ a street-smart approach to investment real estate that works in today's sophisticated urban markets where both buyer and seller are shrewd, and the tenant is as educated and experienced as the landlord. Innovative techniques are needed to survive in today's real estate market. On the pages of this book you will learn our hands-on approach to acquiring, managing, and prospering with real estate as you prepare for a future with independent wealth.

Finding a piece of real estate that is not overpriced, whether commercial or residential, is about as tough as finding a worker who loves Monday mornings. Or so it seems. Real estate properties are just so high today, aren't they? Remember when a house sold for $30,000? In 1970 not only was a house selling for 30,000, a car was selling for $3,000. The bad news was that you were only earning $6,000. A house back then was selling for five times your yearly salary.

Today, as you scan the "houses for sale" section of the daily newspaper you are filled with disbelief. How can anyone in his right mind pay $200,000 for that kind of house? Who could afford to make those mortgage payments? What people fail to realize is that home prices have "gone through the roof" along with salaries. House buyers no longer earn the 1970 salary of $6,000. Salaries have risen more than sixfold to $40,000 a year. Similarly, the 1970 house price has increased sixfold to the range of $180,000 to $200,000 with expansions and extras. Relatively speaking, nothing has changed. Considering the sixfold increase, the house might not seem to be worth the inflated price. But think, are you, as an employee, worth six times more than you were worth in 1970? Are you doing 600% more work now? There is no need for a panic attack. Just realize that house prices and salaries have risen proportionately. When considering current home prices, it is necessary to keep the total picture in mind.

It is apparent that house prices rise along with salaries and other necessities. Real estate has risen over the years. There is and will always be a demand for real estate. To quote Will Rogers, "Land—they ain't making any more." Whether your preference is residential properties to buy, fix up, and sell, rental properties to manage, or commercial properties to own and manage, real estate offers the unique opportunity to financial independence. Over the months and years, increases in rents and the build-up in equity will enable you to become economically well-off. Whether you are interested in split levels in Great Neck or a strip shopping center in Parsippany, the secret to wealth-building is finding a bargain. Bargain properties are in all areas of the country and in all types of investments. In a bargain property, you are buying real estate below the market so that you are guaranteeing yourself a profit, regardless of what the real estate market does. You are locking in your profit when you sign on the dotted line. Just as you learn to become an accountant, movie director, or car mechanic, you can learn techniques to building real estate profits. Using the good-buy approach, you will be able to determine if the row of stores for sale is a screaming buy or a property that will leave you screaming to sell at any price, or if an office building is a once-in-a-lifetime find or a lost cause. Buying the right property at a bargain is the first step in turning dreams of independent wealth into reality. If you put into practice the good-buy principles, you will be able to say good-bye to your full-time job. And even if you choose not to give up your full-time job, life will be much more comfortable than ever before. No where but through real estate will you be given the opportunity to change your life, retire your time card, and travel the road to riches.

Why Invest in Real Estate?

Winners are people who aren't afraid to take a chance now and then. Losers sit around and wait for the odds to improve.

—Rev. G. Hall

LOOK AROUND YOU. THE COST OF LIVING IS RISING. YOU CAN'T AFFORD THE things you could a few years ago. You have too much week at the end of your money. Your paycheck doesn't seem to belong to you anymore. Piece by piece you are giving it away until there is nothing left.

Is this phenomena only happening to you? Not by any stretch of the imagination. We are part of two-income families and we still can't make ends meet. Are prices going to suddenly stop rising so that our paychecks cover the expenses the way they used to? Unfortunately not. The American middle class is gradually disappearing, and our country is becoming two classes—the rich and the poor. Miracles are not going to happen to change conditions. The only way things are going to change is if you change them.

As much as you hate to admit it, you are not going to win the lottery and change your life. It is just not likely to happen. What you are going to have to do is take steps to change your life. A new haircut, a new car, and a new husband or wife are not the changes we mean. You are going to have to find a way to build a sound financial future. God gave us two ends. One is to sit on and the other is to think with. Your financial success depends on which end you use the most.

Most of us work hard at our jobs and have little to show for it. We are not well compensated. We have little control and a poor outlook for the future. With heavy financial obligations there is no way to walk away from the job and change careers. There is only one avenue for the middle class person to travel to change his life. That avenue is real estate.

Real estate investing is not a get-rich-quick solution to changing your life. It is a sound, sensible plan to ensure yourself a steady financial future and allow you to make choices in your life. Real estate is the only means for the average middle-income investor to change his or her life. You can't count on the stock market that catches a cold when a third world country sneezes. You can't count on your bank that could fold as quickly as a cheap umbrella, leaving you in long lines to attempt to collect your money. You certainly can't count on rare coins that you buy at premium prices, only to find that the coin has been overgraded forcing you to take a loss when you sell.

No where but in real estate can you be in control. What happens in another part of the world or to the bank on the corner does not affect the value of your property. The real estate market can be strong or soft, but you are still in control of your property. You have physical possession of your property—no one can take it from you as long as you keep up payments. Can you say the same thing with the stock market where the president of a company can embezzle thirty million dollars of inventory and send a company into bankruptcy? Your real estate investment will not be worth twenty-five percent less in one day because of a world event. With physical possession of your property, you can make a deal anytime you choose. You can be as flexible as you have to be to entice a buyer, or be enticed by a seller.

THE IDEAL INVESTMENT

Unlike any other investment, real estate is an IDEAL investment for the bargain hunter. There is no assurance that you will become wealthy overnight, but through hard work and sound practices it can help you fulfill your dreams. The acronym IDEAL helps demonstrate how successful real estate can be to a wealth builder.

The letter I represents *Income*. As the owner of rental properties, whether commercial or residential, you aim to earn a positive cash flow every month from your investment. By purchasing properties in desirable areas at the right price and on favorable terms, you earn a cash-on-cash profit on your investment. Having property in a desirable location that is in demand by prospective tenants allows you to increase rents as each lease comes up for renewal. You can raise your rents in excess of your increases in Principal Interest Taxes Insurance (PITI). Once your real estate investment is fine-tuned through the selection of responsible tenants, assignment of responsibilities to tenants, and prudent property supervision, it will bring considerable income.

Depreciation is the D word. Your property increases in value each year, if you have bought it below the market. Yet the U.S. government tooth fairy claims that your property is losing its value. It is becoming worth less and less every year. And in 27 years your property will have no value at all. Therefore the Internal Revenue Service allows you to depreciate your property over a period of $27\frac{1}{2}$ years as if it is losing value each year. With this yearly gift write-off of a percentage of your investment, you are able to legally reduce or eliminate your tax liability to the IRS each year you are eligible. Imagine while your property is increasing its value, the government gives you a credit or tax advantage as though the property is decreasing in value. We welcome government gifts; you can too.

The letter E in IDEAL represents *Equity build-up*. If you invest in the stock market and your stock rises five points on Monday due to takeover rumors, it can just as easily decline by the same amount when the company president says that there is no news to account for the price action. Market factors cause wild gyrations in stocks and often irrationally. In real estate, market factors are observable and often tangible. Factors that cause a property to rise include a thriving neighborhood, low crime rate, accessibility to shopping, good schools, and favorable economic climate. These conditions are not reversed overnight. Signs of change are observable. As the years pass, the equity in a property rises with no payment of capital gains taxes. No taxes need to be paid until after the property has been sold. In the meantime you are building up a real estate empire worth hundreds of thousands of dollars, possibly even one million dollars. Over a period of five or ten years, you notice a steady increase in the value of your portfolio, with values climbing faster in some years than in others as the real estate cycle changes. As you take an account of your portfolio, you might decide to borrow on the value of your real estate assets. You are able to make your money work for you instead of working for your money. By borrowing from the equity in your money machine, you can borrow for any major expenses and live off the ever-increasing monthly profit.

The A word is *Appreciation*. Over the long-term, nothing appreciates in value like well-situated real estate. Historically, real estate increases in value steadily, has price spurts, has a slight correction or price adjustment, and then resumes its steady increase. Other investments have more of a roller coaster price history. They spurt to unrealistic price levels and then plummet, leaving the small investor holding the bag and nothing else. If you like excitement, go to Atlantic City and Las Vegas, don't buy real estate. Real estate investing is not exciting most of the time, but it is profitable. In the late 1970s and early 1980s real estate did become exciting as prices skyrocketed, leaving the ''would have, should have, could have" people counting other people's profits and not their own. Skeptics in most sections of the country said it couldn't last, but the rapid rise in real estate prices was lengthy and substantial. Finally, in the late 1980s, prices slowed down as investors sought to cash in on the appreciation in their homes. In some sections of the nation such as the Northeast, the large number of unsold homes put a damper on price appreciation, until the balance between supply and demand could be met. In other areas of the country, real estate prices have resumed increasing, but at more normal levels. The contrast between the go-go days of skyrocketing prices and normal times gave the impression of a slump, with doomsayers predicting a crash in real estate prices.

Over any time period of ten or twenty years, real estate prices have outpaced inflation. The same can't be said for passbook savings accounts or the Dow Jones Industrial Average. One reason why real estate prices outstrip inflation and always will is that the cost of building materials and labor continue to increase. The expense of building materials and labor are factored into the cost of constructing a new building. The price of a new building has a direct effect on the price of existing buildings, with the price of existing buildings rising near the level of the new buildings, as purchasers make comparisons and buy what they perceive as the better value.

Try to pick up a three-thousand-pound car. You can't do it. Now use a form of a lever, such as a jack. Suddenly it is not such an insurmountable task. Leverage works in many different ways to make otherwise impossible things possible. *Leverage* is the L in the IDEAL investment. In real estate you get more bang for your buck than in any other investment. Where else can you earn 100% on your investment in a single year without carrying a handgun and having your portrait hanging in the post office? With real estate you can buy a property for $150,000 by putting down $15,000 and borrowing the rest in the form of a mortgage. Since you always buy real estate below the market, it would not be surprising for it to appreciate in the first year. If the value of the property in the first year rises from $150,000 to $165,000, a rise of $15,000, consider what you have done. You have made a 100% return on your money. You invested $15,000 in cash and the property has risen by $15,000. You doubled your money in that first year. If the property rises by $150,000 to $180,000, you have earned the astounding return of 200%. You invested $15,000 and made $30,000, quadrupling your money. If you buy properties at wholesale prices, as you will learn in this book, you will find that it is possible to earn such returns in real estate without becoming a riverboat gambler. The leverage factor gives you the power to make a little money go a long way, unequalled by any other form of investment.

Real estate, for all the reasons mentioned, is an IDEAL investment. In fact, all the nation's wealth is built on it. Eighty percent of the wealthiest people in the United States made their money through real estate. People might become successful in many different fields, but they invest their capital in real estate. Think about how real estate affects you. You live on real estate. You work on real estate. You have recreation on real estate, as well. Ask any successful person you admire what his or her greatest investment has been and the chances are it will be the home or another piece of real estate property. Investments in real estate lay the foundation for everything else that follows.

No one knows what lies ahead—not one year, not one month, not one day. If anyone knew one day ahead with certainty of what was to be he or she could become an instant millionaire in the stock market or any field of gambling. But no one knows, despite all the economists' and financial analysts' predictions. No one definitely knows what will happen. No one knows how much real estate will appreciate in the future, though certain basic facts exist. Although people have desires, they don't need a diamond, an oil painting or an antique automobile, but people do need shelter. Regardless of what happens to the economy, there will always be a need for housing that people can afford.

AFFORDABLE HOUSING

Affordable housing is the key to a profitable real estate investment, now and in the future. The baby boomers, those middle-aged people born after World War II, are in their prime earning years. They are marrying, having children, and trying to find affordable housing. Many are relocating from their first apartments and are looking for their first home. Well-to-do boomers are seeking to upgrade from a smaller first home to a larger one.

It has always been the American dream to own your home. There have and will always be more people wanting homes than currently owning them—creating a demand for real estate. The outlook for real estate, both residential and commercial is highly favorable. Many areas in our country are at rockbottom prices, as poor economic conditions, lack of jobs or overbuilding have impacted sections of the country. Areas such as Phoenix, Arizona with a lack of jobs; Houston, Texas with the oil market and bank failures; and Southern Florida troubled with condominium overbuilding have remained at depressed prices for many years. The large number of unsold properties present a great opportunity for investors since it will take more years for the supply of unsold properties to be met by demand. It appears that prices can only rise, though no one knows the exact timetable.

Commercial and residential real estate throughout the nation will continue to be in demand for the foreseeable future. The problem of the homeless is a nationwide epidemic. And it is not just economic. There is a lack of affordable housing units throughout the country. It is just a matter of time until jobs open up in the depressed areas, bringing a demand for affordable housing there as well.

Trends signal a strong future for real estate. The impact of baby boomers, as they marry, seek their first home, upgrade, or divorce and remarry will help buoy the market. The strong presence of women in the work force gives clout to women as they seek their own homes without fear of mortgage discrimination. With ever-increasing life spans, people are living longer and remaining independent without giving up their private homes. Elderly people live in single family housing, as they remain where they raised children, move to smaller homes, or relocate to the sunbelt states. Thus, the demand for single family housing remains. Along with the strength in residential housing markets there will be an accompanying demand for commercial, industrial, and recreational properties. Increased residential population brings on a need for retail stores for services, factories to manufacture the items, and recreational properties and areas for the residents to unwind after the work week.

The affordable housing situation has begun to make headlines and is drawing attention from our legislators. The number of housing starts, which is the number of permits for houses to be built, has failed to keep up with the demand for housing. There is simply not enough affordable, quality housing to satisfy the demand. Consequently there has been an exponential growth in illegal housing. Illegal housing has more than one family living in a house, as separate apartments are built into one-family homes and families rent out additional space. Local communities are beginning to recognize the problem, as they find ways to calm the dissent among property owners while easing the housing crisis in the affected areas. Local governments have issued mother-daughter permits and permits for others who register the apartment with local government.

Real estate has been a proven wealth-builder, yet there is no best mode of investment. It is unbeatable because it is something that people will always need. People do not necessarily need stocks, bonds, paintings, stamps, coins, or antiques. But everyone needs real estate because everyone needs shelter. Everyone would like the best housing he or she can afford.

Though it is a basic human need to have shelter, there are other conditions that make some real estate more desirable than others. The factors of supply and demand influence the value of real estate throughout the country. Areas that are in demand and have a low supply of properties on the market will carry a higher price tag than areas that are not sought by purchasers.

Wouldn't it be nice to have a crystal ball and know which areas of the country will be in demand in the next ten years? It would be nice, but it isn't possible. What is known is the trends that are already in place, and the cities that are experiencing the greatest growth. Expectations are based upon the trends in effect and the likelihood of the continuing into the foreseeable future.

According to demographic studies, there are eight cities expected to experience the greatest growth over the next decade. They are, in order of expected growth, Dallas, Chicago, Atlanta, Washington D.C., Cincinnati, Nashville, Denver, and Miami (Florida). All eight cities are considered transportation hub cities, which means that they are the central locations chosen by airlines to base their incoming, outgoing, and connecting flights. Since they are hub cities, manufacturers and distributors find that they manufacture and ship products at lowest cost from these locations. Along with increased business comes good employment possibilities and a growth in population, real estate values, and income.

Real estate investors, both in the United States and abroad, feel that over the long-term American real estate is a prime investment. If you have any doubts read the newspapers and learn about the latest foreign real estate acquisitions in major American cities. Japanese investors in particular feel that the United States is a lucrative investment area for the next decade and beyond. In 1988, for example, the Japanese purchased in excess of sixteen billion dollars of U.S. real estate, with the purchases spread among the hub cities. They have invested in office buildings, resorts, and mixed-use properties. With the enormous imports of goods from Japan by the United States, Japan receives billions of dollars, for which it needs a safe haven for the money. Japan invests large sums of its investment profits back into United States real estate. Taiwan and South Korean investors have also become big players in the United States real estate market. Increased penetration of the American real estate market by the Japanese, Taiwanese, and South Koreans over the next decade and beyond appears likely.

TYPES OF INVESTMENTS

Real estate investing has been a proven winner. Yet ask the average person if he or she invests in real estate. Do you know what the typical response is? ''I don't have time to invest in real estate.'' In truth everyone has time to invest in real estate. There is real estate for people with a great deal of time as well as with limited time. Among the property types are single-family homes, raw land, cooperative apartments, shopping centers, condominiums, recreational property, multiple-dwelling homes, rehab properties, office buildings, farmland, industrial properties, hotels and motels, as well as real estate investment trusts and syndicates.

All these types of real estate can be profitable investments. You must choose the ones that best suit your needs. You know best what your needs are and how much time you have to devote to nurturing your real estate empire. Raw land, for example, requires a minimum of care and can offer a tremendous rate of return, where it is possible over time to double or triple your investment. However, there is no guarantee that your raw land will ever whet another investor's appetite. Simply put, raw land might not be easy to sell.

Although there has always been a special appeal to own your own home, the problem is that not everyone who would like to live in a private home can afford to buy one. Single-family homes require considerable care and time. Like an intern, you are on-call twenty four hours a day and seven days a week. Tenants call for any problem, from a clogged drain to a strange odor. Your time is theirs, or so they think, as long as they are paying rent. The positive cash flow is usually small, unless you buy properties with a large down payment or with a very low selling price. Believe it or not, in many areas of the country there are still single-family homes and condominiums selling in the $30,000 and $40,000 price range. So if you have the time to find the property and manage it, single-family homes can be a lucrative field of investment. In other parts of the country where affordable house prices tip well over the $100,000 mark, note that $1000 plus per month rent is considered affordable to the working couple.

Cooperative apartments offer good news and bad news. The good news is that there is a company that manages and makes repairs on structural problems. You are called only if an appliance breaks down or if the management company is not being responsive to your complaints. The bad news, and it is very bad news, is that the cooperative board seems to want control of everything including the air that you breathe. They usually have approval power over the selection of your tenants. Even though you feel a prospective tenant is responsible and credit-worthy, the management company, which is hired by the coop board, might demand to see the prospective tenant's tax returns and a detailed application before granting approval. Many prospective tenants will be reluctant to undergo such scrutiny and not pursue your cooperative apartment. The cooperative board and its abuses do not stop there. They might also withhold permission from a prospective purchaser when you choose to sell. So over all, owning a cooperative apartment as an investment is a mixed bag. The personal integrity of the board members often determines the quality of your investment. Before considering the purchase of a cooperative, consider the pluses and minuses of its ownership and make sure that you are not left holding the bag. If the board members don't cooperate with you from the outset, don't support them with your money. Invest your money in a comfortable situation. The coop is only as good as its board members.

Condominiums offer more good news than bad news when compared with cooperative apartments. Though management of your cooperative complex is assumed by the management organization, you own the individual unit for which you hold a deed. With a co-op, you do not own the individual unit but rather a number of shares in the corporation that owns all the units and its property. As evidence that you do not own the cooperative apartment, you are given a proprietary lease instead of a deed of ownership. With the condominium, you exercise control over the rental of your property, though the board likes to be kept informed. A condominium retains the right to refuse your selection of a potential purchaser, though if the person is responsible and creditworthy, it will not with-hold approval.

Are you a real estate high roller? Then, recreational properties might be the investment for you. Recreational properties carry a higher risk than single-family homes, cooperative apartments, or condominiums, but offer much higher rewards. One reason is that the cost per acre is low, and you can purchase large tracts of land for a relatively small amount of money. When we are talking about recreational properties, we are not referring to time share, which is anything but a real estate investment. Time shares cannot be easily sold, despite the claims of developers and sales people. Bona fide recreational properties can prove inter-esting and profitable for the person willing to assume above-average risk and hold the property for an indefinite period.

Raw land can be thought of as an unpolished diamond. It offers great poten-tial but only acquires substantial value after something has been done to it. As raw land is developed, you can capture the ultimate value of the land. Be aware that raw land investment is fraught with risk. Parcels of raw land must be evalu-ated by a professional before any investments are made.

Do you have a brown belt in shopping? Whether you do or not, that doesn't qualify you to invest in shopping centers. Shopping centers can be lucrative but are not for a novice investor. Risks are high and so are the rewards. Management is a critical ingredient. Concerns with competitive shopping centers, adequacy of parking, compatible tenants, responsible tenants, and responsive management help determine if a shopping center is a success.

Office buildings, like shopping centers, are not for the unseasoned investor unless you are advised and guided by an experienced property investor. Con-struction costs are prohibitive, as buildings must be modernized or customized to attract and maintain tenants. Attracting long-term tenants and a desirable anchor are important factors. Arrangements of rents and payments of utilities are also critical subjects to be considered in any arrangement. Other commercial ventures such as hotels and motels and industrial properties have their unique investment features and risks, with which you must become familiar before investing.

Less risky than many commercial ventures and very rewarding is the field of rehab properties. There are investors who rehabilitate and sell properties and nothing else. Rehab properties require extensive renovations, some with a total gutting. The field is very lucrative and requires the expertise of professionals, including engineers, architects, contractors, electricians, plumbers, etc.

Many real estate investors feel that multiple-dwelling properties are the greatest thing since lasers. The feeling is that multiple-dwellings mean multiple incomes. The problem is that they also mean multiple headaches from the many tenants, should you choose to manage the property yourself. Good management is essential in a multiple-dwelling. You must be decisive and at times conciliatory.

In the words of Kenny Rogers, "you have to know when to hold them, know when to fold them." The fact of life is that people can't seem to get along with one another in close proximity. You, as the landlord, often have to play peace-maker and assure both sides that they are absolutely right. In terms of your policies, you need to be consistent and fair, though it might ruffle some feathers. A multiple-dwelling can be anything from a two-family to a six hundred apartment house complex and still you have to wear many hats to keep the project functioning without open warfare. As the owner and manager of a multiple-dwelling, you are faced with tenant compatibility, utility costs, parking assignments, sleep and lifestyle variations, as well as the basic supply and demand for comparable apartments.

Real estate investment trusts and syndicates are for the passive investor who doesn't want to get his hands dirty or be awakened by phone calls from tenants. These kinds of investments can offer high rates of return and profit potential, as well as tax advantages, if your income does not exceed levels prescribed by the I.R.S. One drawback does exist with these investments. Not having a hand in management you have neither input or knowledge about operational expenses, salaries paid to management, or other factors that could control the value of your investment. Should there be fraud or mismanagement, which is a common complaint, despite securities laws and accounting audits, you have no idea until it is too late.

REAL ESTATE SCALE

You can build a successsful portfolio with any kind of real estate. Real estate offers a real opportunity to build an asset base to provide for independent wealth and retirement. There are five major types, with varying degrees of value. They are in order of value-commercial, industrial, residential, vacation, and agricultural. The shorter the supply, the higher the selling, which leads to a rise in the property value.

Commercial

Commercial property is said to be the most valuable and desirable. Whether it is an office building, store, diner, hotel, or motel, all have something in common. They operate to make a profit. Don't become confused. Though commercial is more valuable than residential, it doesn't mean that Joe's camera shop is more expensive than Al's waterfront home. What it means is that a 60-×-100 plot, zoned commercial, is more valuable than the same size plot, zoned residential. The potential income from a commercial property will make it considerably more valuable than a residential property in the same area. Buyers will be more willing to pay a higher price for the commercial, due to its appeal as an income-producer. Even in a run-down area, a commercial property will command more money than a comparable residential property.

Industrial

Next to commercial, industrial property is the most valuable. It can be a factory, warehouse, industrial park, truck depot, or manufacturing facility. Industrial is used mainly for manufacturing and storing, while commercial deals with selling.

Industrial property is often built in less desirable areas. As heavy industry expands, the industrial land value rises since there is more competition for land for industrial use. Demand for industrial property does not cause residential property values to rise, since it is a different real estate market. If an auto plant is being built in Phoenix, there will be a large demand for semi-skilled and unskilled workers, as well as a demand for engineers and executives. Other companies will seek to locate there, resulting in a demand for housing, entertainment, medical care, and restaurants, but not necessarily in the immediate vicinity of the auto plant.

Residential

Residential property value is determined by location and factors deemed desirable by investors. In the last decade, single-family home prices have soared while condos in many areas have failed to keep pace, due to overbuilding. In downtown areas, such as Manhattan, the real estate of the luxury coops often cause it to become as valuable as office buildings, since office buildings are in close proximity.

Affordable housing has become a national priority. With the problems of the homeless, and the cost of buying a house, there is a severe shortage of affordable housing. Whatever the variety, there is and will continue to be strong demand for affordable residential housing.

Vacation

Vacation property consists of land for recreational use. It can be ski trails, campgrounds, marinas, parks, or vacation homes. Vacation property can be a second home in the country, as well as land zoned and used for recreational purposes.

What is a vacation home? It could be a one-room shack or a lavish townhouse, a time share or manufactured home. They're properties to get away from it all. Some are rented for the season or weekends. As an investor, you have a welcomed source of income to help pay your expenses, as you rent part of your property.

Vacation homes can sharply increase in value. Many investors initially purchase a one or two-room cabin for weekend getaways. Then over the years, they expand and upgrade with modern facilities and conveniences to meet the needs of a growing family. Rural areas become developed as parkways are built and properties become urban. The best thing that can happen is for your vacation property to become residential as population centers develop.

Agricultural

Agricultural property has the lowest use and value. It is farmland and ranchland. It is considered farmland, whether it is used for farming or lies unworked. In recent years, farmers have not been earning enough money to live on their land investment. Farmland across the Midwest has been foreclosed on as farmers have been hurt by droughts, famine, and diseases affecting their crops and animals. Banks refused to grant loans to farmers. In good times, there would be some demand for agricultural land. During times of distress, there is little or no demand.

SUMMARY

Real estate is the investment upon which everything else is based. Virtually everything you do concerns or takes place on real estate, from the place where you work to the ballpark where you play. Real estate offers investors like you the IDEAL way to change your present status and prepare for a brighter future. With the IDEAL investment, you can finally exercise some control over your work situation, while earning a substantial income, getting tax advantages, and building up tax-free equity, all with a small initial capital investment.

As an investment vehicle, real estate is multi-faceted since there is a real estate investment variety to suit the needs of any investor—from the hands-on type to the don't-want-to-get-fingernails-dirty type. There are as many approaches as there are reasons to call in sick on Monday morning. Among property types there are single-family homes, cooperative apartments, condominiums, recreational properties, raw land, shopping centers, office buildings, rehab properties, multiple-dwellings, apartment houses, and real estate investment trusts and syndicates. There is a hierarchy in the value scale of the five major types of real-estate: commercial, industrial, residential, vacation, and agricultural.

2

Investing in
Undervalued Areas

HAVE YOU VISITED A NEIGHBORHOOD TOY STORE LATELY TO PURCHASE THE HOT toy on the market? If you have, you probably walked away empty handed. Because of media advertising or word-of-mouth conversation, you find a huge demand for that item. It's sold out. The reason—demand exceeds the supply the store can offer. New shipments arrive and disappear almost immediately. To meet the heavy demand, the store raises its prices. You want it, you pay the price.

SUPPLY AND DEMAND

It seems like kid's stuff, but it's anything but. Supply and demand are what control prices on everything that is bought and sold, from Ace bandages to Zen philosophy books. The real estate market also operates through the supply and demand principle. In a hot area where properties are bought within hours of hitting the market, strong demand translates into cash chasing a limited number of available properties. Homes stay on the market for very short periods before they are snapped up. The result is an upward spiral in property prices. Prices continue to rise as long as buyers pay the ever-increasing numbers. When buyers refuse to pay the astronomical prices, the prices level off. No hot market stays hot forever.

Supply and demand not only cause prices to soar, they also cause many an owner to become sore. A lack of demand or absence of bidders on a property will cause a property to be priced well below market value. That's bad news for the owner but great news for you. A property stays undervalued until people realize that it is a bargain. Such a realization could take months or even years.

Areas become undervalued for many different reasons. There could be the cancellation of a defense contract resulting in layoffs. There could be large unemployment or a health scare. What happens in a local economy affects the way people feel about real estate and the fervor they feel investing there. The Houston, Texas area became depressed in the mid 1980s from low oil prices and high unemployment. The savings and loan crisis in Texas and other areas has caused prices in many parts of the country to remain soft, as banks hold and try to sell the millions of dollars of foreclosed property they hold in their portfolios.

Other parts of the country have not had poor economies, yet other factors made them undervalued properties. Orlando and Miami, Florida suffered the results of too much building in the 1970s and 1980s as the market became saturated and overbought. The same can be said for Las Vegas, affectionately known as Lost Wages. Las Vegas continues to undervalued because of its endless desert land and the plethora of building in every part of the city. Undervalued conditions often take many years to correct, when new investors discover the land as an up-and-coming place to invest. When large numbers of people get the idea at the same time and put their money behind their ideas, the marketplace explodes.

Can you predict the future? Unfortunately few people can, though economists were able to predict six out of the last three recessions. Wouldn't it be great if you could tell which property is going to turn around before it turns around? You don't need tea leaves, tarot cards, or anything supernatural. You just need good old-fashioned knowledge. You can spot a turnaround area early if you can recognize the signs. Many of the signs pointing to an undervalued property are listed in the Undervalued Property Inventory. Check the UPI and see how many qualities listed fit your property. The more qualities you can identify the more likely it is that property is undervalued and ripe for a turnaround.

Undervalued Property Inventory

- ☞ Neighborhood is in a path of growth or near a growth area.
- ☞ Trend of large companies to relocate there.
- ☞ Neighborhood with an attractive natural boundary such as lake or park.
- ☞ Neighborhood with cultural or sports attraction.
- ☞ Overcrowded conditions in neighboring areas.
- ☞ Stable areas nearby.
- ☞ Trend of rising property values in nearby areas
- ☞ Short commuting time to growth area.
- ☞ Indications of government funding on federal, state, or local level.

☑ Travel time of less than an hour to business center.
☑ History as thriving neighborhood.
☑ Neighborhood with historic past or architectural uniqueness.

Score

10 or higher—excellent area for turnaround
6 to 9—good possibilities
5 or less—not ready for turnaround

TAKING A NEIGHBORHOOD TEMPERATURE

A neighborhood is much more than people, trees, and homes. It has a life of its own. A neighborhood can be hot, up-and-coming, on the way back, or going downhill. There are many other labels you have heard and used to describe the temperature of a neighborhood. Sometimes a neighborhood has much more going for it than appears on the surface. In fact sometimes good things happen to bad neighborhoods. What happens to the adjoining neighborhood spreads to the stagnant one and makes both come to life.

Consider a neighborhood that is undergoing gentrification. People are moving back from the suburbs to be closer to the inner city. A neighborhood deemed to be desirable has had a huge influx of people and increase in demand for its services, with stores sprouting in every direction. Finally, the neighborhood because of a lack of physical space cannot expand any more. There are no more available lots for houses and there are few vacancies in apartments. In a word, the neighborhood is congested.

But still people want to live near the hotbed of activity. What happens? They move as close to the area as possible. The result is that the neighborhood that is bursting at the seams overflows into adjacent neighborhoods, which have lower housing costs and lower rents. If the surrounding neighborhood has architecturally different houses or historically significant houses the recovery takes hold more readily. There are scores of investors and others who find those designs linked with history to be fascinating and appealing. Such a house is a collectible, like the 1952 Mickey Mantle rookie card or 1909 S-VDB Lincoln Head cent. Impressed by Roman columns or designs from the Civil War period, people become attracted to neighborhoods. Physical boundaries such as beaches, rolling meadows, lakes, and parks are also considered desirable locations to be near.

The average person spends one-third of his or her life working. Combined with one-third for sleeping, that doesn't leave much time for anything else. It's no wonder then that a short commute to an industrial park or business center is so appealing to a home buyer. Some buyers of homes even overlook the fact that there are rundown pockets in a neighborhood, as long as the majority of homes are structurally sound and well located. The feeling is that the resurgence in the adjacent neighborhood will encourage residents to fix up their properties. Peer pressure results in neighborhood revitalization as residents catch the fever. Investors seeing the neighborhood start to turn around begin to buy rundown properties in the hopes of getting on the bandwagon. Smart investors know that big money is made buying in a turnaround neighborhood before the general public is aware that it is turning around.

Down does not necessarily mean out. An area that is depressed does not have to stay that way. Many properties that people wouldn't touch with a ten-foot pole can now only be held with a potholder.

HOW THE CONCENTRIC CIRCLE THEORY AFFECTS REAL ESTATE

Skim a pebble along a lake and you see it, the ripples along the water that start where the pebble hits and extend outwards. The ripples cause circles to become increasingly larger and larger with each ripple. While it doesn't seem that pebbles have much to do with real estate, there is a strong relationship. The concentric circle theory is that a city expands from the outward into bigger and bigger circles. The city of Chicago illustrates the loop theory, where the city developed in the areas that surrounded the loop, a section of the city and then extended outward.

Neighborhoods turn around in that same way from the center outward. A large employer decides to locate in a city. Other large employers follow and it doesn't take long until the area heats up or as investors say "the area gets hot." With strong business conditions and a hot job market, you soon have a hot real estate market. Office rentals rise as landlords sense they can command it from other commercial tenants whose business might be helped by being in close proximity to major employers. Property values rise in the city as commercial and residential investors move en masse to invest. The supply of available property in the immediate area for major employers dries up. Purchasers expand their horizons blocks away from the target area. Surrounding areas become hot as people buy up properties because they see others buying up and rehabilitating properties. Interest in real estate keeps spreading outward and outward until it reaches a point where interest subsides.

Atlantic City was an area in the midst of a financial turnaround. Several large companies decided to invest and refurbish hotels along the boardwalk. Donald Trump refurbished or built several hotels along the boardwalk. Then he decided to own a hotel by the Marina, several miles away. People thought he was crazy, that no one would stay at a hotel that wasn't along the boardwalk, but Trump rebuilt a hotel there. The hotel has been a success. Less than one block away, a major hotel constructed a 750-room casino hotel and that too has prospered. In years to come other hotels are likely to sprout up nearby. There is now a tendency for hotels to build a block or more away from the boardwalk. More and more properties are being bought by speculators for future development. In Atlantic City, you can bet on the concentric circle theory.

The Camden Turnaround

Think of the city of Camden, New Jersey and you might say "m-m good." The reason is Camden is the international headquarters of the Campbell Soup Company. Despite the location of Campbell Soup, the city had been in the throes of a depression for more than ten years. As you drove down Broadway and through side streets it looked like a war zone. However, for the last few years, Camden has been one of the hot investment areas in the country. If Christopher Columbus discovered America, then Sonny Bloch can be credited for discovering Camden, New Jersey. Sonny Bloch is the well-known real estate expert, talk show host and author who introduced Camden to real estate investors. Sonny, who travels hundreds of thousands of miles each year to take the temperature of the real estate markets throughout the country, put the concentric theory into practice. He was quite familiar with the city of Philadelphia, Pennsylvania. Philadelphia had an excellent job market and strong housing market. The problem was that there was not sufficient affordable housing for Philadelphia. There was housing, but it was not affordable. Then, he came upon the city of Camden, New Jersey, a city ten minutes away by car and just across the ridge from Philadelphia.

Sonny Bloch felt that Camden was a city whose time had to come. Though it had been a burnt-out shell of a city for more than a decade it had qualities that a person with vision could appreciate. The proximity to thriving Philadelphia made it interesting. The fact that Camden had a state-of-the-art hospital, Cooper Hospital, an employer of thousands of people, gave it added potential. Cooper Hospital was advertising for large numbers of professional people, and they would need affordable housing. People moving to Camden could easily commute to Philadelphia or work at Cooper Hospital. The hospital, which was located in a sanctioned historical district, would need doctors, nurses, and other employees who would be available on short notice and could work staggered hours.

THE DIAMOND LOOK AT RHINESTONE PRICES

Take a drive down any block in Camden, New Jersey and what do you see? In the historical district near Cooper Hospital, you see brick row houses. Had they been across the river in Philadelphia, they'd be selling for several hundred thousand dollars. But here in Camden, they sell for less than fifty thousand dollars. If a person wanted to buy ten or fifteen blocks away from Cooper Hospital, there would be houses selling in the twenties, some even two-family structures.

As the word spread about the fantastic housing bargains in Camden, the city found itself mobbed with visitors on weekends and real estate offices with investors ready to make offers. Sonny Bloch had exposed the possibilities and investors began bargain-hunting. With the passage of weeks and months, physical changes were evident as houses were being rehabilitated block by block. The immediate vicinity of Cooper Hospital began to take on the appearance of the Georgetown section of Washington, D.C., an affluent section of the nation's capital. Home prices near the hospital took a meteoric rise. The renaissance of the historical district spread to surrounding blocks, with signs of renovation ever-present. "Smart money" has continued to flow into the area, leading to better economic times for a struggling city and riches for real estate investors looking for undervalued properties.

The revival in Camden goes on and will continue for many years. While prices in many parts are no longer at basement prices good undervalued situations still exist, the price appreciation has spread blocks away to areas such as Polishtown, East Camden, and Cramer Hill. The concentric theory is working today in Camden and will continue. Efforts by the local government including the development of the waterfront with the multimillion-dollar aquarium propel the recovery. The proximity to Philadelphia by car, upgrading of the rapid transit system, and expansion of Cooper Hospital ensure many years of continued price appreciation to bargain-hunting investors.

HISTORY UPS THE VALUE

Real estate investing does not seem to have much to do with show business. Show business is fast-paced and exciting while real estate investing is slow and needs cultivating. Yet in New York City the two have started to mix in a very exciting way. As you recall from the Undervalued Property Inventory earlier in the chapter, two of the characteristics of an undervalued property are a neighborhood with an historic past and a neighborhood with a cultural attraction. In the early 1920s and again in the 1940s, there was a Paramount movie studio in operation in Long Island City. In 1981, George S. Kaufman, along with Gregory Peck, Johnny Carson, and Neil Simon invested to modernize the studio and develop it into a major movie studio. Movies such as *Radio Days*, *Moonstruck*, and *The Secret of My Success* as well as many television shows, including "The Cosby Show" have been produced there. Now the Kaufman Studio and the Silvercup Studio have revitalized the film and commercial-making industry in New York. As the Kaufman Studio has continued to expand, major office buildings and a number of prominent companies have decided to locate there. Companies throughout the country have begun to recognize the area as a major film production center once again, as it had been when it was a silent movie studio in the 1920s. The redevelopment of the studio has caused positive changes in the neighborhood, as many dilapidated structures in the neighborhood were acquired by the studio. The neighborhood has been upgraded, and there have been opportunities to participate as an undervalued neighborhood becomes recognized.

What lies ahead for investors in Long Island City? There are many who believe that the recovery and development shall be of monumental proportions. There are those who predict that Long Island City will become the new Hollywood. Predictions are that the development of the neighborhood will continue many blocks to the south and west, and along the East River, with investors reaping the rewards. The renaissance will bring a large number of jobs as radio, television, film, and commercial production continues. There will be a need for large numbers of laborers to make it all possible. For buyers of undervalued properties, there might prove to be no business like show business.

RISKS AND REWARDS OF VACATION PROPERTIES

While the idea of investing in undervalued real estate near a motion picture studio is exciting, real estate doesn't have to be exciting to be profitable. It is a way of becoming actively involved when you have limited resources for investing. When buying an undervalued property, you are purchasing land at a discount and subsequently lowering your risk. There is risk in undervalued properties—the property could remain undervalued for a long period of time before it is recognized. The amount of use for a property determines its desirability to investors and the likelihood that will be recognized by investors as a bargain. Vacation or recreational land is one area that fits into the category of a high risk investment. Not to suggest that you are likely to lose your investment, it just that there is no assurance that the land will be in demand. It could be two years, twenty years, or never. However, while it carries a higher risk than other real estate investments, it also has much higher reward possibilities. Who knows if those twenty acres in the middle of nowhere will ten years from now be overlooking a multimillion-dollar ski resort or shopping mall? Vacation properties have that potential. Are vacation properties for you?

If you think vacation properties are great places for hunting, skiing, swimming, and playing tennis you are right. But they can do more than that. Undervalued vacation properties can also help lead the way to financial independence. With a vacation property, you have a getaway spot from the nine-to-five potboiler. At the same time it is possible to make the ''good buy'' that brightens your financial picture. The trick is to locate a vacation property in an undervalued area with a good deal. Buying at a deep discount from the retail price helps ensure a profit when you decide to sell.

A big problem in considering a vacation property for investment is the cost factor. Buying recreational land is unlike buying residential properties in established communities. Some investors see potential in undeveloped areas while others seek run-down vacation properties in areas undergoing renovation as the better route. Whether vacation property is undeveloped or run-down, you must consider these factors before opening your wallet:

1. Proximity to well-known vacation areas.
2. The cost of large parcels vs. small parcels.
3. The importance of a southern exposure.
4. The need to comply with zoning and building laws.
5. The desirability of waterfront property.

Any investor would want a property adjoining a popular vacation resort. To be five hundred feet away from a well-known ski resort would be a dream come true, but it's not possible unless you have megabucks. The closer you are to a popular resort, the more costly it will be. To keep the property in an affordable range, it is best to purchase property about fifteen to twenty minutes away by car from the attraction.

Everybody loves privacy. It's often repeated that good fences make good neighbors. That isn't because people love neighbors less, but rather that they love their privacy more. Anyone who is buying recreational property should consider the privacy factor. How much land do you need to go with your house? You probably feel that one acre would be all the property you need. But guess what? The cost per acre when you buy ten acres will cost much less than the cost of one acre. You can get a much better buy when you purchase land with more acreage. Besides, if it complies with zoning laws, you might be able to subdivide and sell off additional acres.

Although you might not care in the slightest about it, you must consider southern exposure. A property should have the sun from 10 A.M. to 2 P.M. The property is considered to be more desirable, more salable, and more expensive because such properties can make maximum use of solar heat.

Just because the seller or real estate agent calls the land vacation acreage doesn't mean you can build a ski resort or swimming complex. Like any other property, check it out before you buy it. Ask for a copy of the land survey or lot, block, and section codes. Then call up the zoning department and learn about any restrictions there might be on that particular piece of land. Call the building department to see if there are requirements about the frontage or boundary requirements. Don't assume that you can do what you want with your own piece of the rock. Never assume that because your land is near or adjoining something you'd like to build that the local laws will allow you to do so. Check first.

It can't be said often enough. They aren't making anymore waterfront property. Waterfront property is always more expensive than a similar property that is not waterfront. Still the initial expense pays off. Waterfront property appreciates much faster. In recreational properties, riverfront, oceanfront, and lakefront are prime real estate. Properties containing ponds, streams, and brooks are also in increasing demand. If you have a choice between a property on the water and one that is not, buy the one on the water if you can afford it. It will be that much easier to sell when you make that decision.

PROPERTY TURNAROUND ASSESSMENT

Investors who are interested in vacation properties know that cost factors are to be considered in any purchase decision. Still, they are not unanimous in their approach to vacation property as an investment. There is no right or wrong area of investment in undervalued vacation properties, however there are common factors that identify a property that is ripe for a turnaround. Complete the Property turnaround assessment checklist and count up the number of YES responses. If you have six or more YES responses, the chances are that your area is a turnaround situation. Note that the period of three years is used. That is because extraordinary circumstances could have distorted the statistics in the past year. There could have been unfavorable weather, a health scare, or any number of reasons.

1. Have sale prices shown an average yearly increase of ten percent or more in the last three years?
2. Have rental prices risen at least ten percent per year in the last three years?
3. During the popular season have there been vacancies in the last three years?
4. Have zoning laws been passed to control the amount of new building in the area?
5. Have large resorts in the area been expanding or renovating?
6. As you visit the area does it appear that properties are being maintained or improved?
7. Is local business prospering?
8. Do you see many vacant stores in town?
9. Are the prices of properties rising faster in this area than other nearby vacation areas?
10. Are large corporations making commitments to book events there?
11. Are hotels and motels acquiring property in the area?
12. When properties are put up for sale, do they remain on the market for less than ninety days?

TIME SHARING IS NOT AN INVESTMENT

Watch out. Time sharing is not a vacation property investment. Time sharing or interval ownership gives you the right to occupy a particular property for the same week every year for however long the agreement provides. It is not a real estate investment, but rather a vacation investment. Time sharing is a great place for vacations but a terrible place for your investment money. Time shares cannot be easily sold, and then only at far less than you paid. The deed you are given expires after a certain number of years and doesn't control one hundred percent of the property's ownership. Actual vacation property investment consists of purchasing an entire property for keeps. Buying a well-located vacation property at a good price and on the right terms can help pave the way to financial success. Time shares will only help pave the driveway of the developer.

RAW LAND IN THE DIRECT PATH OF GROWTH

Buying land just because they're not making any more is like buying a boneless chicken for a dance contest. However, buying land that is currently out of favor is a sensible strategy. Quite often you will come upon a tract of land that has been sitting on the market for many months without a bite. Yet directly to the north, raw land is selling briskly. The raw land that is selling could be listed with an aggressive real estate broker who is touting it as a possible hot spot if gambling is legalized or a location for a hotel or a shopping center. As a result of effective marketing, tracts to the north sell at a premium to tracts in the south. Eventually, the interest might spread to areas in the south, east, and west. The problem is that your hair might turn white and your great grandchildren might feel the offer is too low. So buying raw land on the prospect of an eventual gold mine is a long shot.

Hardly anything is certain these days. However buying raw land that is in the process of being rezoned is much less risky than buying parcels in God's country and praying. If the zoning on land is upgraded, the profit potential of the land will increase. If two acres of farmland is about to be turned into residential property, there could be a money tree in your front yard. The trick is to locate raw land that is likely to be developed or changed within a certain time period. There could be a zoning change allowing land in the town to be used for a different purpose than currently. Environment or other restrictions could be lifted. Attending zoning board meetings, which are open to the public, could prove to be both enlightening and enriching. When the land is in its raw state, it is land with potential, similar to the starlet with looks and talent but without a contract. Until the starlet's talent or the raw land's potential is developed, each is just a hope.

Many frustrated landowners will tell you this. Not all vacant land gets developed. Some sits idle while the owner pays finance costs, maintenance and taxes for years and years.

Other factors make raw land less than desirable. For one thing, raw land has no great worth until a developer is willing to buy it and build on it, and there is no guarantee that a builder will make such an offer. If there is change in zoning laws or local planning board laws, your property might become unsuitable for its original purpose. If you had been thinking about keeping part of the land and selling off the remainder, you could be prevented from doing so by new legislation.

Is raw land for you? Raw land is not all negative. There are thousands of people across our country who have made millions through raw land. It is still being done today. People are buying forty-acre parcels in rural areas of the country where the land is very inexpensive. In such undiscovered areas it is possible to purchase land at about three hundred dollars an acre. Then the people sell the land in ten-acre parcels to other land speculators. A forty-acre parcel is difficult to sell, while a ten-acre parcel is easier. Therefore, each ten-acre parcel will sell proportionally per acre for more than the original forty-acre parcel. If an investor can sell all four ten-acre parcels, a handsome profit will be realized. Of course, such ventures are not for the average investor, but it shows how an aggressive investor can profit from raw land.

If you are more familiar with raw oysters than raw land, then you are not a likely candidate for forty-acre parcels. When you buy raw land, you are gambling—plain and simple. You are betting, in the case of rural raw land, that the growth in population in the directional path of your land will make it more popular than it is today.

The value of raw land is determined by many factors. Among them are:

☞ Zoning laws allowing construction
☞ Access to drinking water
☞ Access to drinkable water
☞ Level land
☞ Access to power lines and telephone lines
☞ Convenience to highways and main streets

STAGES OF REAL ESTATE

Raw land doesn't remain in the same state forever. A real estate property moves through six stages in its career. The stages are:

Stage 1—Raw land
Stage 2—Construction
Stage 3—Getting Established
Stage 4—Stability
Stage 5—Decline
Stage 6—Rediscovery

Raw land, as the name implies, is real estate that has not been developed. It is land in its natural state. It has no sewers, no water, no plumbing. Raw land can be compared to the raw talent of a young baseball slugger. He has the power, but until he learns to hit the curveball he will be just a talent with potential. The raw land could be an empty lot in the inner city, a wooded area along the highway, or a forty-acre parcel to be subdivided into ten-acre parcels in Colorado. The raw land is not always valuable or desirable. It might have been in this condition for fifty years and could stay as raw land for another fifty. Whether or not it has use to a builder or developer will help determine how long it will remain raw land.

Construction

If you live in a major metropolitan area suburb, as we do, there is not much vacant land. Every now and then a long-term property owner decides to sell a parcel of his or her land to a developer. The developer applies for the necessary permits and variances, gets the approvals and construction begins. In the Long Island township where we reside, builders in recent years have been acquiring raw land and building multifamily houses. Consumer groups protested the over-development and brought pressure on the local government to combat the population density problem. Town boards responded with legislation requiring minimum plot size and minimum frontage requirements. Intended to stop building, it has not. However developers have found it more difficult to profitably build on the raw land they acquire, due to the high cost of land on Long Island. As long as there is money to be made anywhere, builders will continue to acquire well-situated raw land and build.

Getting Established

Surviving the construction of a home, retail store, or shopping center isn't easy. Until then you thought that living on the edge was not rewinding the video before returning it to the video store. During construction you learn first-hand of the delays, unexpected costs, no-shows, and conflicts when working with builders or contractors. Once the property is in turnkey condition, ready to throw off some income, you must get established.

Getting established means getting yourself in a stable position financially. You must find a quality tenant, set the ground rules, and earn a return on your investment. Through advertising on your own or listing with a broker, you must rent at a positive cash flow. Finding a quality tenant who maintains and improves the property is your goal here. At the same time you'll be earning a positive cash flow that does wonders for your piece of mind.

Stability

Property management has become well established. The tenant knows your expectations. The property seems to be in cruise control. Though it has taken good training and proper planning, properties appear to be running themselves. Having set guidelines on which responsibilities the tenant assumes, you have a minimum of repairs requiring your time and money, as well as few vacancies. With an established, smooth-running operation, you are able to raise rents every time there is a tenant turnover, thereby maximizing your cash flow. By fine-tuning your management strategies, you encourage tenants to maintain properties by themselves and only call you for a major repair. With your properties requiring a minimum amount of your attention, you are able to purchase and develop additional properties.

Decline

Decline is not a pleasant word. Yet all things do decline in condition, some more slowly than others. Despite routine maintenance and delegation of upkeep to tenants, eventually the property falls into disrepair. Trying to maximize your positive cash flow, you postpone the new roof, upgrading of the electrical system, or new heating system. You find yourself with major repairs and a property that is slipping.

To complicate matters a new strip shopping center or apartment building is opening down the block to compete with yours for tenants. To attract your tenants they are offering lower rents and other perks, as well as squeaky clean premises. You decide to hold your ground and reduce costs to maintain profitability. But little by little the property begins to slip, as repairs are overlooked to conserve money. Eventually the property is not up to par, and tenants are not willing to renew.

You have a problem on your hands. What will you do? Either you are going to pour a truckload of money into the property, put it up at a lower than market price to sell, or abandon the property. If you are receiving summonses for violations on major repairs, you cannot afford or obtain financing, abandoning the property is your only option.

Neighborhoods Decline Rapidly

Many neighborhoods of the same age tend to decline at about the same time unless efforts are made to restore them. A neighborhood in decline has burned-out and abandoned houses, and large numbers of vacant stores. The neighborhood gives the appearance of a war zone. Despite the sense of hopelessness, you are looking at an undervalued area. It is undervalued because there is little demand for an area that is falling apart. Buyers and renters are scarce, if they have a choice. The state of decline remains until buyers step in once again to restore properties and make renovations. It could be months, years, or decades.

Rediscovery

Rediscovery occurs in many different ways. It can result from the gutting of entire houses and blocks and building of new structures. It can be major renovations of existing run-down properties. Rediscovery is the final stage of the land cycle, after the land has declined as far as it can.

Rediscovery usually takes many years. Prospect Heights, home of the famous Prospect Park of Brooklyn, New York, is an example of a neighborhood undergoing rediscovery. Prospect Heights in 1981 was a neighborhood of almost 10,000 brownstones and apartments, many in disrepair. The area had been declining for more than twenty years. Despite the presence of 526 acres of Prospect Park, the Brooklyn Museum and the Brooklyn Botanic Garden, Prospect Heights had become a neighborhood of deteriorating houses and an overabundance of drugs.

Property values were at rock bottom. A four story brownstone was selling for the incredibly low price of $20,000. Then gentrification set in. Middle-class people decided they wanted the convenience of Manhattan without paying Manhattan prices. People decided to move back from the suburbs to be closer to the city. People discovered considerably lower rental and selling prices in Prospect Heights. The turnaround had begun.

Eventually you could see empty buildings being rejuvenated on virtually every block. Though change has been slow, almost three thousand of the ten thousand homes were renovated in a five year period. Friends of friends and relatives have remained on waiting lists for housing. To meet the growing need, developers have offered to relocate tenants of dilapidated buildings into renovated apartments in other parts of Prospect Heights.

The change both physical and economic has been startling. Co-op prices have soared as have the prices of condominiums and refurbished brownstones. The brownstones that were selling for $20,000 have risen to the $400,000 range, as Prospect Heights continues in the rediscovery stage.

Commercial Recovery Follows Residential

The rediscovery stage of a neighborhood does not stop or start on a dime. It is a long process. Even with the housing situation of a neighborhood in a steady period of recovery, the commercial area will not undergo immediate improvement. The commercial sector, including the stores and office buildings, experience a slower recovery. In Prospect Heights, for example, the main shopping area has taken a number of years to catch up with the revival of the residential market, though it has been catching up. Secondary shopping areas take much longer to recover. Areas that were drug infested or crime ridden will be the last to show improvement, since investors and consumers will avoid the area.

Getting in on the Ground Floor

The rediscovery period can be a very profitable time for the investor. For one thing, it presents a timely opportunity to get in on or near the lowest prices. If you buy before the big money comes into an area, there are advantages as well as disadvantages. While you might be getting in on the ground floor, the prices could stay in the basement until the rediscovery takes solid hold. In the case of Prospect Heights, the rediscovery period has lasted almost ten years. At the beginning you would have wondered if anything would ever develop. But then when the rediscovery took hold it was evident that big money was pouring into the area and prices would rise substantially. If you had invested once the rediscovery was in full force, you would be paying higher prices, but your money would be working for you from the start.

All during a rediscovery stage there are profit-making opportunities. Following the buy-high, sell-higher approach you can make money, as long as you realize that you are not buying at the absolute bottom and prices might not continue to rise at the same rate. At the beginning you can invest virtually anywhere in the recovering area and sell for a long term profit. The area close to a major park, water, museum, hospital, or major attraction is likely to be the first location to be refurbished and is the best choice for investment. Surrounding blocks are renovated next and are also a good opportunity to share in the redevelopment, at lower prices than the prime area. Once the recovery is in full throttle the primary commercial area shows signs of recovery, as people more economically advantaged spend money in the neighborhood. Investment in the commercial primary area pays rich rewards as increased business volume from improving neighborhood demographics results in higher selling prices on retail properties and increased rents for renters. If you miss the boat on investing in commercial property in the primary commercial area and refuse to pay the inflated prices, you still have considerable time to invest in the secondary shopping areas of the neighborhood. Investing in the secondary areas often requires nerves of steel, as you see boarded-up stores alongside yours and frequently drug addicts hanging out on the corner. It is clearly not for every investor.

Eventually secondary commercial areas do recover. Gentrification causes a demand for stores selling fresh meat, dairy products, take-out foods, dry cleaners, and recreational services. You can invest profitably in the secondary areas if you have a nest egg to finance the investment as it slowly recovers and the ice that is running in your veins begins to thaw. Investing in undervalued areas requires a great deal of imagination, patience, and courage. You must be the kind of person who sees a glass as half-full rather than half-empty to make it work with undervalued properties because there is so much of the down side that you see at the beginning of the rediscovery stage. People will say your elevator doesn't go all the way to the top when you describe or show the properties to your colleagues. If you are thick-skinned with the desire to succeed and are not afraid to wait it out, investing in undervalued areas could be very lucrative.

SUMMARY

Although neither a crystal ball nor Tarot cards will tell you the future of real estate, a knowledge of supply and demand in areas will help. There are more clearcut signs that particular properties are poised for a rise without the use of supernatural powers. You can spot a nearby property that is having a commercial rebirth and invest several blocks from the hot spot, so that you can purchase it before any interest surfaces. Use the UPI to identify qualities in property that can offer you a groundfloor opportunity to real estate fortunes.

Knowing what to look for in undervalued raw land can spell the difference between a great investment and a raw deal. Real estate properties move through six stages of development in their career. The stages are raw land, construction, getting established, stability, decline, and rediscovery. Being aware of the particular area's stage can help in locating areas ripe for investment as well as those to avoid. If you have the desire to succeed and are willing to conduct the research and act on your findings, your investments in undervalued properties can pay rich rewards.

3

Bargain-Hunting Basics

Definition of a Bargain: Something you don't need at a price you can't resist!

YOU MIGHT NOT KNOW EXACTLY WHERE YET, BUT SOMEWHERE OUT THERE waits a bargain property with your name on it.

Of course bargain property is still around because it hasn't been discovered by a street-smart bargain hunter. In a department store it seems to be much easier to spot a bargain. Signs are displayed throughout the store and announcements are broadcast alerting you that the sweater that usually sells for $39.99 is on sale for $19.99. At $19.99 the sweater seems to be a bargain. But what makes it a bargain? Is it because the store claims that the price has been reduced by twenty dollars? Possibly, but not unless the twenty dollar reduction is legitimate, and the product is better than others that can be bought elsewhere at the same price.

FINDING THE GOLD

A mere low price does not make an item a bargain—not a sweater and not a real estate property. A bargain is only a bargain when it compares favorably to a similar product that sells at the same or a lower price. Just as the department store bargain is not always what it seems, a real estate bargain is not always the great buy it appears to be. Many factors help determine whether you are buying a golden opportunity or fool's gold. That bargain really exists, but do you know where to find it?

Painting a Favorable Deal

Have you heard the usual advice that only the best neighborhoods make good investments? Some real estate seminars recognize sound investments by three factors: LOCATION, LOCATION, LOCATION! Yes, it is true that no matter what part of the country you're looking to invest in, the property location is important. Unless there's a local catastrophe, a property with appeal that is in a desirable neighborhood when it's time to buy will have appeal when it's time to sell. A property doesn't have to be beautiful to be a great investment property. Location, while important, is not the most important factor when purchasing investment properties. You are, after all, buying properties for investment profits and not for marriage. You don't fall in love with real estate, you fall in love with the profits they earn.

You can't overlook location. Common sense tells you that a great house facing a meat packing plant is not a good investment. Great house, yes; great investment, no! Certain factors make one block or one neighborhood more desirable than another. Closeness to schools and houses of worship, availability of public transportation, low crime rate, well-run schools, and proximity to shopping are all factors a potential investor should consider before making a purchase. Although you won't be living there, the person who buys or rents your house will seek some of these facets.

Though location is important to an investment, the DEAL is the critical factor. Naturally, if you can make a great deal and manage a terrific location, the deal is just that much sweeter. To paraphrase a popular sports motto, ''The deal isn't the best thing, it's the only thing.'' Buying a property at the right price and on the best terms produces the best deal and the maximum profit opportunity. What good is it to have a great location if you are paying too much for the property? Don't overpay for location. You'll never be able to recoup your investment if you overpay.

When you focus in on the location, it's too easy to lose sight of the entire picture. Think of a painting taking special note of all the details including its frame. You could focus your eyes on just the beautiful frame. Perhaps a charming cottage in the painting catches your eye. The wall where the painting is hung also draws your attention. Yes, these are important details, but you must sit back and focus on the entire picture. Do all the details seem to work for the perfect picture? In the same vein, do all the terms of the real estate deal seem to be favorable to you? Zero in on the deal and not the details. Evaluate the overall deal and whether the terms are favorable to you.

TWO DEALS: IT'S YOUR CHOICE

Consider a split-level house in an affluent suburb. The school is two blocks away and the house of worship is five blocks away. On the next block there is a pool and cabana club. Free club membership is deeded to the house. The seller has no mortgage. No owner financing is available. However, the owner will close the deal and move out at the buyer's convenience.

The second house is a brick row house in a metropolitan neighborhood. The school is several blocks away, while the house of worship is about ten blocks away. The seller needs to sell his house quickly because he has been transferred. He is willing to give back a mortgage at the current interest rate.

From thumbnail sketches you might get through realtors and neighbors, you must learn to overview the picture. Which house probably would provide the better deal? If you pick the first house because of its neighborhood, you could be making a serious mistake. While the first house might be a better selection for a residence because of the location and amenities, you are purchasing it for investment and not for your primary residence. The second house would likely be the better investment. The seller must move. He appears to be flexible because he is willing to take back a mortgage at favorable terms. You are probably buying the house at a better price because the seller must sell. You are also saving thousands of dollars in closing costs by not having to take out your own mortgage through a bank. Bank fees are costly. Add the bank fees onto the purchase price of the property to determine if the deal is really worth it.

When purchasing investment property many investors lose sight of the fact that they will not be living in the house. Buying at a deep discount and making cosmetic improvements and cost-effective repairs will transfer your investment into a success in every deal. An average location can offer superior profit potential if the price and terms are favorable. Having an elevator is no guarantee of a gold mine but not having good judgment is a guarantee of the shaft. Beware.

HOW MUCH IS ENOUGH?

Keeping in mind that you must zero in on favorable terms, let's make a deal. Answer three questions and you're ready to deal:

1. In your region, you must put down a certain percentage of cash for a down payment. How much cash will you put down?
2. How much in closing costs and legal expenses will you encounter? Deduct them from the above amount.
3. Now putting down that amount in number 2, what is the maximum price you will be able to pay?

Knowing our highest price line figure was $139,000, we contacted a realtor with whom we had done considerable business. While we were insistent on a particular neighborhood, she was aware that our primary concern was the deal. We sat down in her private office where she opened her multiple listing books for us to browse. Familiar with our needs, she removed a half dozen listings from her book and explained the particulars. All were in the price range we specified. At our direction the realtor called the sellers to see if the houses were still available. Some had been sold; others had been taken off the market. Still others had been reduced in price.

One house sparked our interest. It was a house priced at $149,900 in a neighborhood where houses were priced in the $400,000 range. We were realistic enough not to delude ourselves into believing it was a $400,000 house, but we could see that the house would offer affordable housing in an affluent neighborhood.

One look at the house and anyone could see why it didn't have any takers. The house faced a busy street and had no garage. Upon more careful inspection you could see beyond the obvious flaws that the house was a "diamond in the rough." First of all, the house was situated on large property, approximately 50×150, with definite expansion possibilities. In one direction, it faced a thriving restaurant with inadequate parking. In another, it faced a $1,000,000 all-electric waterfront house with inadequate parking. For the icing on the cake, there was a marina down the street that was under contract to build condominiums within a two-block radius. Although we could see from the date on the listing that the house had been on the market for many months, there seemed to be little interest in the property. But to us the potential seemed intriguing in many directions. Three potential developments made this property a special situation. Anyone could lead to a purchase offer at a substantial profit. Though there were no assurances, there were several possibilities: the condominium could purchase our property for a business office or model home, the restaurant could seek additional parking, the million dollar home would seek to build the pool and cabana and health club facility they had informally mentioned to us, and business zoning might be a future possibility. The only drawback seemed to be bluntly— the house was ugly. Yet this house was a solid buy on its own merits. It was a winning situation. By buying the house and renting to a tenant, we could receive a positive cash flow each month, even if nothing further developed. And if something did develop, we would make a large capital gain to augment the positive cash flow we had earned.

It doesn't take a rocket scientist to figure out what we did. As long as we could buy below the market this house was a must. Because of the heavy traffic outside the house, the house had been on the market for several months and drawn no bids. The asking price was $150,000. Since the rule of successful investing is to avoid paying retail, we offered less. Our bid of $138,000 was turned down, but our subsequent bid of $139,000 was accepted. Even though our bid was well below the asking price, the realtor was under an obligation to submit all bids. All realtors are required to. In any case, terms were agreed on and the deal was completed over the ensuing months.

Perhaps it seems as if we counted on too many long shots to happen if our deal was to hit. However, we didn't feel that way at all. We calculated our costs before making the bid. By checking the local houses and departments for rent in the classified ads, we were able to determine what rent would be expected for such a house in the neighborhood. And we know how much our monthly mortgage payments would be. We would have a positive cash flow. With a positive cash flow we could wait forever for any of the developments to take place. We would take a deal like this any day of the week.

USING REAL ESTATE AGENTS

Yes, we used the real estate agent for this deal because she had the house and was able to cement the deal through negotiations. Deal with professional real estate agents with whom you feel comfortable. It is the real estate agent who holds the deck and deals the cards. The real estate agent who puts the deal together often means the difference between a deal that flies and a deal that falls apart. The real estate agent knows the condition of the house, having seen it, the reason the house is being sold, how much the seller needs from the house, etc., etc. Even though the real estate agent represents the seller and not you, the agent can tell you if your submitted bid is in the ballpark. As with any profession some real estate agents are more competent and more experienced than others.

To find out if the real estate agent you are using is the top of the heap or just a heap, fill out the Real Estate Agent Checklist. There are positive as well as negative attributes listed. A positive attribute earns one point, while a negative attribute earns none. A score of seven or higher qualifies a real estate agent as the right person to represent you. A score of less than seven would suggest that the real estate agent might not be right for you. Though the agent is the seller's broker and not yours, the person can still be an irreplaceable aid in putting together a good deal for you.

Real Estate Agent Checklist

1. The real estate agent has been local resident for three years or more and is active in the community.
2. The agent has at least three year's experience in sales.
3. The agent works in the office on a full-time basis.
4. The agent shows you houses in a price range that is appropriate for you (the price range you requested).
5. The agent previews property and screens it before showing it to you.

6. The real estate broker has a knowledge of finance and has connections with lenders.
7. The broker knows the car routes and visits properties in an organized way.
8. The real estate agent discloses faults and potential problems.
9. The agent allows you time to evaluate without undue pressure.
10. The real estate broker does not criticize other brokers.
11. Flexible or negotiable commissions are common practices.

Don't seek out a wheeler-dealer who promises to make you a fortune. If he could, he would not be sitting across the desk trying to earn a commission by selling to you. You want someone with information and negotiating skills. If we could step out of the pages and hold your hand, we'd point you in the direction of your first goal. Goal: find at least one real estate sales person with a high enough score who you feel comfortable with in conversation.

Your Agent

With the agent you have chosen through our guidelines, make an appointment to look through the multiple listing books. Making an appointment is a wise move. It saves you time and allows the broker to match properties with your needs before you get there. The real estate agent in many cases is personally familiar with the property and has met the seller or spoken by phone. The agent has broken the ice and perhaps learned the seller's current situation. Though agents can't ethically disclose the information to you, the agent can intelligently put together a deal. The agent will know whether the seller is looking for a quick deal, has turned down many bids, or doesn't immediately need the proceeds. Knowing what the seller needs from the sale is important information for you.

A wise real estate agent knows how and when to compromise. A foolish broker plays take it or leave it games. Since good agents often have an idea of the bottom line figure the seller will accept, the agent will have to create money to bridge the gap between what you are willing to pay and the minimum the seller will accept. To some agents it is known as the forbidden C word. In other words it is cutting commissions and some brokers refuse to acknowledge that it exists. Smart brokers cut their commissions whenever necessary to make a deal, figuring that three percent of something is a lot better than seven percent of nothing.

What is the truth about real estate commissions? The truth is that real estate commissions are not fixed. There is no standard commission. However, some large chain real estates that reach across the U.S. try to operate on a fixed rate commission. They can continue such practices because they deal with major corporations that pay their commissions to relocate corporate executives.

If you are not a large corporation, don't pay commissions as they do. All commissions are negotiable. Knowing the market, the customers, and the lenders, and having the good sense to compromise, a real estate agent can be one of the best bargain-hunting sources available to the buyer.

Personal Checking

Although an agent helped us find that diamond in the rough, many of our deals we found and nurtured without agents. You must be able to find the for sale signs, but also to read the signs of the owner. What financial and emotional signals is the owner sending?

SIGNS TELL A STORY

Watch out for those signs. A motivated seller must be flexible in either price or the terms of the sale. The seller could offer a second mortgage, provide owner financing at or below market rates, accept nothing down as a down payment or accept merchandise or other property as a down payment. Where there's a will to sell there's a way to make a deal. Obviously, the more desperate the seller the more willing the seller is to compromise on the terms of the sale. Looking for the right signs will make you aware of good opportunities. Strange as it might seem, there are houses being offered at wholesale prices in your neighborhood and mine today. Ride up and down your streets. If your neighborhood is like ours there are more FOR SALE signs than STOP signs. Not long ago a string of FOR SALE signs would have been the first sign of a deteriorating neighborhood. That is no longer the case. For various reasons people have decided to sell their homes. It could be the large price appreciation of the last ten years and the desire to cash in profits. It could be that children have grown and moved out, leaving the nest empty. Maybe there has been a divorce, a marriage, a job transfer, or a decision to roll over the profits into a more expensive house. Whatever the reason, it is a fact that one of every five Americans moves every year. Another statistic states that the average American moves every seven years.

As you look at houses make mental notes about the properties. There are always exceptions, but in general, a house in disrepair will have an owner willing to deal. That person will have little time, little money, or little interest in holding onto the house. The seller's headache might become your blessing. Let your fingers do the walking and the seller do the talking. Try to find out diplomatically why the owner is selling and what is being done with the money. No one can tell you the exact way to ask the question because each of us has a unique personality. However, it does matter why the person is selling. If the person is being forced to sell because of circumstances, that person will be more likely to meet your terms. As far as learning what the seller will do with the money, you will learn if the person needs the money to make the move. It is possible that money is not the reason the seller is moving. The person might just want to have the financial and custodial responsibility removed. By learning about the proceeds of the sale you might be able to help the seller and yourself.

Anyone can ask tactfully why the person is selling and what will be done with the money. Why ask? By asking you will discover if the person needs the money to make the move. If the seller doesn't need the money, you might want to rent out the property from the seller and find a tenant. You will use a Lease with an Option to buy form that will give you the responsibility of paying the monthly rent as well as the opportunity of purchasing the property at an agreed-upon price within a specified time period. A Lease with an Option to buy form can be found at the back of this book in the last chapter. The seller profits because he or she is able to meet the payments without watching over the property. You profit because you are able to tie up the property at today's prices without spending your own money.

No one is exactly like you, so no one knows exactly how you think, feel or speak. Just as a guide, here is a conversation that could take place between a potential buyer and a seller. Sellers don't always make for easy conversations.

Buyer—"I passed by your house and found it very interesting. May I ask you a few questions?"

Seller—"Sure, what would you like to know?"

Buyer—"How long have you had the house up for sale?"
    (If it has been many months or a year the person is likely to be flexible).

Seller—"About three months."

Buyer—"About how many offers have you received?"

Seller—"About five or ten."

Buyer—"Could you please tell me why you haven't accepted any?"

Seller—"I don't really want to discuss it."

Buyer—"Excuse my questions, but I'm just trying to see how I can help. Could you just answer a few more questions?"

Seller—"All right."

Buyer—"Are there any major repairs that will have to be made in the next six months?"
    (If the person makes a false statement he or she will be held responsible).

Seller—"No."

Buyer—"If we can reach a deal, what are you going to do with the money?"

Seller—"I'm not sure. Why?"

Buyer—"I only want to see how we can work things out."

If you meet with reluctance to answer, try to explain that you are trying to find out how you can reach a deal and solve her problem. Never lose sight that the motivated seller has a problem, and you have the solution.

SELLER PROBLEM SOLVER

Here are some of the common problems that you could encounter from a motivated seller. Note some of the ways you can help solve the problem.

Illness or death	Price reduction for a quick sale
Job transfer	Ability to make a deal on price and terms if money is not needed to move
Divorce	Less negotiability in price because of need for cash
Foreclosure	Offer of several thousand dollars and take-over debt
Second home	Need for quick deal Offer large amount of cash for quick closing
Retirement	Possibility of getting financing by seller if paying full price

READING THE CLASSIFIEDS

HOUSE FOR SALE signs are not the only way for sellers to market their houses. A useful source of information for street-smart bargain hunters is the classified ads in the daily newspaper or Pennysaver. Listed under the heading REAL ESTATE FOR SALE many anxious owners advertise their houses for sale. The term FSBO indicates that the property is For Sale By Owner. It is a statement to you that the owner is selling without a broker and without a commission. Investors often refer to people who are motivated to sell as Don't Wanters. As the name implies they don't want the house and want out. For any number of reasons a Don't Wanter wants to unload an unwanted burden, soon!

How do you spot a Don't Wanter? While the person doesn't wear a sign saying "Take my house, Please," the signs are almost as clear. The wording of the newspaper ads offer clues to the desperation of the seller. Look for these terms in the ads to help you identify the motivated seller's willingness to deal. It shows the seller wants to deal faster.

The Deal Faster Reference

☑ Desperate
☑ Empty, vacant
☑ Assumable loan, no qualifying
☑ Little down, nothing down
☑ Flexible, will consider all offers
☑ All offers
☑ Sale by owner
☑ Transferred, moving out of state
☑ Equity participation
☑ Rent to buy, lease with option

Classified Ads

Below are actual listings from a daily newspaper. The names of the towns have been changed, as have the phone numbers. Read each listing and see if you can locate the word or words that show the seller is motivated and seem to advertise a Don't Wanter. Not every ad listed has a motivated seller.

1. *Parksville.* 5% down. 115,900. 3-bedroom ranch, dining room, garage, fenced, low taxes, full basement, den. Owner anxious. Broker—475-5500.

2. *Plaindome.* Busy corner building, 8 rooms, zoned commercial, owner must sell, possible rental, $225,000. 988-5000.

3. *Roseville.* $129,990. Adorable 3-bedroom ranch, dining room, garage, fenced, low taxes, won't last, 757-2552.

4. *Woodside brick building for sale.* Gigantic store, 1400 sq. ft w/3 br apt., owner will take back 2nd mtge. Best offer. 221-4944.

5. *Meadowlawn.* Vacant split-level, walk to R.R., eat-in-kitchen, 3 bedrooms, 2 baths, family room, $179,990. 541-3900.

6. *Los Ranchos.* 3-bedroom townhouse, parklike grounds, owner retiring, 878-6921.

7. *Corning.* 99,990. 100% financing available on 3-bedroom cape. Owner will help with closing costs, only $7,000 cash needed. 878-6885.

8. *Newport.* Unique 2-bedroom condo, brick with fireplace, 2 baths. Must see. $259,000 firm. 678-4992.

Let's compare your answers to ours and see if you identified the Don't Wanters.

1. *Parksville.* ''Owner anxious'' tells you that the owner is willing to make a quick deal on favorable terms to you.

2. *Plaindome*. "Owner must sell" is a sign of the owner's need for quick action. "Possible rental" tells you that the owner is so anxious to sell that if you don't buy it, he'll even rent it.

3. *Roseville*. "Won't last" is not a sign of motivated seller. It usually is a sales pitch. Could it really mean that the house will fall down if you blow on it?

4. *Woodside*. "Owner will take back a second mortgage" is a sign of flexibility that shows she is anxious to sell.

5. *Meadowland*. "Vacant" tells you that the person couldn't get a buyer and moved out. Now he is stuck with it. Paying taxes and mortgage on a vacant house is not a seller's idea of fun.

6. *Los Ranchos*. "Owner retiring" tells you that the owner wants to get out and get on with her life.

7. *Corning*. "100% financing available" means just take it off my hands, so I don't have to make any more payments. "Owner will help you with closing costs" means I'll even pay your expenses if you take it.

8. *Newport*. "Must see" does not indicate that the seller is motivated. It is only a real estate buzzword. "Firm" indicates the owner is not willing to negotiate.

Read and evaluate the ads in Fig. 3-1. Try to determine why particular ones appeal to you.

SOHO Area Investor-Property
Owner anxious-ridiculous price! 2BR, 1bth. Low mtg. 212-555-6430.

87 ST/MADISON BY OWNER
Spacious 1 BR, huge clsts, 24-hr drmn, immed. Make offer $195K. 203-555-2097

BALDWIN DISCOUNT CO-OPS
Builder offers deal of a lifetime-name your price. Hurry. Financing avail. Call 516-555-0017

$REDUCED$
MERRICK NORTH-Expanded Cape, EIK, LR, DR, 3-4 BR, 2 full baths. Potential. Principals. $170,000. 516-555-8555.

PRICED TO SELL
MERRICK-Colonial
Living room, dining room, den, 1½ baths, garage. $189,900. 516-555-1000

HICKSVILLE 150's
OWNER RETIRING
Maint free 5 rm Ranch, formal DR, new custom kitchen. lo taxes. "OWNER SAYS SELL"
Broker 516-555-2900

HUNTINGTON-BRICK CAPE
REDUCE DRASTICALLY $155,900 516-555-6475

FARMINGVILLE $137,200
OWNER MUST SELL. 4 BDRM COLONIAL, NEW KIT, NEW WINDOW, WON'T LAST. Broker 516-555-3800.

NORTH SHORE OFFICE BLDG. Prime location. 5,200 sq ft. newly renovated + sep. bldg plot. Guaranteed rents over $90K/yr, triple net. Must accept best offer by 9/1. Owner. 516-555-5600.

SEAFORD-Reduced Thousands.
Dual Ranch features 3 bdrms, eik, din rm, bsmt w/ outside entr, gar, deck, owner transferred. offered at $169,990. Broker 203-555-7880.

I DON'T WANT IT YOU CAN HAVE IT

Sometimes the house shows itself as a Don't Wanter. By examining certain tell-tale signs of a neglected property, you can often spot a Don't Wanter. How many of these signs are present?

☞ Peeling paint on the exterior
☞ Seriously cracked driveways and sidewalks
☞ High grass and weeds
☞ Broken windows and storm doors
☞ Vehicles parked on the lawn
☞ Cars without license plates on the property
☞ Debris scattered on property
☞ Property appears vacant or abandoned
☞ Overgrown trees and shrubs obstructing windows
☞ Appearance of missing roof shingles, leaders, and gutters in disrepair

Don't get the wrong idea. Just because a house has one or two of these characteristics, it doesn't necessarily mean that the person is a motivated seller. It just might mean that the person is a slob. It could also be that the person was on vacation for two weeks and didn't have time to mow. Maybe a storm cracked a few windows and the owner didn't have the time to do the repairs. It is important that you don't jump to conclusions. However, if half or more of the signs are evident there is an excellent chance that the owner is motivated to sell.

ESTATE SALE BARGINS

Another form of Don't Wanters are estate sales. Now that your appetite for real estate bargains has been whet, here is one more source that is little known by many real estate investors. *Estate sales* are the sales of real estate owned by deceased people who died without leaving a will. Where there's a will, there's a way, but where there's no will, there's an estate sale. As with the foreclosure sale, an estate sale is advertised in the newspaper well before the date of sale. Also, as with foreclosures, there are investors who specialize in investing at estate sales. They know their business just as carpenters or systems analysts know theirs.

Shortly after the death of a home owner, the local government conducts an appraisal of the property to determine its value. Professional real estate appraisers establish a minimum or *upset price*. The auction sale is advertised in the newspaper and a professional auctioneer is hired for the sale. Before the auction sale, the properties are open to inspection, but are sold "as is." The fact that no warranties are made about the condition of the house eliminates all but the adventurous from attending the estate sale. An estate sale usually consists of a number of houses auctioned rather than one. Several estate sales are held over the course of a year. Once the upset price is met, the auction begins. The house is sold to the highest bidder. If the upset bid is not met, the house is withdrawn from bidding at the sale and is carried over to the succeeding auction held later in the year.

What happens if you bid successfully at an auction sale? Relax, you don't have to bring a suitcase full of hundred dollar bills. All you are required to do is present a certified bank check or cash totaling 10% of the value of your successful bid. Then depending on the rules of your locality, you have anywhere from 30 to 60 days to close on the house. Sometimes the sale has to go through the courts and attorney general's office, but eventually you are issued clear title to the property. Did you ever wonder what happens to the money that you paid for the property since the owner did not have a will? The local government administrator searches for heirs. If heirs are found, the proceeds go to them. If there are no heirs, the proceeds go into the state in which the house is located.

PLACE YOUR OWN CLASSIFIEDS

There are said to be three types of real estate investors. There are those that make things happen. There are those who watch things happen. And there are those who ask what happened? If you are aggressive you are probably the first kind of investor. Rather than wait for an ad with terms that indicate a person is a Don't Wanter, you might choose to place classified ads of your own. If you advertise people will offer you the deals. Place a well-worded ad in your daily paper or weekly Pennysaver. Results could prove to be very rewarding. There is not one approach that works. You must try a format or approach that you are comfortable with.

How do you discover an ad that works? Do you ask a friend? Possibly. But there is a foolproof way to find out if an ad works or not without investing even one cent out of your pocket. Here is what you do. Pick up a copy of the latest newspaper or magazine where you see ads from private investors offering to buy real estate. Make a note of the exact ad. Pick up a copy of the same periodical from three months ago. Is the ad in that edition too? Pick up a copy from a year ago. Is the ad in that issue too? If the ad can be found in all three issues, you have just found an ad that works. If an ad works, investors will use it again and again.

BUYER BUYBACK ADS

"I BUY REAL ESTATE"
"I'LL BUY YOUR COMMERCIAL PROPERTY"
"I'LL PAY YOUR PRICE IF YOU MEET MY TERMS"
"I'LL PAY FULL PRICE FOR FLEXIBLE TERMS"
"I SOLVE SELLER PROBLEMS"
"I'LL HELP WITH YOUR BACK PAYMENTS"
"WHEN YOU NEED TO SELL YOUR PROPERTY, CALL ME"
"PRIVATE INVESTOR WANTS TO BUY YOUR PROPERTY"
"YOUNG COUPLE LOOKING FOR A FIX-ME-UPPER"

The Buyer Buyback ad ideas work well in classified ads, at a relatively low expense. An inexpensive ad in the classifieds can reach one million readers or more. If you prefer the personal touch you can have business cards printed. In that way you have personal control over the people who are seeing your ad or business card.

If you want to keep your message simple you can try a flyer. It is less wordy, but still gets across your message.

USING THE DIRECT-MAIL LETTER

Did you ever think that you could get to work with your eyes closed? Your car seems to be on auto-pilot as it somehow gets to the workplace without your conscious effort. The reason is that we are all creatures of habit. We have been doing the same thing in the same way for so long that we do it automatically. We get a letter, take a quick glance and toss it into the circular file. What you must do is find a way to quickly grab the reader's attention before it swims in marinara sauce. There are things you can do to avoid having your letter quickly discarded. Here are some techniques you can use to make your letter effective and to get the person to consider offering the property to you.

There are several important parts of your direct-mail letter—the headline, the letterhead, and the body.

Headline—summary that captures the reader's attention and gets the person to read the body of the letter. The headline is placed under the letterhead, but above the words, "Dear Investor."

Letterhead—the identification with or without a logo. It should be simple.

Introduction—a startling statement to grab the reader's interest.

Body—the principal part of your message. It includes all the information you wish to convey.

Conclusion—the action step that draws together the facts. The action step could be something as simple as, "SO IF YOU WANT IMMEDIATE CASH FOR YOUR PROPERTY AND TO CLEAR UP YOUR BACK PAYMENTS, CALL ME AT 555-1234."

A direct letter is sometimes beyond the means of the average investor. It takes time, effort, and great expense. But if you choose to buy in a particular area, you could reach every home. If you have access to a particular mailing list, you could reach the right people. If done properly, a direct mailer includes an outer envelope, the letter, and a self-addressed stamped envelope or post card. You will not receive responses from a large percentage of the letters, but the few that respond probably are motivated sellers.

There is a variation to the direct-mail letter that is far less costly and conveys the same message. It is the flyer. The flyer can be mailed, handed out in person or with the Pennysaver placed on car windshields or even on front doorknobs. The windshield idea is not the best since people tend to immediately discard anything on their windshields. Figure 3-2 a sample of a flyer that could be used to promote your real estate interests. You can either use the exact wording or change it to your individual tastes.

I BUY PROPERTY!!

I buy real estate in any condition.

If you or someone you know is thinking about selling a house or other real estate property, call me before you list with a real estate agent. I just might be able to save you a commission and the anxiety of waiting for the right buyer to come along.

Call: 201-388-6081

The choice is yours. Whether you prefer a flyer, newspaper ad, business card, or direct-mail letter, every investor needs to get the word out that he or she is looking for properties. Everyone can use a little self-promotion. In promoting yourself, you shouldn't lose sight of the human factor. There are numerous motivating factors in a person's life that can propel a person into action. Most every person wants to get the most out of life. Many want to become independently wealthy to escape from the daily rat race. Sellers of properties want their goals to be met as well. If you can meet your goals while helping others with theirs, you have an unbeatable combination. With a variety of motivating factors and formats to promote your real estate efforts, certain basic things must be realized. In any contact, written or oral, don't forget to include your phone number. No matter how motivated, most people just don't seem to have the time to write a letter. A letter is a time-consuming process, from finding the stationery, formally organizing their thoughts, the stamp, and running to the post office. A phone call, on the other hand, only takes a moment. A person responding to your ad is more likely to call than write. And one last thing, the money you spend for a few ads will prove to be the bargain of a lifetime if it leads to a deal. Your purpose in all the self-promotion is to uncover those motivated sellers who must sell.

THE MAGIC TENS RULE

The Magic Tens Rule is a way for you to judge if you are paying too much for a property. Simply put, don't pay more than ten percent interest for a mortgage and don't pay more than ten times the annual rent to purchase a property. By adapting the two parts of the rule, you protect yourself from high mortgage payments or an abnormally high purchase price that will prevent you from realizing a healthy profit when you sell.

Let's assume you have found a property that rents for $1000 per month. Multiplying by 12 you reach a yearly rent of $12,000. You should not pay more than $120,000 or 10 times the $12,000 for the property.

SUMMARY

Finding a bargain is more important than the location of the property. What truly counts is the deal. Buying a property at the right price and on the best terms produces the best deal.

There are a number of excellent sources of bargains. Riding up and down the neighborhood in search of "For Sale" signs is effective, as is reading the classified ads of the newspaper. Learning to identify key phrases that show a person is motivated can be very helpful.

The real estate agent is often a fine resource for finding bargains. She knows if the seller desperately needs the money and is negotiable. She has the multiple listing books that contain key information about the property, including price, taxes, and amenities.

There are many bargains in real estate available right now. Regardless of whether you shop through a broker, read the classifieds, or respond to "For Sale" signs, there are bargains awaiting you if you apply the bargain-hunting basics.

4

How to Guarantee a Good Buy

BUYING REAL ESTATE CAN BE HIGHLY PROFITABLE OR HIGHLY TREACHEROUS, depending on the action you take. If you make the right moves you move toward financial freedom. Make the wrong moves and you are face-to-face with an alligator. And you know what alligators do? They devour human flesh.

Any time you purchase a property, you are faced with four choices. You can hold onto the property and rent it out while getting a positive cash flow. You can hold onto the property and take out financing. You can sell it right away for a profit that investors refer to as *flipping it*. Lastly, you can trade it for another property. Sounds simple enough with only four alternatives. Then why do so many investors go astray with their investments?

Real estate investors are unsuccessful when they commit any of the Eleven Deadly Sins of Buying Real Estate. Each can be hazardous to your wealth.

ELEVEN DEADLY SINS OF BUYING REAL ESTATE

1. Thou shalt not buy any property at the asking price.
2. Thou shalt not fall in love with any property.
3. Thou shalt not accept any representation or claim from a seller or real estate agent without written substantiation.

4. Thou shalt not accept a mortgage with negative amortization.

5. Thou shalt not buy any property because of tax benefits, unless it is a good buy on its own merits.

6. Thou shalt not purchase any property without a real estate attorney.

7. Thou shalt not buy real estate you can't personally manage or oversee.

8. Thou shalt not purchase a property if it has to be sold within a time period.

9. Thou shalt not buy a property without a professional inspection.

10. Thou shalt not enter into any contract to purchase without weasel clauses.

11. Thou shalt not enter into any agreement with a partner unless you maintain total control in writing.

Thou Shalt Not Buy at the Asking Price

A seller or real estate agent prices a property above the price the seller actually expects to accept. It is a reasonable expectation that the seller will be willing to compromise a bit on the price and accept less. It is your right to offer anything you want and the seller's right to turn down your offer. You might be pleasantly surprised to find that the seller accepts your offer or makes a counter-offer. In either case, you will be able to purchase the property for less than you had expected. Furthermore, paying the full asking price adversely affects your chances to turn a profit should you need or choose to sell the property quickly. So bid lower than you would expect the seller to accept. If the seller is motivated enough, she might accept your offer.

Thou Shalt Not Fall in Love with Any Property

Everyone has seen a property that he or she finds breathtaking. It might have an open bay view, sunken living room, or a kitchen with every convenience ever thought of. Take a picture of it, tell your friends about it, but don't marry it. Real estate is not comfortable to sleep with. It doesn't cook, clean, balance the checkbook, or know how to party. It is an investment and only that. It is just a means toward becoming financially independent so you can make the choices in your life instead of others making the choices for you. If a property is a sound investment that will make you money, buy it. If it doesn't offer profit-making possibilities, walk the other way. With a real estate investment the only thing that matters is if the numbers work.

Thou Shalt Not Accept Any Statement from a Seller or Broker without Substantiation

It is often said that figures don't lie but liars figure. There is some truth to both. It is possible to stretch and even reformulate the truth using statistics. And don't lose sight of the fact that there are people who would say just about anything to make a few dollars. Where does that leave you as an investor? It leaves you in deep gunk unless you are ready to deal with the unscrupulous. Assume the prospective seller who seems like an upstanding person in conversation states that she is leaving all the lighting fixtures because she has no use for them in her new place. Do you take her words at face value and assume it will be done? Not if you don't want to be kept in the dark. Even if the seller is moving to Alaska and has no use for her air conditioners, you had better make sure that any promise or offer made in conversation is put into the written contract. Household items frequently are sold for quick cash or given away to friends before closing. Unless it is put in the written agreement, you have no recourse if the seller at closing says she never made any such promise. If the items are missing, and you have them written into the contract, you can request cash payment for them at closing. Get it in writing whether it is from the seller, real estate broker, or even your attorney. Remember, and you can tell the person involved, "if it is worth saying it is worth putting in writing."

Thou Shalt Not Accept a Mortgage with Negative Amortization

How would you like to borrow a thousand dollars from a friend, make monthly payments on time and then be told you owe eleven hundred dollars? You would think that your friend is trying to pull a fast one on you. Well, the neighborhood lender loves pulling these kinds of fast ones on borrowers if you let them. They call it negative amortization. With a negative amortization the amount you are paying on your mortgage is not the total interest expense. You might be asked to make constant monthly interest payments of $500, while the actual monthly interest expense is $525. In effect, every month your equity in the property decreases by $25, as the size of your mortgage debt increases. In the long run, with negative amortization, you might find that your mortgage outstanding will be larger than the original mortgage.

Why would anyone take out a mortgage with negative amortization, you wonder? The reason is that the borrower doesn't know. The mortgage broker or loan officer sweet-talks you and explains that your payments will not be going up for full year, no matter what happens to interest rates. Boy, you feel like you have a piece of the rock and something better than Mom's apple pie. But what have they offered you? Absolutely nothing. They told you that your payments will stay the same for one year, no matter what. They didn't tell you that your expenses will stay the same no matter what. There is a world of difference between expenses and payments. An expense is the amount you actually owe and are being billed for. The payment is how much of the expense you are actually paying. The lender is not being truthful as he or she glosses over the negative amortization feature of the mortgage to emphasize the low payments and their continuation for the course of a period of time.

The word *amortization* is derived from the Latin word for death. Negative amortization gives you a good idea of what will be happening to your personal finances if you agree to a mortgage loan containing it. The policy is common with both banks and finance companies. Be sure to ask any bank or mortgage representative if there is negative amortization in the loan. If the person says there is none, ask the person to state in writing that there is no negative amortization. Do not accept negative amortization and don't let anyone tell you not to worry about it. It can be something very hazardous to your financial well-being.

Thou Shalt Not Buy a Property Only for Tax Benefits

Discuss finances with any friends and you are likely to hear gripes about the amount of taxes they are paying. No one likes to pay taxes. The problem arises though when you allow taxes to get in the way of your good sense. Many people get involved in real estate because of the heavy tax bite and seek a tax deduction to offset their high taxable income. This is a costly mistake. Buy zero coupon bonds, tax-exempt bonds or Double E savings bonds, but don't buy real estate. Buy real estate only if you are getting a good deal. After all, the objectives of investing in real estate are earning a positive cash flow while you hold the property and realize a capital gain when you sell. If you save on your taxes by reducing your taxable income, that is a bonus, but it shouldn't be your sole reason for investing.

Thou Shalt Not Buy without an Attorney

In many states, it is common practice for deals to close without an attorney. In others, an attorney is a fixture just like the ceiling fan. Remember what they say about the person who acts as his own attorney—he has a fool for a client. Whether or not you think you need an attorney, you do. You are putting hundreds of thousands of dollars at stake in a transaction. The thousand dollars or less for the attorney to read over the papers, draw up the contracts, and gain concessions is a small price to pay, when you consider the potential hot water in which you can find yourself.

As a youngster do you remember what happened when you and the fat kid on the block got on the see saw? It made the see saw unbalanced, as your part of the see saw was thrust into the air. If in a transaction the seller is represented by an attorney and you are not, the same thing happens. It becomes a shoot-out where only one of the parties is armed. So an attorney is a must. You need someone to, at the minimum, examine the documents to make sure they represent your interests and not only the seller's. Never, never use the seller's attorney. No matter what is promised the seller will be protected, but you won't be.

When one magnificent house in our neighborhood was advertised for $150,000 below market value, buyers lined up. The ultimate buyer was in such a rush that he used the seller's attorney. The buyer had no idea that the tenant was selling a house that he didn't own. The tenant skipped town with the buyer's $30,000 bank check. The buyer would not have been taken for a ride if he'd used his own attorney. Never use the seller's choice and expect protection.

If you are concerned with keeping down your closing costs, you can hire an attorney to read over the documents and advise you of anything adverse in the agreement before signing. To have a handle on your expenses, have the attorney agree to a fixed fee for checking over your paperwork. Ask him or her to send you a statement confirming your agreement, or write one out on the spot requesting a signature. Admittedly, there are going to be many attorneys who will not be amendable to these arrangements. But if an attorney balks at either giving you a flat fee or putting the agreement in writing, simply thank him for his time and look elsewhere.

Thou Shalt Not Buy Properties You Can't Manage or Supervise

In baseball it is said that managers are hired to be fired. In real estate, it is not much different. Property managers have a strong reputation for not spending an investor's money as if it were her own. There are often questionable discrepancies between the amount of income the investor is expecting and the amount he finally receives. Though many investors disagree with us, our modus operandi is not to invest in any G.U.—any property that is Geographically Undesirable. To us, a G.U. property is any property more than one hour away from your residence. As hands-on managers, we inspect any situation personally before calling in a professional to make a repair and try the obvious things such as plugs and circuit breakers. If the oil burner or furnace breaks down at 11 P.M. on a frigid February evening, a twenty minute commute to the property is inconvenient but manageable. An hour or more ride is a no-no and if it happens too frequently can turn you into a don't wanter.

Not everyone agrees with our rule of thumb. There are investors who invest two or three hours away from their primary residence and hire someone to take care of their properties. To us that seems like hiring a fox to watch over your chickens, but for some people it seems to work. Some investors hire a Certified Property Manager (CPM). The CPM is placed in charge of screening and securing tenants, making repairs, maintaining the property, and collecting the rent. Face it, how many people outside your family would you trust to be in control of hundreds of thousands of your hard-earned dollars? Probably not many. Investors as well as most homeowners familiar with contractors know how unreliable they can be, with incomplete jobs, dubious billing, and shoddy workmanship.

If you are a passive investor, one who does not actively manage your own properties, you should be extremely careful before placing your property in the hands of a manager. First look up Real Estate Management in the yellow pages of the phone book. Look or ask for the CPM designation after the person's name. The CPM designation indicates that the person is a member of a professional management organization with standards for continued membership. Membership is not a guarantee of complete integrity but it is a first step in the weeding-out process. You will have to ask a number of questions of a prospective property manager before hiring him or her. Any negative responses, bad vibes, or a reluctance to fully cooperate should disqualify the person. Remember that you are the employer, and the person will be working for you. You make the final decision. Read through the checklist before making that decision.

The CPM Checklist

1. Is the certified property manager bonded?
2. Is the CPM willing and able to give you the names and addresses of properties currently managed?
3. After visiting those properties, are you satisfied with the physical appearance and maintenance?
4. After interviewing current clients, do they seem to be satisfied with the management?
5. After interviewing current clients, does it seem that the CPM is working on their behalf to keep down costs?

Whether you are managing properties yourself or hiring a property manager, remember that properties run themselves but only one way—into the ground. Properties need care and maintenance. If you can't personally supervise, maintain, or hire someone responsible, you are making a date with financial disaster.

Thou Shalt Not Enter into Any Contract without Weasel Clauses

A *weasel* is not a four-legged animal. What it is in real estate language is an insertion in a contract that allows you to back out if certain conditions are not being met. Weasel clauses or escape clauses are needed in a contract to enable you to cancel the contract legally and receive back your down payment when certain events have not taken place. A buyer might have many different reasons for escaping from a contract. A better deal might come along. You might be unable to get financing at affordable rates. You might have become aware of costly repairs or improvements the property needs. Maybe you just changed your mind. If you have weasel clauses in your contract you can likely use one of the clauses to escape from the contract without legal ramifications. You can usually recognize them by their wording. They usually begin with the words, *subject to*.

☞ Subject to the approval of my attorney.
☞ Subject to a professional termite report.
☞ Subject to a professional home inspection.
☞ Subject to obtaining a written mortgage commitment within sixty days of signing of contract.
☞ Subject to a professional appraisal.
☞ Subject to the sale of my other property.
☞ Subject to obtaining a current Certificate of Occupancy (C.O.).

Weasel clauses are musts for you as a buyer, even if you have every intention of going through with the deal. No one ever knows what lies ahead. It is advisable to be prepared for any developments. You can tell that the term weasel clauses was not coined by a buyer. It has an unfavorable connotation, probably first used by an attorney or real estate agent who saw his dreams of a Jaguar turn into a Pinto. Regardless how others feel about them, without weasel clauses in your contract, you are not fully protected.

Thou Shalt Not Purchase a Property if You Have to Sell within a Time Period

Someone once said that the only sure things are death and taxes. You pay sooner or later. When you buy real estate and have to sell within a time frame, you are asking for trouble. No one knows what market conditions will be in three months, six months, or whenever you have to sell. Should you find unfavorable market conditions at selling time, a costly problem could result. In a soft market, you might not only have to accept twenty percent less for your property, but also have to wait several months and agree to the buyer's terms. A buyer's market occurs when a small number of buyers choose from a large number of available properties. Be the hammer and not the nail in the transaction. But only when you do not anticipate a need for the money for an indefinite time period.

Thou Shalt Not Buy a Property
without a Professional Home Inspection

Buying a property without a professional inspection is asking for trouble. No one but a professional can look at the property and know if it is in tiptop condition. The professional makes a hands-on inspection, climbing, probing, testing, measuring, and evaluating. The inspector has been trained to spot potential problems before they become a problem to the buyer. Unless you have x-ray vision, you can't tell what is inside a wall or ceiling or if any of the roof rafters are rotted. A professional home inspection is a must.

Professional home inspections are not only useful before the closing. They can be a big money-saver after the closing. Let's assume that the inspector examines the boiler, finds it in good condition, and states so in the written report. Being a prudent investor you take out a guarantee with the home inspection firm. It costs no more than one or two hundred dollars. Since the inspection attested to the fact that the boiler was in good condition, and issued a guarantee policy against defects for a time period, usually one year, should a major problem arise it is responsible for repairing or replacing your boiler, at no expense to you. For the little that the guarantee costs, you shouldn't be without it.

Thou Shalt Not Enter into Any Partnership Agreements
without Maintaining Total Control in Writing

Everyone at one time or other hears of a great deal but doesn't have enough cash or credit to swing it. Should you take in a partner? The answer is a definite maybe. It depends on who is in control. If your partner is willing to remain silent, putting up his capital but not his "two cents," an agreement is workable. But if you have entered an agreement where you have to have a meeting to consult before every decision, you are headed for trouble. As with any kind of business, a real estate investment requires daily attention. It does not run itself. Often there are emergency situations that require immediate action. A roof collapses. A tree falls through the living room. A pool collapses. What do you do? Do you call a handyperson from the local newspaper, supermarket bulletin board, or a well-advertised firm from the yellow pages? When you make the decision, you likely choose the person you feel can get the job done at the lowest cost. However if E.Z. Spender is your active partner you might find yourselves at loggerheads over which firm to hire, E.Z. might only want to hire a nationwide company to do the repair, which charges three times the cost of the person you would choose. Furthermore there might be a disagreement over which costs are necessary and which are not.

Partner interference brings your effectiveness to a halt. Problems also result when one partner wants to sell and the other doesn't. If one partner needs the money for a car, a wedding, or even a divorce, your investment becomes a Don't Wanter. Frequent squabbling over day-to-day operations often results in the break-up of the partnership. Properties are liquidated on less than favorable terms, and losses result this way. Your capital is eroding and there is little you can do because you haven't maintained total control.

FIVE GOODS EQUAL ONE GOOD BUY

The Deadly Sins can be thought of as eleven ways to get poor quick in real estate. Some practices can be modified to suit individual preferences, but others are lethal. Years of successful real estate experiences by others and us turn up the same caveats. Preparation is vital before entering any real estate transaction, from knowing your available finances to knowing what you want to do with the property, how, and why. A wise person once said, "Those who fail to prepare—prepare to fail." Proper steps must be taken even before taking the checkbook out of your pocket. Without proper preparation you don't have a fair chance in real estate investing.

What is a good buy? Is it a property that sells at a low price? Is it a property that the real estate agent says won't last? Maybe. Is it a property that sells for less than your friend paid? That depends. Many factors are involved in determining whether or not a property is a good buy or a so-so buy. Our philosophy is that if a property is not a good buy, then good-bye. There are always good buys around. If they are not in your town, they might be in the next town or a town an hour's drive away. The thing to remember is that there is never a time you can't get good buys. And there is never a bad time to make money in real estate.

A good buy is not always the lowest-priced property in an area. It could be, but it does not necessarily have to be. Other factors are equally important as the asking price. In fact, the lowest-priced property could turn out to be anything but a bargain if it requires extensive repairs to get it into turnkey or move-in condition. Five major factors qualify a real estate investment as a good buy. The factors are good terms, good property condition, good location, good price relative to the previous three, and good features.

Good terms are very beneficial to a buyer. They make the deal flow more smoothly by simplifying the details. Consider these terms. The seller will take back a mortgage so you don't have any closing costs. The seller will accept a small down payment and possibly nothing down if you agree to pay the full asking price. The seller will close at your convenience. The seller will allow you to show the house to prospective buyers or tenants before closing. The seller will agree to make the deal contingent on your being able to sell a property to raise the necessary cash. The seller will allow you to flip the property before closing if you find buyers. In the contract you would list yourself as John Buyer or his assigns, enabling you to assign the contract automatically to another buyer while selling the property for more than you paid. Many skeptical real estate people will say that nobody is going to give you terms like those mentioned. Possibly, you are right, but it doesn't hurt to ask. The worst the seller can say is "no." The willingness of the seller to agree to any of your terms depends on market conditions and how badly he or she wants to make the deal. The willingness of a seller to be accommodating is appreciated by any prospective buyer. The terms of endearment help cement a deal by making the buyer select one property over another.

A *good location* is another must for a property to be a good buy. What makes a property location a good location? There are many qualities. Look through the good location checklist and see how many of the qualities described fit your property location.

Good Location Checklist

- ☞ Appearance of property
- ☞ Climate
- ☞ Drainage
- ☞ Exposure
- ☞ Physical hazards
- ☞ Health services
- ☞ Shopping nearby
- ☞ Transportation available
- ☞ Street traffic patterns
- ☞ Utilities

Just as there are qualities that make a property a good location, there are qualities that make a neighborhood a place to avoid. We call the list of negative qualities, The Neighborhood No-Nos.

The Neighborhood No-Nos

- ☞ Avoid property near a cemetery.
- ☞ Avoid property in a low-lying area subject to flooding.
- ☞ Avoid property bordering on a school playground.
- ☞ Avoid property adjacent to a sewage plant or town dump.
- ☞ Avoid property that has heavy traffic.
- ☞ Avoid property near factories.
- ☞ Avoid properties that have a public garage as a neighbor.
- ☞ Avoid property if you see emissions from factories.
- ☞ Avoid the most expensive house on the block.
- ☞ Avoid property on a block where most of the properties are rented.

A *good price* is certainly appealing to any buyer, but it must be evaluated along with the other factors. A good price alone does not make a property a good buy, though many buyers are overly influenced by the asking price. If you are offered a strip shopping center for $50,000 and it is alongside a toxic waste dump, nuclear power plant, or drug-infested war zone, the deal suddenly doesn't seem like the terrific buy it appeared to be in the real estate broker's office. A good buy should be judged by what comparable properties have sold for in the most recent sixty to ninety days. You could hire an appraiser to do the homework, check the multiple listing books yourself at a friendly local real estate agent with whom you have a good working relationship or visit the county clerk's office to check the books that show the actual sales prices of properties in your area of interest.

Appraisals are a tricky subject. Appraising is part art and part science. Don't leave it up to the real estate agent who drops off the card in your mailbox offering a free, no-obligation appraisal. Hire an appraiser with a professional designation such as MAI, ASA, or SREA. An appraisal will cost a few hundred dollars at the most, but what is a few hundred dollars when you are investing hundreds of thousands? There is even such a thing as a drive-by appraisal that is less detailed and also less costly if time and money are of the essence.

Good features are important to a deal because properties are bought to be sold. Any time you buy, you have to consider an ultimate sale, whether it is two years or twenty years. When you buy, consider why another person would find it an attractive property to purchase. If you can't objectively find a half dozen desirable features or positive attributes, you might be buying the wrong property. The good location factors listed previously are some of the factors appealing to a buyer. In addition, a property should offer convenience to a prospective purchaser. A house should have such features as an eat-in-kitchen, central air, and electric garage door opener. Since most families spend a major portion of the day eating, reading, and chatting in the kitchen, it had better be large enough for the family to gather. More than one bathroom is also a must. For a commercial property, there must be sufficient parking. The property must be situated on the optimal side of the street and be attractive for shopping, visiting, and working.

There is never a bad time to buy real estate as long as it is a good buy. Through careful negotiating you can obtain good terms. Through smart shopping you can uncover property in good condition with a good location at a good price with desirable features. With these factors you have a good buy. And with a truly good buy, you will never lose money on a real estate deal.

THE BUYER'S TWO STEP

Now watch your step. In fact, watch both of your steps. We are talking about the Buyer's Two Step. The Buyer's Two Step has nothing to do with the Texas oil baron's ball. It is a street-smart way for you to avoid being romanced without foreplay. Through the Buyer's Two Step, you arrange for two-property inspections. The first is by a professional home or property inspector who is a member of the American Society of Home Inspectors (ASHI). Many home inspectors during the inspection welcome you to accompany them and ask questions. There couldn't be a better opportunity to question the inspector about anything of which you are unsure or have doubts. You might notice cracks in the foundation, water stains on the ceiling, floors that creak or are obviously uneven. Ask anything. You are paying for the inspection, the inspectors are amenable, and you have the right to completely understand anything of which you are unsure. The fact that you are being billed by the hour surely doesn't discourage the inspector from being thorough and patient.

Of course, you previously learned the value of the weasel clause "subject to a professional inspection." Therefore any unexpected major surprises discovered in the inspection will not bind you to the deal, should you choose to cancel. Street-smart investors usually ask the inspector to estimate the cost of the repair in the written report. You present the defects with a copy of the inspection report and ask that the repair be discussed before closing, with an amount set aside at closing for the repair or a downward adjustment in the selling price. If the seller or the seller's attorney refuse to make any repair or price concessions, you might decide to cancel the deal, be free of legal obligations, and receive a refund of your down payment. Usually there will be some compromise, since an inspection at a later date by any professional would have turned up the same result. Realistically, the defect would be more costly to repair at a later date.

The second part of the Buyer's Two Step is completed by you. A week before closing, call up the sellers. Arrange to visit the property to make certain everything is in working order. A standard clause in every contract is that plumbing, heating, and electricity are in working order and that the roof is free from leaks. Test out appliances, light switches, and outlets; turn on the hot water in the kitchen and the water in the shower at the same time. Flush all the toilets. If any defects were spotted in the first inspection by the professional, you could ask the inspector to re-inspect before closing. As your walk-through inspection is carried out, take notes of anything that is not functional and present it to your attorney before the papers are signed at closing. Frequently the seller's attorney has a list of expenses for you to pay at closing, such as prepaid taxes and reimbursement for oil in the burner. Your presentation of defects helps offset your out-of-pocket expenses at closing.

The Buyer's Two Step is both a timesaver and moneysaver. It is the key to avoiding annoyances and expenses after closing, when the seller would be half a country away. Your attorney has already been paid, so you can imagine that he won't be anxious to follow up in post-closing problems.

Do you have an uncle or brother-in-law who claims to be handy? Everybody does. But don't count on a family member for the Buyer's Two Step. Only a professional should be counted on. So where do you find a qualified professional? The best way is through word-of-mouth, asking someone who has recently hired a professional engineer or home inspector and recommends the person. If you don't have a recommendation, consult the yellow pages under the heading, House Inspections. Remember that a good house inspection doesn't cost money, it saves money. Uncovering a problem before closing when they can more easily be rectified is better than discovering problems later when you have to foot the bill.

Regardless of whether your property is residential or commercial, a qualified inspector can be the greatest thing since the mute button on the music channel. A commercial property inspector can uncover faulty or antiquated wiring, a roof needing replacement, or an assortment of hazardous conditions, each of which could be very costly.

Check Out Your Own Taxes

As valuable as the professional inspection is, it is not the only investigation to save you money. Of all people, the tax collector can be your ally. By having the section, lot and block number of the property, you can obtain the current school tax and town tax from the tax collector's office. In your town, the tax collector's office might have a different title. In our town, it is called Receiver of Taxes. With the current taxes in hand, you can compare the figures with those given by the seller or real estate agent. Don't depend on what they tell you. It's not guaranteed. You must verify the amount of taxes. You can also verify that the taxes are not in arrears for nonpayment. If there is a serious discrepancy in the taxes, you can ask for an adjustment in the sales price or a cancellation of the deal. After all, a material difference in taxes affects your financial health. A larger-than-expected tax bite can turn a positive cash flow into a negative cash flow and make a bargain into a not-so-great deal. Frequently a seller will be willing to compromise on the selling price, since it will take weeks and possibly months to find another buyer, unless you are in a hot market (seller's market).

Check Your Own Zone

When is a good buy not a good buy? It is when a purchase is not what it appears. When a residential or commercial property is not as it was represented, you will be caught in a financial mess. If the multi-family house is not a legal two-family, and you discover that there is no certificate to make it so, you could be required by the town to dispossess one of your tenants. In dollars and cents, you will be losing one of your rental incomes. Similarly, if the apartment building you purchase is designated as a legal three-family dwelling and there are five apartments in operation, you could be required to close down two apartments preventing you from renting them. The resulting loss in your income could be staggering.

You are most likely not an attorney. How then do you know what is legal and what isn't when purchasing a property? You could have your attorney demand such documentation in writing from the seller's attorney. Of course this must be done before closing. If the property is purported to be a legal two- or three-family, ask for proof in the form of a certificate. Nothing is legal unless a government authority specifies that it is.

Regulations for zoning and building vary from area to area and from town to town. To find out the laws for your municipality, visit or call the zoning department. Each building department has a set of laws or ordinances that specify the types of occupancy permissible in a particular area. In one town's ordinance there could be only single-family residences permitted. In another's, multifamily residences are permitted with special permission under certain circumstances. A legal two-family in places is deemed legal only if it is owner-occupied. In other places, permissions were granted twenty or thirty years ago, and the historical precedent continues in grandfather clauses. Where there is an owner-occupied status, you must be very cautious. If you purchase a legal two-family from an owner with a valid certificate and do not plan to live there, your certificate is not valid for occupancy by two unrelated families. You have an illegal situation that could be hazardous to your wealth if you are forced to comply with local regulations. One rule of thumb in real estate is never to assume any situation is legal or complying with any ordinances just because someone claims it to be. Felix Unger of "The Odd Couple" was no real estate expert, but he knew one important principle. He said "Never assume anything—because when you assume you make an ASS of U and ME." Believing something to be true without checking the facts leads to needless and costly complications.

SUMMARY

Just as there is never a bad time to make money, there is never an easy way. We all know that when something appears too good to be true, it usually is. Many precautions are taken to assure you that a purchase is a good buy. If it is not a good buy, you should say good-bye to the deal. Even if the seller is your next-door neighbor or your lifelong friend, be careful. Certain practices should lead you to walk away from a deal. They were detailed in the Eleven Deadly Sins of Buying Real Estate. If you can't manage your own property check the CPM checklist to find one that is qualified.

For a deal to be a good buy certain conditions must be met. In any deal there must be good terms, good property conditions, good location, good price, and good features. Good terms make payments easier and, therefore, a deal less complicated to complete. Good property conditions are essential unless you have hands of gold or contacts with people whose hands custom-fit screwdrivers and hammers. A good location is important but can be put on the back burner if the terms and other features are favorable. Making money doesn't have to be pretty. A good price is essential, because if the price is right in relation to comparable value, the location, property condition, and terms can be de-emphasized. A bargain price will be attractive to an investor as long as the problems are manageable. Desirable features help facilitate selling but are not as crucial to a purchase as terms and a good price, since the property is not being bought as your primary residence. With properties bought for investment, positive cash flow for as long as you own and capital gains when you sell are the primary concern. Remember not to accept sellers' and real estate agents' verbal promises. Check out your own taxes, zoning, and home inspections. If you don't spend the time, expect to spend the money.

5

Buying Rehab Housing

A prudent person is like a pin; his head prevents him from going too far.

—Morris Mandel

IF YOU ARE AN INVESTOR WILLING TO ASSUME ABOVE-AVERAGE RISK, THEN you should consider rehab housing. The risks are high, but the potential rewards are astronomical. One thing to bear in mind—rehab housing is not suited for the investor with shallow pockets or impatience. There are just too many things that can go wrong.

When real estate markets soften, and all markets do eventually, there are often tremendous buying opportunities. People lose their jobs and often their homes. Properties are taken over by banks, mortgage companies, RTC, FDIC, IRS, and HUD. From years of neglect and a lack of maintenance, properties fall into disrepair. Often facing foreclosure they are abandoned. Following foreclosure, houses sit boarded up for months, perhaps years, until a buyer steps in to purchase and rehabilitate the property.

Rehabilitated housing or rehab housing as an investment is suited towards one person—the person with a green thumb and hands of gold. If you are a person who is handy and able to make most repairs competently without calling outside help, then rehab housing might be your road to riches. Remember that it is fraught with traps and dangers. There can be rotted roofing rafters and sheathing, aluminum wiring that requires pigtailing, foundation problems, and other potential wallet-busters.

What are the characteristics of a property ripe for rehabilitation? According to many real estate experts, these are the characteristics most frequently mentioned:

☞ A house that is structurally sound in a neighborhood with rising prices.
☞ A handyman's special in a turnaround neighborhood.
☞ The worst house on the best block.
☞ An old home with character or historical appeal.
☞ A property on or near the water or having water rights.

If you live in one of the areas that has been hot in the last few years such as San Francisco, Las Vegas, and Washington D.C., it is unlikely you will find great rehab housing. Soaring prices have led to a building boom, with few promising tracts of land untouched. Even though other previously hot areas, such as the Northeast, have normalized and are no longer appreciating by twenty percent annually, they are not prospects for rehab housing. Though prices have stabilized and even fallen, they are still substantially higher than before the boom.

There are investors who wouldn't touch rehab housing with a ten-foot pole. They are not necessarily wrong. You should only invest in the type of real estate with which you feel comfortable. One negative aspect of rehab investing is every property is in as-is condition and probably requires substantial renovation. Another is that because of the poor condition of the property, it is difficult though not impossible to get a mortgage. The modus operandi to save time and financing costs is to, whenever possible, buy the properties for "all cash." In that way you are in control of the circumstances, without having a lender dictate to you or having to raise capital each month to pay financing costs. If you decide to make repairs immediately or hold off on cosmetic improvements, you won't feel the stranglehold of a mortgage.

PROFESSIONAL INSPECTIONS

Before signing on the dotted line for any rehab deal, it is necessary to find out from a professional what the costs are likely to be. An inspection by a licensed home inspector or professional engineer before can avoid headaches after.

Many real estate investors we know look up licensed inspectors in the yellow pages of the phone book, under the category of Home Inspection Services or Building Inspection Services. Listed are professional engineers with the designation P.E. after their name, or inspection firms employing a professional engineer. The professional organization to which many professional engineers belong is the American Society of Home Inspectors (ASHI), which sets standards of performance for its members. We have hired P.E.s as well as home inspection firms with satisfactory results. Recently for convenience purposes we have favored nationwide inspection firms over individual or local home inspectors. Though the quality of the inspection is often comparable, the nationwide firms are not dependent on the fortunes of an individual proprietor. In other words, if three months after purchasing a property, for which you have a one-year guarantee, the roof that had been reported in good condition, collapses, and the single proprietor has died, moved out of state, or gone into chapter XI, what do you do? You can't dig him up and sue for damages. He is beyond damages and so are your chances of recovering money to pay for the roof.

What if you had hired a nationwide home inspection firm? Perhaps they aren't as responsive as a sole proprietor who wants recommendations would be, but their guarantees have nationwide backing. Among reputable nationwide inspection firms are Housemasters of America, AAA Nationwide Real Estate Inspectors Service, and Tauscher Cronacher Professional Engineers. Many local firms that operate in a bistate or tristate area are also worthy of consideration.

Home inspections are not inexpensive when you write the check. They are the bargain of a lifetime when serious defects turn up after contract. If serious defects appear before closing, you can demand that repairs be made or the selling price be reduced by the amount of the repairs. Of course, the seller has the option of refusing to make the repairs and canceling the contract.

Is it possible that problems can be overlooked or understated by the inspectors? Sure. That is why many investors take out an inspection guarantee with the inspection firm. In that way, if problems are not diagnosed before closing and disaster strikes, you are covered. For an investment of a few hundred dollars for a home guarantee, you have protection for one year from closing. If anything breaks down and needs replacement and you weren't forewarned, you are protected.

How much does a home inspection cost? It usually costs about $300 for a structural check. The firm we use invites you to accompany the professional engineer on his inspection to ask questions, and we do. You should do likewise. After all, it's your money and your investment.

The first part of the inspection is the meeting between the inspector and the owners. Pertinent questions are asked about the house, such as age, type of heat, how long they have owned the house, etc., etc. He walks through the house looking for obvious signs such as leaks, windows that are cracked or don't open, floors that sag, faulty plumbing, and electrical problems. Entering the bathroom, he turns on the hot water in the tub full force simultaneously with the kitchen faucets to make sure there is sufficient hot water. Similar demands are made on electricity by testing out several appliances at the same time. He notices if the outlets are grounded and if safe wiring is used throughout the house. Entering the basement, the inspector checks out the electrical service to make sure there is sufficient amp capacity for the house. A physical inspection is made of the attic to determine if there is sufficient insulation and to inspect the condition of the roof and chimney. While making the physical inspection, the inspector makes notations on his checklist. At the end of the inspection the inspector seeks a quiet place to collect his thoughts and his findings. The physical inspection takes between sixty and ninety minutes. The write-up of the report consumes another forty five minutes to an hour. The billing for the inspection is based upon the time expended. At the conclusion of the write-up of the report, you pay the fee and are given one copy of the report, which the inspector discusses with you. Written comments are provided for any deviations or defects with qualifiers. If the house is an older one, as was our recent purchase, the inspector will qualify many things as average, for their age.

Home inspection firms, like all professionals should make preparations before beginning work. Ours did. Our inspector, who was a real estate investor himself, had rehabbed a one hundred-year-old house personally. Therefore, he was familiar with building codes, as he checked out the plumbing, and electrical work. He noted the need to upgrade the electrical lines and plumbing to comply with local law. Furthermore, at our request, he included ballpark figures on the cost of each improvement. In this way, we could present the estimated repairs to the seller for negotiation purposes, as well as to judge whether the deal made sense for us. The total inspection took longer than expected and was slightly more expensive, but it was well worth the expense. We gained an understanding of the reasons why various procedures were taken and the possible ramifications. Had we not questioned the inspector, we could have had a less meaningful and useless piece of paper called an inspection. Take the time, be there and learn about the property from the expert.

THE COSMETIC KISS

It goes without saying that all rehab projects are not the same. There are rehabs where bathrooms and kitchens are merely modernized. And there are rehabs where an entire interior needs to be gutted. Obviously the degree of work determines whether or not the deal makes sense for you. There are many approaches to making money in rehab housing investments. If carried out with an eye to controlling costs and the other to complying with standards and local laws, all can lead to success.

One approach to rehab investments is the *cosmetic renovation* approach. The strategy is to purchase a structurally sound property that is physically unattractive, at below market prices. Basically you are buying an eyesore that you feel can be made presentable and salable. You give the property a physical makeover and then sell at or above market value. The plan works if you purchase the property well below market value and can either do the work yourself or hire competent people at reasonable rates. The strategy has been used for decades by the small investor, as well as by the multibillion dollar insurance companies that manage properties.

Skeptics are likely to think that if the cosmetic renovation approach is that easy, why doesn't every investor use it? The answer is that there are many problems with the approach. First of all, how do you find a property selling substantially below market price? In healthy real estate markets, speculators with links to real estate brokers are constantly snapping up bargains as soon as they hit the market. What you have to do is to keep looking until you spot an eyesore and make a bid to take the property off the market. If it is a rental property, check on the rent by speaking with the tenant. Tell the tenant you are thinking of renting in the area and would like to know how much an apartment like hers rents for. Compare her rent with rents in the area in comparable properties in creampuff condition. The rent should be 45-50% below other rentals, which is the potential that the property holds if you restore it to creampuff condition.

John Reed, who publishes the Real Estate Investing Letter, has a rule of thumb in tackling rehab situations. His motto is "Paint it. Clean it. Cover it. Don't replace it unless it's really cheap to replace." You have purchased the rehab as an investment, not as a bride or groom. Your goal is a profit, not a lifetime companion. If it has to be replaced, then you have no choice, but if you can make cosmetic improvements that increase property value and rentability, so much the better. If the property needs a new bathroom or kitchen, reconsider whether this deal makes sense for you. Bathroom and kitchen overhauls can easily turn into tens of thousands of dollars in repairs. Ask yourself if you really need it. Unless you are experienced at such overhauls and are willing to pour in sweat equity by doing the work yourself, forget it.

Ask anyone what the biggest mistake in rehab housing is. The stock answer will likely be "trying to make things perfect." Bear in mind that you are not going to live there. Don't do all kinds of fancy things because the person who rents your place might not share your taste. Our rule of thumb is KISS rehabilitation. We don't mean R-rated rehabilitation. KISS stands for Keep It Simple, Stupid. Try to stick with situations that can be improved dramatically with a coat of paint and a roll of wallpaper.

The surprise factor is one of the biggest problems with extensive rehabilitations. Once you open up a wall, you never know what you will find. We own a high ranch where the downstairs level had been converted into a separate apartment. The situation was considered illegal, so when we purchased the property we had the second kitchen dismantled. We hired a contractor to remove the kitchen wall and restore the den to its original size. In removing the wall, the contractor uncovered three live wires, which could have set fire to the house at any time. Fortunately the situation was corrected without a major calamity, for which we considered ourselves lucky. Had we not dismantled the wall, we would have had a ticking time bomb and not been aware of it.

DEMOLISH OR RENOVATE?

Though the KISS technique is the most sensible from a dollars and sense perspective, some rehabs cannot be cured with a bucket of paint. Some need extensive renovations. As the purchaser you face a monumental decision. Do you tear down only what needs to be replaced or do you gut the entire place? Increasingly, investors are choosing to knock down the entire interior and sometimes even the exterior to start over.

The consensus among general contractors, who rehab, 99% of the homeowners who have rehabs have the houses leveled. The feeling is that with the house leveled, you can get things done exactly the way you want them. Conversely, if you leave parts of the house intact, you have to build around it. Furthermore the feeling is that opening an old wall is like opening a can or worms. The reasoning is that you just don't know what you will find. When problems pop up, it takes time to correct the unexpected as you watch the costs escalate. That is why general contractors prefer to level and start from scratch.

Starting from scratch is the preferable move. In addition to avoiding the unexpected and keeping down costs, total gutting can sometimes be a moneymaker. Where zoning laws permit, many homeowners have their homes repositioned on the property and have large tracts of land subdivided. By selling off the parcels, you often discover that the money realized from the sale of the subdivided land will pay the construction costs.

Before you hire the bulldozers, stop. There are drawbacks in the total demolition approach. First of all, zoning laws might have changed in your locality, allowing you or prohibiting you to make drastic alterations. You might not be able to build a new structure in the same location and with the same dimensions as the original structure. You might only be permitted to build a smaller home, which would command less money than a larger one. With a teardown, you can't earn any rental income, whereas with a renovation, work can be done while the house is being rented, taking into account convenient hours and a tenant's right to peaceful living. In many areas, keeping a portion of the original foundation or structure allows you to maintain the original tax base of the existing house that will be substantially less than newer construction.

When does it make sense to tear down a property instead of renovating it? You probably should not answer that question alone. It is preferable that you call in licensed contractors for an estimate of the repair. Don't rely on one or two estimates. Get at least five or six estimates. In that way you will have a more realistic view of your expected costs. Expect a wide range of prices, from dirt-cheap to astronomical. Try to select contractors who are a member of NARI, the

National Association of Remodelers Industry, a national organization that strives for quality work and integrity from its members. An architect, in addition to a licensed contractor, can guide you in your decision to tear down or renovate.

Don't Renovate an Older House . . .

☞ If you have 10-amp electrical service and outdated plumbing
☞ If kitchens aren't eat-in and can't accommodate microwave ovens and dish-washers
☞ If the house does not have a foundation

FINDING THE CONTRACTOR

Whether you decide to finance a demolition or renovation, be realistic. Not only will you have to do a thorough analysis of the financial requirements, remember to expect the unexpected. Our experience has been that whatever price you start with, double it, and that is probably what it will cost when you're finished. And if it somehow costs less, consider yourself lucky. Who is going to do the work? Are you doing it yourself or hiring a contractor? Naturally, if you are hiring the contractors, the job will be substantially more costly than if you are going to put in your sweat equity. Finding reliable help is never easy. Days and often weeks are spent in making appointments for estimates. You call people with ads in the yellow pages and local newspapers and expect them to be responsive. All too often you leave a message on their answering machine and your call is either not returned or returned weeks later, when you have already made a decision. Eventually you find a contractor who seems responsible, though you don't really know. It is advisable to interview each contractor who appears reputable before signing any contract.

The Contractor Top Ten List

1. Is he licensed and what is his license number?
2. Is he a member of the NARI?
3. Can he give you the names and addresses of three people in the area for whom he has done work in the last ninety days?
4. What are the names of the lumber yards in the area from which he buys materials?
5. Will the contractor be subcontracting or having his workers do the work?
6. Will the contractor be on the job?
7. What will his payment schedule be?
8. What will his guarantee for parts and labor be?

9. Will he agree to clean up and cart away the debris?

10. How soon will he get started and how long will it take to finish?

References

If you are able to find a number of satisfied customers who have used the contractor recently, it is likely that his work will be satisfactory. Ask the people if you can visit and see the work to judge for yourself. Contact a few people to make sure he is not sending you to his relatives.

Lumber Yards

Ask for the names of the contractor's suppliers. If the contractor won't give you the names of local suppliers from whom he buys, there might be a reason. Check out the recommendations by visiting the suppliers. It is possible that if he does not buy from local suppliers, one or more might have a mechanic's lien against him for nonpayment in the past.

NARI Membership

If he is a member of the NARI he likely upholds its principles and will be trustworthy. If there is a problem with the work, you can tell the NARI to intervene and see that it is completed satisfactorily.

Licensing

Is the contractor licensed to operate in the locality? If he is licensed, he might have had to put up a bond to work in the area. The bond protects customers from disreputable contractors. It is against the law to be unlicensed in an area that issues a license for the performance of certain types of work. If you hire an unlicensed contractor, you have no recourse if things don't work out as planned.

Subcontracting

Will the contractor have his regular employees do the work or will he hire workers for your particular job. If you are relying on his firm's reputation, you want the people who have done quality work for him. You don't want people who are answering the want ads. You don't know the quality of their work.

Contractor on the Job

Ask if the contractor will be on the job. If the contractor will not be present on the job site, there is no one to oversee the work. A contractor who is not personally involved in the project might not be the one you want for the project.

Many years ago we hired a contractor to do renovations on our primary residence. Every day there would be different workers but no sign of the contractor. He never checked out the quality of the work and only appeared to count his money. When we asked the workers about the revolving door of new faces, we were told that some had not been paid and quit. Upon closer investigation we learned that it was the contractor's policy to fire the workers right before payday and not pay anyone. If they demanded payment, he would file a police report accusing the worker of stealing his equipment.

Payment Schedule

Ask the contractor what the payment schedule will be. You should not have to pay more than one third for him to start. After all, he has your property as collateral. If you can get him to agree, try to pay no more than a few hundred dollars. Payments should be paid by check and made out to the company's escrow account. In states, such as New York, a contractor might only take money from the account as work is done. The remainder of the money owed should be paid in stages, as certain parts of the work are completed and approved by local government inspectors, if their approval is required. You don't pay the full bill until the entire job is completed and approved by government inspectors or another professional contractor.

Guarantee

Have the contractor write down exactly what is guaranteed and for how long in the contract. Remember the NIWIN principle. If it's Not In Writing It's Nothing. You must have parts and labor guaranteed. It should be for at least two years if it is a major job.

Clean Up

Many contracts specify that it is the owner's responsibility to clean up. Cleaning up debris from a major job can cost up to one thousand dollars, when you consider the cost of renting dumpsters. Make sure that you specify in the contract that the company will clean up and cart away the debris.

What to Do When the Contractor Won't Finish the Job

Every once in a while, despite all precautions, you employ a contractor who is disreputable. Before the job is completed, the contractor asks for full payment. Of course, as a street-smart investor you know better than to turn over all the money. You inform him that you will pay the final amount upon completion. He finds your idea unacceptable because of all the money he claims to be losing on your job. It has cost him more than he agreed and he still needs to purchase materials. You wisely refuse to meet his demand. So what does he do? He walks off the job.

What do you do? You can call the department of consumer affairs in your city and ask for assistance. It might or might not work. Another plan seems to work when nothing short of hiring an attorney will help. These contractors have a well-planned strategy. They walk off every job before the work is completed. They have received the bulk of the money and don't have to complete the work or clean up. Many homeowners call to complain a few times and then forget about the situation, leaving the unscrupulous contractor to prey on other consumers, without being stopped.

According to nationally known consumer advocate Bernard Meltzer, the plan that works best is the paper trail. The scenario is that the contractor who has walked off the job expects you to hire someone else to complete the job. When you do, the original contractor sues you for breach of contract. Bernard Meltzer advises you to send a certified letter with a return receipt notifying the contractor that you expect him to honor the contract and complete the job. If the contractor does not return to the job or respond to your letter, wait two weeks and send another certified letter with a return receipt. In this letter, refer to the first letter you sent and notify the contractor that unless he completes the job as per contract within five business days, you will be forced to hire someone else to complete the job. If the contractor still fails to contact you after your deadline, he has put his cards on the table. It is obvious that he is fraudulent. You can have the job completed by a reputable contractor and then sue the original contractor for breach of contract.

When You Don't Comply with the Law

Never buy a property with additions to the original structure unless you have proof in writing that they comply with the law. Illegal additions can be costly. You could be subjected to costly fines by the local building and zoning department, as well as be forced to remove the structure at your expense. It is necessary to make sure that any property you purchase has a Certificate of Occupancy (C.O.) and Certificate of Completion (C.C.) for any additions to the exterior of the structure. Some times the terms C.O. and C.C. are used interchangeably. When an attorney asks for the C.O., he or she really wants the C.C. to show if any improvements have been made to the original structure.

Many property owners have renovations done without filing permits and then later learn that the work is illegal. Others buy property that way because their attorneys were not judicious or knowledgeable. In both cases, the purchaser gets hurt in the wallet. Once a building department learns of an illegal structure, it can require that it be torn down, regardless of the expense or inconvenience to you. The rationale is that it should not have been built, and it was your responsibility to know. What do you do when you discover after making a purchase that there are illegal structures on your property?

The best thing to do is call up or visit the local building department. The local building department is usually located in town hall or city hall. Speak with a building inspector about your situation and ask for his recommendation of a contractor with whom he is familiar. If the building inspector can recommend a contractor it means that the individual meets with the approval of the building department, knows the codes, and can work to gain the approval of the building department expeditiously. It also might mean that the contractor and the inspector are members of the same good-old-boy network. And that is good news for you. Hire a contractor recommended by the building department, and ask him to make sure all his alterations comply with the requirements of the building department. And if you're worried about it costing you a few hundred dollars more, think how much it would cost you to tear down the structure. How would the loss of this structure affect the property value?

Holding a Deal Together

Local building department recommendations can be quite productive. We have used them to alleviate our difficulties. In our first investment we bought a wide-line ranch home. The house featured a huge eat-in kitchen. In our purchase, we were represented by an uncle, a highly successful corporate attorney—mistake number one. At closing, he asked for a C.O. but never requested a Certificate of Completion to legalize the enlargement of the kitchen. We, as novices, put our trust in our attorney. We did not learn of our error until eight years later when we decided to sell. We couldn't sell because the buyer's attorney demanded a Certificate of Completion.

We found a legitimate method to correct the problem. First we went to contract with the buyer, guaranteeing to supply a C.O. We set aside the sum of $10,000 to be held in escrow for the obtaining of the certificate. We proceeded to visit the town building department and were given a set of procedures to follow, as well as the name of an architect who was familiar with town regulations.

Since the structure was already completed, the architect had to pretend that the structure did not exist. He had to draw plans as if the kitchen were going to be constructed. Having worked with the town for decades, he was well versed with procedures. With great diligence and a vivid imagination the architect completed plans and submitted them to the building department. Shortly thereafter the plans were approved, the structure was inspected, and the certificate was issued. Closing on the sale proceeded on schedule, and the escrow money was released to us.

What lessons can be learned from our experience? Don't buy properties without checking if they have illegal additions. Don't hire an attorney who doesn't know real estate law inside and out. Remember that the local building department can be a valuable source of information. Any time renovations are being done, whether by you or a contractor, remember there is accountability and the need to comply with the laws. In your case, you have to answer to the building department and the zoning department codes.

The Nuts and Bolts of Contracting

Not everyone is a born general contractor. The problem is that it takes some people thousands of dollars and dozens of grey hairs to find that out. If you have a job where you are on the road for days or weeks at a time, are behind a desk from nine to five without a phone, or are otherwise inaccessible for the entire work day, you should not be a general contractor. There are going to be times when your input is needed to make an urgent decision or when you should be there to make certain the project is proceeding on schedule or within budget. If you can't be there when your presence is required, you should hire a builder to oversee the project.

It can't be overemphasized how important it is to know exactly what you want to do and how you want it to be done. Detailed plans must be made before construction begins. Subcontractors, the people you hire to complete each segment of the entire job, must understand thoroughly your plans, goals, and expectations. As the work progresses you must maintain accurate records, obtain necessary permits, approvals, and documents, as well as make sure sufficient insurance is in force. As the general contractor, you have to size up potential subcontractors and determine if each has the necessary skill, reputation, appropriate price, and compatibility with you and other future employees. You will evaluate the subcontractor based upon recent work he has done in the area, as well as his price, since the lowest-priced person is not always the best choice. You will keep an open mind and an open checkbook to allow for the unexpected and added expenses. With the right attitude, the necessary preparations, sound judgment, and sufficient financing you can avoid many headaches and make general contracting a success.

Should you be your own general contractor? General contractors who operate their own construction firms don't think you should. The reason is not surprising. You can save at least one-third of the cost by contracting yourself. And that cuts into their business as general contractors where they hire all the subcontractors and parcel out the work. It doesn't matter if a wrench doesn't fit your hands, since it is not necessary for you to do the physical labor. You can still be the general contractor, without taking a test or having exceptional mechanical ability. In fact, most states don't even require a license or exam to be a contractor.

Organization is a must in becoming your own contractor. Most importantly, you must be able to coordinate the project. Will you be able to make sure the subcontractor and workers show up for work every day? Can you oversee the shipment of materials and make sure you have sufficient quantities to complete the job? Will you be able to do each of the following—obtain the work permits before work begins, hire the necessary personnel, meet the payroll, set up the work schedule, keep in contact with building and zoning departments as problems arise, and arrange for periodic inspections by the building and zoning departments as conditions warrant?

If you think being a general contractor is within your grasp, stop and consider these questions:

- ☞ Do you have the time to oversee the job and stay until completion?
- ☞ Will you be able to make frequent and unplanned trips to the work site?
- ☞ Can you make detailed plans and follow them through to completion?
- ☞ Can you maintain accurate records and comply with all regulations?
- ☞ Can you delegate responsibility to each contractor and oversee the work?
- ☞ Will you be able to set aside a substantial sum of money to allow for unexpected expenses?
- ☞ Do you have working relationships with suppliers for materials?
- ☞ Do you have a substantial line of credit?
- ☞ Can you get along with a variety of people?
- ☞ Are you willing to hire and pay for additional help if the project becomes unmanageable or overwhelming?

If the answers to fewer than seven questions are YES, becoming a general contractor might not be the right move for you. Read on and find out why.

COMPLYING WITH LOCAL ZONING AND HOUSING LAWS

Most people who become wealthy with rehab housing do it through sweat equity. Simply, they do most of the labor themselves, saving the cost of hiring laborers. The cost of hiring workers is prohibitive and cuts deeply into any expected profit. If you are handy or know someone who is, the best way to profit with rehabs is with the do-it-yourself approach.

Rehabbing is more than tearing down and building back up. There are regulations that must be obeyed. Zoning laws and building codes vary from city to city and even town to town. Visit city hall or the local library and check out the local residential zoning laws. If they are written in gobblygook, visit the zoning department and ask questions. Meet with the building inspector and ask questions about your proposed project, learning the steps required to comply with the laws of the city or town. Inquire about the regulations governing your project.

We have always been told that money doesn't grow on trees. If you are doing rehabs or other construction, you might learn differently. Trees might cost you large sums of money. In your locality, there could be laws dictating where trees should or should not be placed. More importantly, local regulations can prohibit you from removing trees from a plot. The inability to remove trees can make construction or rehabbing more difficult and costly, as the law dictates even how far from the property line you can build.

Quite possibly a building permit will be required for your project. Building permits are both costly and complicated. Along with a building permit, there must be detailed information about the project, drawings, and photographs. An architect or draftsman could charge hundreds or even thousands of dollars for the professionally-drawn plans submitted to obtain the permits. Other varied fees are paid to obtain the permit. In fact, in New York State, the building code requires a registered architect or licensed engineer to prepare construction plans for any project in excess of $10,000. Check in your locality for laws governing construction.

There are other factors to be considered, as well. If there is an addition to the structure, which could affect neighbors, people living within a certain radius of the property must be informed. Zoning board meetings are held to air any objections from neighbors in a public forum. People have the right at zoning board meetings to protest the construction and even prevent it if it will affect their property with any losses or disruptions. To ease neighbor's anxieties, sketches, photos, and sample models are presented at board meetings to gain approval of the project. Following the testimony, the members of the zoning board vote their approval or disapproval.

Zoning board meetings are by no means a piece of cake, unless you have broken bread with some of the board members prior to the meeting. You can, without violating any improprieties, speak to a board member in an attempt to gain insights about your project and a guesstimate about its chances. Frequently to smooth things over, an investor hires builders, architects, or engineers with a good reputation in the community. Requesting the name of a well-respected person from a zoning board member can be productive. That person might agree to accompany you to the zoning board meeting to answer any questions posed.

Timing is always important. When you obtain a building permit, you must remember there is a time limit. It is urgent to start building before the permit expires. If you don't, you must start all over again, applying for a new permit and paying the necessary fees. Once construction begins, expect visits from the building inspector to make sure everything complies with the laws. If the carpenter or architect know the building inspector and have worked with the local building codes, the project flows more smoothly. You might even be able to sleep nights.

COST-EFFECTIVE REMODELING

Remodeling is more than meets the eye and the wallet. The toughest part, besides paying the bill, is deciding how much to renovate. As a real estate investor concerned with the bottom line, you have to be concerned with improvements that will build value in your investment. Of course, certain repairs have to be done just to make a building usable. Not all improvements will add to the resale value when you choose to sell, but are a must anyway.

One of the wisest improvements you could choose would be insulation. Adding insulation is a double-edged sword. It not only increases property value, it also reduces heating and operating costs. Local utilities encourage energy conservation by visiting and offering a free energy audit, while informing you of the amount of insulation needed. Insulation can be expected to cost between $1500 and $2000, including labor for an average house. In resale value, about 80% of the cost will be recovered.

Remodeling a bathroom can be appealing to the eye, and it is rewarding to the balance sheet. A remodeled bathroom can be expected to cost between $6000 and $10,000. Of course, with frills it can cost many times that. In the northeast, prices are considerably higher. There are many components to a bathroom remodeling job as listed in the list of typical expenses. Yours can vary, as construction costs differ in parts of the country. The prices in the list merely demonstrate the extent of labor and materials required in a bathroom renovation. They are not actual prices. A person desiring a more lavish remodeling might include marble sinks and vanities, hot tubs, etc. Such would not be advisable for a person doing a rehab and seeking to flip the property. To be kept in mind however, research shows that a remodeled bathroom added to an existing home increases the selling price by the cost of the bathroom. A ten thousand dollar bathroom renovation will get the seller an additional ten thousand dollars at selling time. So a bathroom remodeling is a cost-effective project.

Typical Bathroom Remodeling Costs

Carpentry—$2500
New wall—$1800
Electrical—$500
Drywall—$400
Paint—$100
Tile—$1200
Toilet—$300
Shower—$500
Mirror—$200

Kitchen remodelings are also cost-effective projects, though with kitchens the KISS approach works best. As simple as you can keep the remodeling, the better. Smaller remodelings increase the value of a house, as do major remodelings, though neither will gain back the full investment cost as a bathroom remodeling will. A kitchen remodeling should be considered more of a comfort enhancer than a profit enhancer.

Skylights and swimming pools, like the kitchen modernization, make a house a more attractive and comfortable place to live. However, unlike the kitchen modernization, they are not as cost-effective. A skylight increases the value of a house by a little more than half its cost, while a swimming pool only recaptures a small portion of its investment in a resale. The reason is that not everyone wants a swimming pool in the backyard, unless the house is situated in the southeast or southwest. In most parts of the country, an in-ground pool will only enhance the value of a house by about twenty-five percent of its cost. In many cases, the presence of an in-ground pool will make it more difficult to sell the house.

If you hate to have your investment dollars go up in smoke, there is one rehab job to consider. The fireplace. Research shows that a six-foot wide fireplace and mantle will enhance the resale value by more than its cost. Not only will you enjoy the warmth of the fireplace but also the warm feeling of a higher selling price.

Unquestionably major renovations add beauty and value to a home. Some offer dollar-for-dollar value, while others pay back a portion of the investment. One decision every investor faces with renovations is how to pay for them, especially when you have a total rehab situation, and the banks won't give you the time of day. Real estate investment expert Sonny Bloch suggests a plan to win over lenders and gain needed rehab money. He suggests that you hire an appraiser who belongs to the SREA, ASA, or MAI to appraise the house. First, you want him to appraise the house as it is before renovations. Then you want the appraiser to furnish you with an appraisal reflecting what the house will be in showplace condition. Of course, the house will appraise substantially higher with the house renovated than when it looks like a bomb site. Meeting with a lender, you present both appraisals, so the lender can gauge the intrinsic value of the property as estimated by professionals. If you are looking for $60,000, and you have a house that will appraise for $200,000 in showplace condition, there will be little problem obtaining financing.

HUD

Now that you have the information about the costs of rehabbing, ways to obtain financing, and methods of locating an ideal rehab property, what do you do with it? The information has no use unless you know where to find a rehab project? One way is to read through the daily newspapers in search of HUD listings.

HUD is the Department of Housing and Urban Development, a branch of the Federal government, which encourages new home construction through the Federal Housing Administration (FHA). It deals with lenders, such as banks, savings and loans, and mortgage companies, and insures the lenders against losses from homeowners who cannot meet their mortgage payments. HUD, as the lender of last resort, sometimes takes over the loans from the lending institution.

When you read an ad in the newspaper offering HUD homes for sale, there are minimum bids required. Homes are shown through local real estate brokers with the key to the home kept in a lock box. Sealed bids are submitted to the broker, with the highest bidder obtaining the property. Particular terms and information are contained in each advertisement.

Investors don't often think of HUD when seeking out bargain properties, but HUD can be an important source of financial assistance and properties to purchase. HUD offices are located in all fifty states plus the District of Columbia and Puerto Rico. Larger states have more than one office. New York, for example, has three offices, California has six, and Texas has five. To find the location of your nearest HUD office, open to the white pages telephone directory. Turn to the blue pages on the last pages of the directory. Find the pages with the heading United States Government Offices. Under the letter H locate HOUSING & URBAN DEVELOPMENT. Contact either the Public Information Officer or General Information to be put in touch with the office to suit your particular needs.

For your convenience, if you want to contact HUD offices outside your calling area you might contact regional HUD offices throughout the United States.

HUD Regional Offices

States—Arkansas, Idaho, Oregon, Washington State

1321 2nd Avenue (Arcade Plaza Bldg.)
Seattle, WA 98101
(206) 442-5414

States—Alabama, Florida, Georgia, Kentucky, Mississippi, North Carolina, South Carolina, Tennessee

75 Spring Street S.W. (Richard R. Russell Federal Bldg.)
Atlanta, GA 30303
(404) 331-5136

States—Arkansas, Louisiana, Texas, New Mexico, Oklahoma

1600 Throckmorton (mailing address: P.O. Box 2905)
Fort Worth, TX 76113
(817) 885-5401

States—Arizona, California, Hawaii, Nevada

450 Golden Gate Ave. (mailing address: P.O. Box 36003)
San Francisco, CA 94102
(415) 556-4752

States—Colorado, Montana, North Dakota, South Dakota, Utah, Wyoming

1405 Curtis Street (Executive Tower Building)
Denver, CO 80202
(303) 844-4513

States—Connecticut, Massachusetts, Maine, New Hampshire, Rhode Island,
Vermont

10 Causeway Street (375 Federal Building)
Boston, MA 02222
(617) 565-5234

States and Districts—District of Columbia, Delaware, Maryland, Pennsylvania,
Virginia, West Virginia

105 S. 7th Street (Liberty Square Building)
Philadelphia, PA 19106
(215) 597-2560

States—Iowa, Kansas, Missouri, Nebraska

1103 Grand Avenue (Professional Building)
Kansas City, MO 64106
(816) 374-6432

States—Illinois, Indiana, Michigan, Minnesota, Ohio, Wisconsin

626 West Jackson Blvd.
Chicago, IL 60606
(312) 353-5680

States and Territories—New York, New Jersey, Puerto Rico, Virgin Islands

26 Federal Plaza
New York, NY 10278
(212) 264-8053

HUD Loans

In addition to HUD being the source of low-cost properties in need of rehabilitation, it is also a provider of home improvement loans. HUD has a number of programs available to investors and other homeowners. The first is the Section 312 Loan Program that offers loans at single digit interest rates to qualified borrowers. To qualify, the money must be used to enable the house to comply with local building codes. If there is additional money lent, it is to increase property values. To qualify for the loan the house must be located in an area considered a designated revitalization area. The government decides to encourage rehabilitation of an area by making low-cost loans that are not otherwise available for investment in other areas.

Another HUD home improvement loan program is the Title I program. The purpose of the Title I program is to improve the habitability of houses in urban areas. Through this program, you can obtain a loan up to $15,000 for fifteen years at a below-market rate specified at the time by the bank. Even though this is a HUD program, it is overseen by the local banks. You apply to the bank for a home improvement loan and based upon your credit rating, it is granted or denied. HUD does not actually make the loan. It backs ninety percent of the loan, so that if you don't pay back the loan, HUD will pay the bank ninety percent of the proceeds. The remaining ten percent remains a thorn in the lender's side. Since the bank does not have the full amount of the loan guaranteed by HUD, and it might have suffered considerable losses in recent years, it becomes overly careful in extending loans. The result is that many well-qualified borrowers might not be approved for Title I loans. A good working relationship with a neighborhood bank can make Title I approval more easily attainable.

Guide to HUD Offices

Many investors prefer to deal with bureaucrats on a face to face level and feel that is impossible if dealing with a regional office. Should you want to contact a local office of the Department of Housing and Urban Development instead of a regional office, a listing of HUD offices in each state has been provided.

Alabama

The Daniel Building
15 South 20th Street
Birmingham, Alabama 35233
(205) 254-1630

Alaska

701 C Street
Box 64
Anchorage, Alaska 99513
(907) 271-4170

Arizona

Phoenix Branch
The Arizona Bank Building
101 North 1st Avenue, Suite 1800
P.O. Box 13468
Phoenix, Arizona 85002
(602) 261-4434

Tucson Branch
The Arizona Bank Building
33 North Stone Avenue, Suite 1450
Tucson, Arizona 85701
(602) 629-6237

Arkansas

The Savers Building
320 West Capitol, Suite 700
Little Rock, Arkansas 72201
(501) 378-5401

California

San Francisco Branch
The Philip Burton Federal Building
450 Golden Gate Avenue
P.O. Box 36003
San Francisco, California 94102
(415) 556-4752

Fresno Branch
1315 Van Ness Street, Suite 200
Fresno, California 93721
(209) 487-5036

Los Angeles Branch
2500 Wilshire Boulevard
Los Angeles, California 90057
(213) 688-5973

Sacramento Branch
545 Downtown Plaza, Suite 250
P.O. Box 1978
Sacramento, California 95809
(916) 440-3471

San Diego Branch
The Federal Office Building
880 Front Street
San Diego, California 92188
(619) 293-5310

Santa Ana Branch
34 Civic Center Plaza
Box 12850
Santa Ana, California 92712
(714) 836-2451

Colorado

The Executive Tower Building
1405 Curtis Street
Denver, Colorado 80202
(303) 837-4513

Connecticut

1 Hartford Square West
Hartford, Connecticut 06104
(203) 722-3638

Delaware

The IBM Building
800 Delaware Avenue, Suite 101
Wilmington, Delaware 19801
(302) 573-6300

District of Columbia

Universal North Building
1875 Connecticut Avenue NW
Washington, D.C. 20009
(202) 673-5837

Florida

Coral Gables Branch
The Gables One Tower
1320 South Dixie Highway
Coral Gables, Florida 33146
(305) 662-4510

Jacksonville Branch
325 West Adams Street
Jacksonville, Florida 32202
(904) 791-2626

Orlando Branch
The Federal Office Building
80 North Hughey
Orlando, Florida 32801
(305) 420-6441

Tampa Branch
700 Twiggs Street
P.O. Box 2097
Tampa, Florida 33601
(813) 228-2501

Georgia

Richard B. Russell Federal Building
75 Spring Street SW
Atlanta, Georgia 30303
(404) 221-5136

Hawaii

300 Ala Moana Boulevard
P.O. Box 50007
Honolulu, Hawaii 96813
(808) 546-2136

Idaho

The Federal Building
P.O. Box 042
550 West Fort Street
Boise, Idaho 83724
(208) 334-2561

Illinois

Chicago Branch
300 South Wacker Drive
Chicago, Illinois 60606
(312) 353-5680

Chicago Branch
547 West Jackson Boulevard
Chicago, Illinois 60606
(312) 353-7660

Springfield Branch
524 South 2nd Street, Suite 600
Springfield, Illinois 62701
(217) 492-4276

Indiana

151 North Delaware Street
Indianapolis, Indiana 46204
(317) 269-6303

Iowa

The Federal Building
210 Walnut Street, Suite 259
Des Moines, Iowa 50309
(515) 284-4512

Kansas

444 SE Quincy Street, Room 297
Topeka, Kansas 66683
(913) 295-2683

Kentucky

539 4th Avenue
P.O. Box 1044
Louisville, Kentucky 40201
(502) 582-5251

Louisiana

New Orleans Branch
1661 Canal Street
New Orleans, Louisiana 70112
(504) 569-2301

Shreveport Branch
The New Federal Building
500 Fannin Street
Shreveport, Louisiana 71101
(318) 226-5385

Maine

The U.S. Federal & Post Office Bldg.
200 Harlow Street
Bangor, Maine 04401
(207) 947-8410

Maryland

The Equitable Building
10 North Calvert Street
Baltimore, Maryland 21202
(301) 962-2121

Massachusetts

John F. Kennedy Federal Building
Room 800
Boston, Massachusetts 02203
(617) 223-4066

The Bullfinch Building
15 New Chardon Street
Boston, Massachusetts 02114
(617) 223-4111

Michigan

Detroit Branch
Patrick V. McNamara Federal Building
477 Michigan Avenue
Detroit, Michigan 48226
(313) 226-7900

Flint Branch
The Genessee Bank Building
352 South Saginaw Street, Room 200
Flint, Michigan 48502
(313) 234-5621

Grand Rapids Branch
2922 Fuller Avenue NE
Grand Rapids, Michigan 49505
(616) 456-2225

Minnesota

220 2nd Street South
Minneapolis, Minnesota 55401
(612) 349-3002

Mississippi

The Federal Building, Suite 1016
100 West Capital Street
Jackson, Mississippi, 39269
(601) 960-4702

Missouri

Kansas City Branch
The Professional Building
1103 Grand Avenue
Kansas City, Missouri 64106
(816) 374-2661

St. Louis Branch
210 North Tucker Boulevard
St. Louis, Missouri 63101
(314) 425-4761

Montana

The Federal Office Building
301 South Park, Room 340
Helena, Montana 59626
(406) 449-5205

Nebraska

The Braiker/Brandeis Building
210 South 16th Street
Omaha, Nebraska 68102
(402) 221-3703

Nevada

Las Vegas Branch
720 South 7th Street, Suite 221
Las Vegas, Nevada 89101
(702) 385-6525

Reno Branch
1050 Bible Way
P.O. Box 4700
Reno, Nevada 89505
(702) 784-5356

New Hampshire

Norris Cotton Federal Building
275 Chestnut Street
Manchester, New Hampshire 03101
(603) 666-7681

New Jersey

Newark Branch
The Military Park Building
60 Park Place
Newark, New Jersey 07102
(201) 645-3010

Camden Branch
The Parkade Building
519 Federal Street
Camden, New Jersey 08103
(609) 757-5081

New Mexico

625 Truman Street NE
Albuquerque, New Mexico 87110
(505) 766-3251

New York

New York City Branch
26 Federal Plaza
New York, N.Y. 10278
(212) 264-8068

Albany Branch
Leo W. O'Brien Federal Building
North Pearl Street and Clinton Avenue
Albany, New York, 12207
(518) 472-3567

Buffalo Branch
The Statler Building-Mezzazine
107 Delaware Avenue
Buffalo, New York, 14202
(716) 846-5755

North Carolina

415 North Edgeworth Street
Greensboro, North Carolina 27401
(919) 378-5363

North Dakota

The Federal Building
P.O. Box 2483
653 Second Avenue North
Fargo, North Dakota 58102
(701) 237-5771

Ohio

Cincinnati Branch
The Federal Office Building, Rm. 9002
550 Main Street
Cincinnati, Ohio 45202
(513) 684-2884

Cleveland Branch
777 Rockwell Avenue—Second Floor
Cleveland, Ohio 44114
(216) 522-4065

Columbus Branch
200 North High Street
Columbus, Ohio 43215
(614) 469-7345

Oklahoma

Oklahoma City Branch
The Murrah Federal Building
200 NW Fifth Street
Oklahoma City, Oklahoma 73102
(405) 231-4891

Tulsa Branch
The Robert S. Kerr Building
440 South Houston Avenue, Room 200
Tulsa, Oklahoma 74127
(918) 581-7435

Oregon

520 Southwest Sixth Avenue
Portland, Oregon 97204
(503) 221-2561

Pennsylvania

Philadelphia Branch
The Curtis Building
6th and Walnut Streets
Philadelphia, Pennsylvania 19106
(215) 597-2560

Pittsburgh Branch
Fort Pitt Commons
445 Fort Pitt Boulevard
Pittsburgh, Pennsylvania 15219
(412) 644-2802

Rhode Island

330 John O. Pastore Federal Building
Providence, Rhode Island 02903
(401) 528-5351

South Carolina

Strom Thurmond Federal Building
1835-45 Assembly Street
Columbia, South Carolina 29201
(803) 765-5592

South Dakota

119 Federal Building
400 South Phillips Avenue
Sioux Falls, South Dakota 57102
(605) 336-2980

Tennessee

Knoxville Branch
1 Northshore Building
1111 Northshore Drive
Knoxville, Tennessee 37919
(615) 558-1384

Memphis Branch
100 North Main Street, 28th Floor
Memphis, Tennessee 38103
(901) 521-3367

Nashville Branch
1 Commerce Place, Suite 1600
Nashville, Tennessee 37239
(615) 251-5213

Texas

Fort Worth Branch
221 West Lancaster
P.O. Box 2905
Fort Worth, Texas 76113
(817) 870-5401

Dallas Branch
1401 Slocum Street
P.O. Box 10050
Dallas, Texas 75207
(214) 767-8293

Houston Branch
2 Greenway Plaza East, Suite 200
Houston, Texas 77046
(713) 954-6821

Lubbock Branch
The Federal Office Building
1205 Texas Avenue
Lubbock, Texas 79401
(806) 743-7265

San Antonio Branch
Washington Square
800 Dolorosa
P.O. Box 9163
San Antonio, Texas 78285
(512) 229-6800

Utah

125 South State Street
Salt Lake City, Utah 84138
(801) 524-5237

Vermont

110 Main Street
Fairchild Square
Burlington, Vermont 05402
(802) 951-6274

Virginia

701 East Franklin Street
Richmond, Virginia 23219
(804) 771-2721

Washington

Seattle Branch
The Arcade Plaza Building
1321 Second Avenue
Seattle, Washington 98101
(206) 442-5414

Spokane Branch
West 920 Riverside Avenue
Spokane, Washington 99201
(509) 456-4571

West Virginia

The Kanawha Valley Building
Capitol And Lee Streets
Charleston, West Virginia 25301
(304) 347-7036

Wisconsin

The Henry S. Reuss Federal Plaza
310 West Wisconsin Avenue, Suite 1380
Milwaukee, Wisconsin 53203
(414) 291-1493

Wyoming

The Federal Office Building
P.O. Box 580
100 East B Street
Casper, Wyoming 82601
(307) 261-5252

SUMMARY

Rehabbing properties can be a rewarding field of real estate investment for the investor who considers the risk, is sufficiently financed, and is willing and able to make or finance the necessary repairs. The field is filled with traps, from unscrupulous contractors to projects requiring a never-ending supply of capital. Careful planning and diligent supervision avoids many of the problems.

Many insightful investors hire a professional before becoming involved in a costly rehab project. Without a thorough inspection by a home inspector or professional engineer, you might be entering financial quicksand. With a detailed report of the drawbacks and the cost to correct them, you can make an intelligent decision about whether the job is worth undertaking.

Experienced rehab people know that no two rehabs are the same. Though all require work, and the degree of work required varies. The general consensus among successful rehabbers is to only do what is necessary. Only replace what needs to be replaced. Try to stick with situations where painting and wallpapering can improve the situation dramatically. The simpler the improvement, the better it will be.

Not every house should be renovated. If a house is old and has antiquated electrical service, plumbing, lacks a foundation, and has a kitchen that cannot be eat-in and accommodate a microwave oven and a dishwasher, think twice about the advisability of rehabbing the house.

There are many pitfalls to avoid in rehabbing. You have to be prudent in checking out, hiring, and overseeing the work. Care must be paid in adhering to the building and zoning codes in any renovation. Failure to comply with the laws could subject you to dismantling the work at your expense. If you are planning to function as your own general contractor, you must make sure you have the time, money, organization, and persistance to follow the project to completion.

In planning a rehab, beyond the painting and wallpapering, certain projects recover more of their cost than others when you sell. Cost-effective repairs are a fireplace, bathroom remodeling, and a kitchen remodeling. Less cost-effective are swimming pools and skylights.

The Department of Housing and Urban Development is an excellent source of rehab properties. They are shown through your neighborhood real estate broker, who can obtain a key to show it from a lock box. If you are interested in a property, you submit a bid for it. The Department of Housing and Urban Development also offers home improvement loans that can be used in doing rehab work. Among the programs are the Section 312 loan program and the Title I program.

Rehabbing is not for everyone, but it could be for you. If it is, it offers one of the most rewarding ways to make large sums of money on a small amount of money invested. The trick is to choose the property carefully, finance it wisely, and manage it prudently.

6

Buying Foreclosures

Opportunities are never lost. The other person takes those you miss.

—Anonymous

FORECLOSURE REPRESENTS ONE OF THE BIGGEST BARGAIN-HUNTING techniques in real estate today. It is also one of the best-kept secrets. Your real estate agent does not usually know whether or not a property is in foreclosure. Unless you check at the county clerk's office, read the newspaper legal notices or subscribe to one of the foreclosure newsletters, it is unlikely that you are apprised of the foreclosures in your geographic area. There are three stages in which foreclosed properties can be bought. They can be bought before the sale, at the sale, or after the sale.

Before the sale means that you buy the property from the owner before the bank actually sells the property at auction. The holder of a mortgage files a notice of default at the county courthouse. The notice of default puts the homeowner on record that he or she has missed a number of payments and will have the mortgage foreclosed on unless back payments are made. You can visit the county courthouse and read through the file of notices of default. Then you can contact the owner and make offers. A homeowner who has just been served with a notice of default is not likely to be in a festive mood, but it is always possible he might be willing to negotiate a deal to get some money for his house before he loses everything. Furthermore, if you are the first or one of the first people to contact a financially-troubled homeowner, there is the chance he or she will sell to you on favorable terms when the reality of foreclosure kicks in.

NOTICE OF DEFAULT

Foreclosure is a lengthy and complicated process. After missing a first payment a friendly letter is mailed to the homeowner. With each succeeding missed payment the situation becomes more crucial. After the third payment, the notice of default is usually sent, and the ninety day clock begins to tick. During that time a homeowner has the opportunity to catch up with missed payments, penalties, and legal expenses. If the homeowner fails to pay off the accumulated payments within the time period, the next step is reached. A notice of sale is mailed to the homeowner and advertised three times before the date of the auction sale.

Before the sale, there are numerous ways of acquiring bargain properties. After reading the notice of default, you can look up the homeowner in the white pages of the telephone book and do the following:

1. Call up the seller and ask how much cash is needed to save the house and the owner's credit.
2. Design a general flyer and mail it out to everyone who has received a notice of default within the last month.
3. Personalize a letter and mail it to every recipient of a notice of default within the last month.
4. Have business cards printed with ''I BUY HOUSES'' and deposit them in mailboxes of financially-troubled homeowners who received a notice of default.

A notice of default can be a financial death sentence to a homeowner but a window of opportunity to you. A notice of default is a written notice stating that a loan is delinquent and is on its way to be foreclosed and sold. The notice of default is mailed to everyone involved and recorded by a mortgageholder with the county clerk's office in the county courthouse. The filing of the notice of default starts a ninety-day period. The notice does not appear in the newspaper, but it is sent to the nonpaying homeowner. The papers are frightening and lengthy. The nonpayer is bombarded with phone calls and letters from people offering to save him from disaster. Sensing that desperation, these good samaritans offer deals that often appear too good to be true. It seems that everyone has an interest in the property.

Three monthly mortgage payments were missed before the notice of default was recorded. No payments were received by the lender. The time clock is still ticking as the fourth monthly mortgage payment is missed. Many homeowners sense the imminent disaster. With four missed payments, it is becoming increasingly difficult to save the property. Within days, all second and third mortgageholders will receive a copy of the notice of default. Before this, they might have had no knowledge of financial problems, if they were getting paid. These mortgageholders are likely to contact the nonpayer and make matters more uncomfortable. Not able to cope with the pressure cooker, many nonpayers abandon their homes and walk away from the situation.

The fifth mortgage payment has been missed. It is the point of no return. Five months of missed payments plus thousands of dollars in bank attorney fees make the situation virtually hopeless. If the nonpayer was unable to make one payment initially, how can he now pay five payments plus thousands of dollars in legal fees? The only thing the nonpayer has now is time. One month remains to make all back payments and become reinstated.

If the sixth monthly payment has been missed, the clock stops ticking. Ninety days have passed since the notice of default was filed in the county courthouse. Everything is about to hit the fan. Within a matter of days, the chance to be reinstated will have passed. The only options remaining are to get the bank's permission to sell or wait until being forced out. (In some areas there is a forty-five-day period to stop foreclosure, rather than the ninety-day period that has been described here.) If the person is able to sell, it might be just for moving costs or a few dollars for food. If the person is fortunate, he might be able to have the lender agree to accept the house back before the official foreclosure. The agreement is called a *deed in lieu of foreclosure*. Though the person loses the house, he does not have his credit rating ruined. By assigning the house back to the bank legally, he does not have a default on his credit rating. The all-important credit rating is saved.

If the lender refuses to take back the property with the deed in lieu of foreclosure, the nonpayer has to face the music. One week after the ninety-day period expires, a notice of sale is published in the newspaper and mailed to the nonpayer and all holders of mortgages and liens against the property. Seven days later a second notice of sale is published in a newspaper. Seven days after that, a third notice is published in the newspaper. Finally, the date of sale arrives and the house is sold at auction.

Below is the Foreclosure Timetable. It does not apply to all foreclosure situations. Remember that some states do not allow ninety days for a nonpayer to be reinstated. Some lenders also do not file a notice of default until months after the third month. Therefore the date at which the notice of default becomes effective is well beyond the sixth month. The table below is to serve as a guide to show how foreclosure takes place.

THE FORECLOSURE TIMETABLE

Missed Payments	Course of Action
1	Sent friendly letter.
2	Receive inquiry from lender to determine if problem exists.

Missed Payments	*Course of Action*
3	Foreclosure letter. Notice of Default is recorded. Ninety-day clock begins to tick.
4	Clock still ticking. Junior lienholders are to be notified.
5	Ninety-day clock on back payments, high legal fees doom owner.
6	Ninety-day clock is about to stop. Little time to reinstate. Notice of sale to be published in papers and sent to junior lienholders (Fig. 6-1). House to be sold at auction.

How to Help a Nonpayer

You have heard about foreclosures. You have read the Foreclosure Timetable. But what can you do about it? How can you get started? If you are a regular visitor to the county courthouse to check on notice of default filings, you become aware of them shortly after they are filed. At the time of filing, the homeowner is still in the early stages of financial problems. While three missed payments does not seem like an insurmountable obstacle to you, it is an albatross around the neck of a troubled homeowner. The homeowner has been warned that the house will be foreclosed, and however well-meaning the homeowner might be, there seems to be no way out. That is where you step in. The person feels helpless, expecting to lose his entire investment in the house. Though the person probably does not know it, he is also about to gain an unfavorable credit rating as the property is foreclosed upon for nonpayment. The default will stay on the credit report for seven years, making future borrowing near-impossible. You can step in as a white knight.

Taking the First Step

From reading the notice of default, you have learned who the lender is, as well as the identity of the owner and other pertinent information. The information is listed in the filing. You uncover how much is owed to correct the notice of default and the amount of legal fees owed. You visit the title company and pay for a commitment letter, making sure that there are no other liens on the property. Then, you determine the market value of the property. By checking current ads, inspecting the MLS books, or getting an appraisal, you can then estimate the value of the house and begin to approach the homeowner. If you know a real estate agent, you can check at what price comparable houses have sold in the last ninety days.

Calling for Action

By doing your homework, you are a step ahead of everyone else. From visiting the county courthouse and checking the notice of default lists, you know the owner and address. Consider opening up the white pages of the phone book and contacting the owner. Don't shoot from the lip. Prepare you questions in advance, remembering that the situation is touchy for you and the owner. No one feels comfortable discussing another person's financial problems.

There is an alternative to the in-person approach. The word processor can offer a personalized approach without face-to-face discussions, at least at first. In a personalized letter, explain that you are interested in buying her house. Mention that you will not only pay off all the debts on the house, but also will pay the moving expenses. You will be able to save her credit rating.

Dear Mrs. Homeowner,

Recently I learned that you are having problems with your house payments. I think I can help. I am not a rich corporation. I am a working person like you. I am a person who likes to help people with their problems. I would like to buy your house. I will pay all your back payments and even your moving expenses. If you would like to stay in your house, I think I can still help.

Please think things over. If you are interested in saving your credit rating and maybe your house, please give me a call. My phone number is 555-7259.

Sincerely,

Donna Paltrowitz

If you feel that this letter is not for you, fine. It is only a guide. Feel free to personalize it. Remember that it won't work all the time. People in financial trouble are not very trusting. You have to gain the person's trust. That is why your letter emphasized that you are a working person, not some heartless corporation.

What do you do if the person responds to your letter? The best thing you can do is invite the owner for a cup of coffee. You can meet at the local diner or coffee shop. If the person invites you to her house, of course accept. But don't invite the person to your house. It will destroy your plans because the person will see you as well-to-do. This will drive a wedge between you and probably shatter all your chances.

On the other hand if you meet at a diner or in her home, the owner will feel more at ease and unthreatened. She will be more receptive to discussing her problems and ideas. Try to listen carefully and allow the owner to open up to you. You can learn all about her needs and gain insight into ways you can help yourself and her. It is then you can ask probing questions in a nonthreatening atmosphere. Questions you could ask would include:

☞ How much cash do you actually need?
☞ Do you need the money to move or to pay off debts?
☞ Would you like to stay in the house if you could?
☞ What would you say if I offered to pay your expenses, buy the house, and let you rent it from me?

Preparing a Flyer

Would you like to reach more people in a shorter period of time? You might want to consider a flyer. You can design your own and then photostat copies. Let the troubled homeowner know that you are looking to buy a house and will pay all back payments. Stress that you are a responsible individual and not a multi-million dollar company. People like dealing with a real person, not a faceless corporation. Here are several suggestions to show how it can be done. You probably have many more ideas. Look in the classifieds under Houses Wanted, and you will find a variety of approaches with different workings.

YOUNG COUPLE LOOKING FOR A HOUSE. WE WILL PAY YOUR BACK PAYMENTS. PLEASE CALL US AT 555-6972

IF YOU MUST SELL I WILL BUY. I WILL PAY ALL YOUR BACK PAYMENTS AND BUY YOUR HOUSE. PLEASE CALL ME AT 555-6972.

This flyer can be an $8^1/2$-×-11-inch piece of paper. Once prepared to your satisfaction, with your first name and phone number, an offset printer will make one hundred quality copies for less than ten dollars. So for less than ten dollars, you can reach one hundred potential customers.

When you compile a list of people who have received a notice of default from the county courthouse or assemble names from a foreclosure newsletter, you might decide to mail each homeowner a copy of your flyer and wait for results. Though this approach is "hit or miss" and does not guarantee results, if your efforts result in even one deal, your efforts will have paid off smartly.

The Clock Continues to Tick

Although the notice of default is received by the homeowner and is recorded at the county courthouse, it is only the beginning of the foreclosure process. Many homeowners still believe they are holding a gold mine, despite the fact that they have already missed three back payments. Rather than sell to you, they will more likely list with a real estate agent. If the house is priced right for the market, it will sell within a reasonable period of time. However, if the homeowner is inflexible and unrealistic in price or terms, a sale will take much longer.

Sellers who are in the foreclosure process too often overestimate the time they have to sell and the ease in which they will sell. Time and bank attorneys wait for no one. The ninety-day notice of default has passed, and the bank is running with the ball. With another missed payment, the second mortgage holders will be applying the pressure. They are becoming concerned with their investment. They have begun to call, write, or visit to find out the true situation. That is bad news for the homeowner and good news for you. Not having sold the property through the realtor and now being many months in arrears, the house is almost history, as well as the homeowner's credit rating.

With six months elapsed, six payments have been missed. Along with the accumulation of thousands of dollars in legal costs, the situation is crucial. The ninety-day reinstatement period as a result of the notice of default has passed. That means that the homeowner can no longer make the back payments and have the mortgage reinstated. The house is most probably a goner. Besides, the amount of back payments owed is prohibitive. A week or so later, the first notice of sale will appear in the local newspaper. While it might seem that your chances with the homeowner have improved with the passage of time, they have not. The reason is that the notice of default has been public knowledge for several months. Any of the hundreds of thousands of daily readers could have seen the legal notice. To complicate matters, the notice of sale has appeared in the daily newspaper, as well as two other public places. It is possible that the notice of sale could have listed in three different newspapers.

Foreclosure newsletters publish this listing, as well as thousands of other foreclosures. Don't give up hope yet of buying a foreclosure. Though you are competing against other potential bargain hunters, it is still worth pursuing the deal if there is substantial equity in the property. Statistics show that most properties at a foreclosure sale do not even draw bidders, unless the properties are in a hot or recently hot area. Your hope is that no one shows up at the foreclosure auction.

By reading a foreclosure newsletter or the notice of sale in your daily newspaper, you may uncover vital information about a foreclosed property. The information might make it possible for you to negotiate a favorable deal.

Sale date, time and place
Address of property
Action (who is suing who?)
Original mortgage and filing date
Judgment amount

Index number (you can examine all the documents at town hall by looking up this number)
Plaintiff's attorney with telephone number
Section, lot and block number (you can find the exact location of the property)

FORECLOSURE AUCTIONS

In areas where real estate markets are or were recently hot, you cannot reasonably expect to pick up a bargain foreclosure property. It can happen, but it is a rare occurrence. In flat market areas, it is much more likely. The "good old boy" network prevents foreclosure bargains in hot areas. Our case in point is that several years ago, we read a notice of sale in the newspaper advertising a house to be sold at the courthouse steps on a particular date at a particular time and price. The price appeared to be at least thirty to forty percent below the market. Since the address was listed in the notice, we passed the house and viewed it from the outside. The notice listed the bank that was foreclosing name, address, and phone number of the bank's attorney. The day of the sale we arrived at the courthouse with a checkbook ready to bid. No more than three or four people waited in the vicinity. Finally when it was time for the sale, all interested parties looked at each other, gazed at their watches, and dispersed. We curiously entered the courthouse and made inquiries. With no one to answer our questions about the auction, we phoned the bank's attorney directly. We were told that the case was settled. Questioning further, we were informed that the homeowner paid off the loan. But had they really? The owner who couldn't make one back payment for all those months suddenly had enough money to pay all back payments and several thousand dollars in legal fees? Possible, but unlikely. Or could the attorney have made a sweetheart deal with the bank? No one can be sure what happened but it appears that two good old boys did business, and the public was deprived of the opportunity to get a bargain.

There was no auction that day, but foreclosure auctions do take place and real estate investors are able to purchase properties well below the market. The trick is to prepare for the auction and know how to find the foreclosed property auctions. One thing to keep in mind is that more than 90% of foreclosed properties are settled or postponed before the auction sale.

It really is not difficult to find the foreclosed property auction. Just look for the ads in the newspaper. The auctioneer will be listed in the ad. Before the auction, call or write the auctioneer and ask for a brochure. Included in the brochure will be pertinent information about the physical and financial condition of the property. With the information in hand, you can better decide if you really want to bid on the property.

No guarantees come with a foreclosed property. What you see is what you get. You are buying the property in as-is condition. You are permitted to inspect the property before the auction, so by all means do so. A good idea is to bring along a contractor or home inspector so you have a better idea of the condition and worth of the property.

Though you don't need to bring your friendly banker to the auction, you should have your financing in place in case you are successful in your bidding. You will be expected to close in forty-five to sixty days. A line of credit is a handy thing to have in reserve.

Don't leave home without it—your checkbook, that is. Bring either cash or a bank check to the auction. For safety sake, a bank check is the better choice. Have the check made out to you, so that if you don't win the bidding, you can redeposit the money in the bank on the next business day. You usually need 5% of the estimated sale price before you can bid. If you are successful in winning the bidding, you are expected to increase your deposit to ten percent within the next week.

Get to know the auctioneer. It is not necessary to invite him or her to dinner. Read the newspaper ads and follow his auctions of any type. Attend as many as possible before the auction at which you intend to bid. In that way, you will be familiar with his techniques, terminology, body language, etc. The auctions are free, and the insights you'll gain are valuable.

Before you attend the auction decide what will be the top price you will bid. Write that price on a 3-×-5 card, and place it in your breast pocket. At the auction hold the card in your hand, and promise yourself that you will not exceed that bid. Good luck.

Whoever wins the bidding pays the trustee. The trustee prepares the deed in your name. When the full price is paid, whether in cash or in mortgage form, the deal is closed. The trustee records the deed in your name. The house is yours.

After the Foreclosure Sale

Many bargain hunters interested in foreclosure properties skip the auction sale. They head right to the bank. Bank robber Willie Sutton when asked why he robbed banks said "because that's where the money is." Banks are also where the real estate is. Banks are sitting on billions of dollars in real estate that is not paying them interest. They call the property on their balance sheets Nonperforming Assets. You call it potential bargains.

When there is a foreclosure sale and no one shows up to make the minimum bid, the bank remains the owner of the property. Banks might be hungry and love money, but they don't love real estate. Banks aren't in the business of owning and managing real estate. Their business is lending money. They aren't real estate investors and are actually embarrassed to be holding real estate that isn't earning money and paying them any interest. The more properties that a bank lists on its company balance sheet as nonperforming assets, the more inept and poorly managed it appears to its stockholders and bank regulators. So the bank is anxious to unload its real estate-owned properties, known as REO properties. This sets the stage with the bank as a great motivated seller or Don't Wanter that offers you an opportunity to purchase property on favorable terms.

REO PROPERTIES CAN BE GREAT BUYS

There are many advantages for you in buying an REO. Being so anxious to sell a property, the bank not only sells it for only the auction price, but also makes sure the property is in livable condition. That is a substantial improvement over a property that is sold in as-is condition. Whatever repairs are needed will be made at the bank's expense. Remember too, that all junior liens were eliminated with the passage of the auction, even though there were no acceptable bids. If there was a $150,000 first mortgage and a $30,000 second mortgage prior to the auction sale, now there remains only the $150,000 first mortgage. Pay off the first mortgage, and the property is yours—free and clear.

It is easier said than done to just pay off the mortgage. You probably don't have $150,000 lying in your dresser drawer, and neither do we. Still you can complete the deal. The bank being anxious to deal will give back financing on favorable terms, with a low down payment. One bank in Florida, was asking for 10% down on investor-nonowner-occupied properties and 5% down on owner-occupied properties.

Everything sounds good so far. The trick to doing anything with which you are unfamiliar is knowing how to get started. You want to contact the lender, but you don't know what to say. If you don't know what to say, bankers can easily make you feel foolish. So you have to work out a plan. Prepare a list of questions to ask the lender and practice them before visiting the bank branch. Visit, don't call on the phone, if you want to be taken seriously. Start with a bank where you have an account so you can work into your approach that you are a depositor at the branch. It is probable that if the bank is a suburban branch, you will be directed to the main branch.

When you enter the bank, ask to speak to the officer in charge of REO properties or nonperforming assets. Expect to receive puzzled stares as bank personnel try to make you feel uncomfortable as you explain what nonperforming assets are. After you have given a good account of yourself, a bank officer will be summoned, and you will likely have to do your song and dance again. Ultimately either the officer will direct you to the person in the bank to assist you or an officer in another branch. No one ever said it was easy dealing with banks. Persistence will pay off.

Once you speak with the officer in charge of nonperforming assets, be sure to mention that you are a depositor or stockholder at the bank. A bank is more amenable to people with whom it has a working relationship. Make it known that you are interested in purchasing several of the REO properties, even though at the moment you will be more than satisfied with one. In that way, it is a win-win situation, where the bank perceives you as helping it with its problems. You will be given a list of REO properties. Examine the data carefully, and visit the properties before making any offers. Make a low offer on a property, at least twenty percent less than the asking price. If the bank turns down the offer, diplomatically tell the officer that the property is interesting, but it is more than you are willing to pay. Return the following month and remain professional. Ask to see the list of REO properties again. If you notice that the property on which you made an offer was not sold, make the same offer or one slightly above. See what the reaction is. There is nothing lost in trying to obtain a better bargain. The worst the bank can do is say no. And there is the possibility that the bank will accept the same offer it refused last month. Remember that it is thirty days later, and there are no payments coming in on the property.

What happens if the bank officer turns down this offer? You have two workable alternatives. You can raise your offer a few thousand dollars and begin a new dialogue. If the new offer is turned down, you might ask a question such as "how much money would you need to take it off your books?" If you are adamant and refuse to raise your offer, ask to speak with the officer's supervisor. An employee never wants a supervisor to intercede because it gives the impression that the person is unable to handle her job competently. As a long shot, the officer might approve your offer or suggest a compromise price. In either case, the thing to bear in mind is that you currently have no deal, so there is nothing to lose and quite a bit to gain.

NOBODY ASKED US BUT . . .

Many foreclosure investors seem to prefer investing after the sale. It is a much simpler procedure to buy after the sale unless you are on the inside of a deal with the bank's trustee. In our case, we were the holders of a second mortgage, who had been paid monthly for two and one half years, with no missed payments. One August evening, there was a loud knock at the door of our primary residence. Upon answering the door, we were served with a summons attached to a notice of default. The summons had been sent by the bank's attorney for the bank holding the first mortgage. One hour later, we were visited by our trustors to whom we issued a second mortgage. Visibly upset, our trustors confessed to having missed several payments. They approached us because they wanted to work with us and to continue to live on the premises. We had previously owned the property before the trustors purchased it from us. The trustors agreed to sell the house back to us with the understanding we would allow them to continue to live there. Working through an attorney and with the trustor's consent, we petitioned the bank to allow us to assume the mortgage, clear up back payments and all legal fees owed. After several weeks of credit checking and other investigations, we were approved by the lender. The lender presented us with a list of back payments and legal fees owed. Our attorney conducted a title search to make sure there were no large liens attached to the property, and prepared the necessary papers for the trustors and us to sign. Among them was a *letter of understanding*, a deed transferring property, and various tax transfer documents. Within one month we had finalized the transaction. The trustors became our tenants and were able to remain in their residence. Their credit rating was kept intact because the house did not actually become foreclosed. It was a win-win situation. We became successful acquirers of a valuable residence in a top neighborhood for a total of fifteen thousand dollars out of our pockets.

OTHER SOURCES OF FORECLOSED PROPERTIES

When most people think of purchasing foreclosed properties they think of banks. Banks are large sellers of such properties but they aren't the only source. There are private corporations, such as Skyline Companies. Private companies hold large portfolios of REOs and are ready to deal, especially with the soft markets of the late 1980s. Not as closely regulated as banks, private companies are able to operate across the nation. By having a geographic distribution of properties you can select a market to fit your financial needs. The softer the market is, the more flexibility in price and terms.

With billions of dollars in their portfolios, companies such as Skyline have the zeal to deal. Their investment doesn't earn them money sitting in their portfolio. Rather than continuing to hold these cash drains, such companies set up their own mortgage banking arms offering below-market rate mortgages customized to the needs of the prospective buyer. Many government agencies sell real estate they have acquired. Read the chart below for a listing of government sources where you can find additional information.

Real Exciting Opportunities

Federal National Mortgage Association
Source—white pages of phone book

Federal Home Loan Mortgage Corp.
Source—white pages of phone book

Veteran's Administration
Source—white pages

U.S. Bankruptcy Court
Source—public notice in daily papers

Federal Deposit Insurance Corp.
Source—offices in Washington D.C.

Sheriff Sales
Source—public notice

Internal Revenue Service
Source—public notice in daily papers

Resolution Trust Corp.
Source—offices in Washington D.C.

HUD
Source—public notices in daily paper

Foreclosures in the Mail

Though we do not currently subscribe to any foreclosure newsletters, there are many excellent ones throughout the country. Some concentrate on one geographic area since research must be done in the county courthouses. By attending real estate seminars and joining nonprofit real estate investor organizations, you can become informed of foreclosure newsletters in your areas of interest. In the New York City metropolitan area including counties in upstate New York and northern New Jersey, for example, there is the *Foreclosure Review*. It is published monthly. Each listing identifies the property, the name of the lender, property address, the age and amount of the mortgage, as well as the lawyer to contact. To find out more, you could write to Foreclosure Review, Inc. at 2 Penn Plaza, Suite 1500, New York, NY 10117. Publishers will frequently send a back issue to acquaint you with their publication.

SUMMARY

Buying foreclosures can be a very profitable way to make money in real estate, though it is not an easy way. The foreclosure process is a lengthy process, as many payments must be missed before a lender can foreclose and either sell or take back the property.

The foreclosure process begins with the first missed payment when a friendly letter is sent to the homeowner. The second month the lender begins to inquire if there is a problem. With the third missed payment, the lender threatens the homeowner with foreclosure and records a notice of default. A ninety-day clock starts to tick, giving the homeowner time to straighten out his missed payments and other costs incurred by the bank. Shortly after the ninety days have passed, if the debts have not been paid, the lender holds a public sale to auction off the property.

Many investors invest in foreclosed properties, in any number of ways. Some invest *before the sale* by learning which homeowners have missed payments. Some invest *at the sale* by bidding against other interested investors. Some invest *after the sale* by either visiting the lending institution or making offers to the officer in charge of nonperforming assets. Nonpayers can be approached via mail, flyers, or even classified ads. Interested investors can contact any of the variety of government or private organizations that hold Real Estate-Owned properties, known as REOs. Among sellers of foreclosed properties are Federal National Mortgage Association, Federal Home Loan Mortgage Corporation, Federal Housing Administration, Veteran's Administration, Internal Revenue Service, HUD, Sheriff's sales, Federal Deposit Insurance Corporation, U.S. Bankruptcy Court, and the Resolution Trust Corporation. Listings of sales are usually found in the local newspapers. Additional information can be found by consulting the back sections of the white pages of the phone book.

7

Profiting from the Savings & Loan Bailout

THERE IS A NEW BARGAIN SOURCE OF REAL ESTATE THAT IS BEING OFFERED TO you by Uncle Sam. Under the Resolution Trust Corporation, set up in July, 1989, this federal agency has taken over $100 billion in real estate from insolvent savings and loan corporations. The Resolution Trust Corp. sells and clears out as cost-effectively as possible the real estate acquired from failing thrifts' portfolios. It will be a monumental task as it is expected to dispose of more than one hundred billion dollars of real estate.

One thing is for sure under the Savings and Loan (S&L) bailout and the creation of the Resolution Trust Corp. There will be tremendous opportunities for real estate investors as the corporation prepares to unload the properties as expeditiously as possible. Although no one verbalizes the thought, the Resolution Trust Corp. is a motivated seller, a don't wanter. It has hundreds of thousands of properties all across the nation to be put up for sale. When you put up a property for sale, you try to maximize your sales price because the proceeds flow into your asset management account. When the government sells a property it is one of thousands being sold. If the property sells for less than it should, it is of no great importance. With the monumental task of clearing up the boondoggle, the primary task is getting the best price possible as quickly as possible.

Properties being sold by the Resolution Trust Corp. are located throughout the nation. There has never been a real estate liquidation sale as the one we are seeing. Though the majority of the properties are in Texas, Florida, Colorado, California, and Arizona, properties can be found throughout the country as banks become insolvent and are taken over by the Resolution Trust Corp. There is not one particular type of property held in the portfolio, but all types. Available are strip shopping centers, office and industrial buildings, Florida condos, beach-front real estate, hotels, motels, waterfront lots, ski lodges, and California development land. The enormous quantity of land for sale will decimate markets that are already depressed, as more properties hit a market where there was already an overabundance of properties for sale. The result could be properties selling for twenty and thirty cents on the dollar, compared with the price at which they once sold.

On the surface it seems that the Resolution Trust Corp. is bad news for real estate. In truth, it is a once in a lifetime chance to profit from bargain-priced properties in your selected area of the country. Never again will market forces cause such bargains to become available in real estate. The agency presents opportunities for the single investor looking for bargains, the cash-strapped investor looking to pool resources with partners, a person looking to purchase his first home, and real estate professionals who will help market properties, perform inspections, represent clients on legal matters, and manage properties after closing. The Resolution Trust Corp. might be the opportunity you have been seeking to set up a sound financial future in real estate.

The Resolution Trust Corporation (RTC) has numerous problems facing it. What should it do with the properties, and how can it most efficiently sell them? In the meanwhile the government is incurring enormous expenses as it implements its strategy. Upkeep expenses continue to mount as properties remain in the portfolio. If the RTC moves too quickly, it might sell properties for too little or too much. If government sales don't realize enough money, the end result will be an increase in federal taxes for all taxpayers. And no one wants that.

So the RTC has worked slowly. It has compiled a catalog of its properties for distribution. Field offices are in operation in cities across the country including Dallas, Philadelphia, Kansas City, Denver, Tampa, and Burnsville, Minnesota, with more to open as the need arises.

GUIDELINES FOR RTC OPERATION

Without a doubt, the RTC faces an enormous task. It has had to establish guidelines for operation. Here are some expressed by Gary P. Bowen, deputy director for asset disposition:

1. Most properties are being sold as-is. While that doesn't mean it is being held together by tape, it also doesn't mean it is a cream puff in broom-clean condition. In general, whatever cosmetic repairs that will make it more salable will be done. The RTC does not offer warranties on the structure.

2. The properties are often sold without financing. Any financing is the purchaser's to obtain. The RTC has the power to issue mortgage-financing assistance, but prefers to do so where properties are difficult to sell.

Economically-distressed areas might have financing available, whereas prime properties may not. The RTC fears that without financing, it might be almost impossible to sell in certain areas.

3. The RTC feels it has a mission to help low- and moderate-income home buyers. Under the savings and loan bailout law, individual low- and moderate-income home buyers can qualify for a first-right of refusal on certain single-family homes and apartment complexes in the Resolution Trust Portfolio. In that way, before certain properties can be sold to a multi-million dollar consortium, it must first be made available to low- and moderate-income home buyers. After being advertised and listed for an appropriate time, if properties don't attract bidders from the target group, then others can apply.

4. Investors are able to obtain properties at realistic prices, based upon their current appraised values. Regardless of the amount of the mortgage outstanding on the property, the RTC will sell the property for less relying heavily on the current appraisal. Appraisals, as you recall, are based upon the prices that comparable properties have sold at within a recent time period. Therefore, current appraisals are deemed to be the true market value of a property.

A LOOK AHEAD

In the last few years, newspaper articles revealed the failed thrifts in distressed states such as Texas, Arkansas, Colorado, Louisiana, Oklahoma, and New Mexico. A matter of public record shows billions of dollars in real estate from these states in the portfolio. Does that mean you will be able to purchase the properties for pocket change? Absolutely not. Properties can be sold for as little as ninety-five percent of the current appraised value. That differs with the full current value for which all other properties will be sold. To make sales in distressed states the RTC knows it must act like a motivated seller and make the deal interesting to buyers.

Despite the ninety-five percent appraisal rule, it seems that investors in distressed states will be getting a better deal than it appears. Appraisers in these states bore severe criticism in recent years for overinflated appraisals. Their overly high appraisals helped cause the multibillion-dollar loan crisis by encouraging banks to offer loans on overvalued property, upon which purchasers later defaulted. To counter criticism, they have now become extremely conservative.

As a result of the appraisal conservatism, appraisers in states such as Texas are offering very low appraisals. The result is low selling prices for real estate in affected areas. The government's stipulations are that all properties must have two appraisals. Then, the property cannot be sold for less than ninety-five percent of the average appraised value. Real estate investors such as Philip Montgomery of Montgomery and Company, a Dallas real estate firm puts the RTC efforts in perspective. "People are buying a future when they are buying that property. There's a market for those assets—but it's at a price." Selling the properties has been difficult; the RTC has lowered prices though it will still take many years to market. Aggressive investors will get a piece of the action. Wise investors don't wait to buy real estate. They buy real estate and wait. Buy through investment companies, brokerage houses with funds holding RTC properties, or individual properties. But be sure to investigate before you buy.

HOW TO GET STARTED

If you have an idea where you would like to invest and the type of property you are seeking, the RTC might be able to assist. The RTC suggests that you write a letter in place of calling. The letter will get your name and particular needs onto their books, so that they can contact you with particular investment situations. You might want to say "My name is _____ and I am interested in _____ type of properties in the state of _____." It is suggested that you write to: Lamar C. Kelly Jr., Director—Assets and Real Estate Management Division, Resolution Trust Corporation, 550 17th Street N.W., Washington, D.C. 20429.

SUMMARY

With assets of more than $100 billion, the Resolution Trust Corporation over the next decade will be selling the real estate it acquired from failed savings and loans throughout the country. In all, there are hundreds of thousands of properties. The RTC has been selling strip shopping centers, office buildings, industrial buildings, condos, hotels, ski lodges, and development land. Never again will the government be selling such an enormous amount of real estate.

The RTC has set up guidelines to manage the real estate sales. They are:

1. Most properties will be sold in as-is condition.

2. Some properties will be sold without financing.

3. Low- and moderate-income home buyers will be given the first opportunity to buy.

4. Selling prices will be based upon current appraised values.

By contacting the RTC directly you can have your name put on the mailing list and receive mailing. Once you have informed the RTC of your particular areas of interest, your needs can best be met.

8

A Guide to Smart Financing

A banker is like a friend who will gladly lend you an umbrella on a bright sunny day.

—Walt Disney

IF THE LAW AGAINST ARMED ROBBERY WERE STRICTLY ENFORCED, MANY mortgage bankers would be serving time. Bankers, with vivid memories of the credit crunch of the late 1970s and early 1980s, have been preying on an unsuspecting public with offers of pie-in-the-sky mortgage terms. For large numbers of unsuspecting borrowers, the likely result is pie in the face.

Enticements vary from low teaser rates to fixed payments to convertibility from adjustable to fixed. The smooth-talking mortgage consultants gloss over details that might prove costly to homeowners over many years. They promise low payments, a more stable index and better terms than the next bank or mortgage company.

CHOICE OF MORTGAGE TYPE

Before selecting a mortgage, there are many factors to consider. When you shop for a mortgage, you learn that interest rates aren't everything. They are only one of the factors to be considered. First, you must decide whether you want a fixed rate mortgage or an adjustable rate mortgage. Are you certain that you want an adjustable rate mortgage just because it is less expensive at the start? Will you be prepared for the periodic increases? If you want the security of knowing that the interest rate will stay the same for as long as you own the house, you will prefer the fixed rate mortgage. If you are a risk-taker willing to take a gamble that interest rates won't rise much, have the prospect of steadily increasing earnings, or don't intend to hold onto the property for more than a few years, then the adjustable rate mortgage, known as the ARM, might be your best choice. Just keep in mind that when the second year of your mortgage comes, there is a good chance that you'll be raised $100 per month or more. Financial problems often result from owners who are unprepared for interest shock.

Investors frequently choose the ARM. It usually offers a lower first year rate than the fixed, and purchasers prefer to pay as little as possible for the first year. They have already been bombarded with the endless closing costs. The ARM is keyed to an index that moves up or down with interest rates. The interest rate on the ARM is adjusted up or down after the time period specified in the terms of the mortgage. With most ARMs, the interest rate and monthly payments change either every year, every three years, or every five years. The period between rate changes is known as the adjustment period. A loan with an adjustment period of three years is called a three-year ARM, with the interest able to change once every three years.

THE INDEX

The majority of lenders tie the ARM rate changes to an index rate. As interest rates climb and fall, so do the indices. If the index rate rises, your mortgage rate will most likely rise. If the index rate falls, your mortgage rate will likely fall too.

The ARM interest rate changes as a result of the movement up or down of an index. How has the index been performing? Ask the lender to show you the rate history of the index for the last ten years. Make sure you understand what you are reading. If not, ask questions. Study it overnight with someone impartial who understands. You spend hours or days shopping for a suit or a car. Spend at least as much time for a major purchase such as a mortgage. Don't lose sight of the fact that the initial rate will definitely rise the second year since the initial rate is not the actual market rate. If you plan to hold the property for three years, consider either a fixed mortgage or a 3-year ARM.

THE MARGIN

If your mortgage is tied to the one-year treasury bill, and the treasury bill rate published in the Wall Street Journal is nine percent, that does not mean that your mortgage will be nine percent. To determine the interest rate on any ARM, lenders add on a few percentage points to the treasury bill rate. The number of percentage points added to the treasury bill or other index is called the *margin*. The margin is really an additional fee charged by the lender. Just as not every lender uses the same index to set the mortgage rate, not every lender uses the same margin. In recent years lenders have come up with many different ways of enticing borrowers. Some offer ARMs with interest rates adjusted once a year, while others adjust them every six months or monthly. Only if you have ice cubes in your veins would anyone select a mortgage with rates adjusted monthly.

FIRST YEAR MORTGAGE RATES OR ARMED ROBBERY

For a few years, lenders offered something known as *teaser rates* on the first year of a mortgage. Recently they have been becoming less popular. Banks could not afford to incur the losses of lending money at below market rates for the first year. First-year rates were often three or four percent below the actual market rate, after adding the margin onto the index. Teasers become squeezers for the purchaser as well. With low first-year rates and subsequent low first-year mortgage payments, purchasers find they can qualify for homes they could not ordinarily afford if rates were set at the market rate. When interest rates rise, they are squeezed as rates are adjusted substantially higher in the second year. In the years 1987 and 1988, lenders offered low teaser rates of seven and a half percent or less to entice borrowers to accept ARM mortgages. For the first year, borrowers had a low monthly mortgage payment, budgeted accordingly, and became accustomed to meeting expenses. But then in the second year, according to the terms of the mortgage, the interest rate can rise by as much as two percent. If the first-year rate was seven and a half percent, the rate became nine and a half percent. On a $100,000 mortgage, the monthly payment without taxes jumped from $700 per month to $840 per month. The third year, the monthly payment likely is raised by another two percent to eleven and a half percent, as interest rates rise along with the index to which it is tied. In dollars, the mortgage payment jumps once more from $840 per month to $990 plus whatever the taxes are. It is apparent by the third year that the mortgage is costing an ARM and a leg.

THE GRADUATED PAYMENTS MORTGAGE (GPM)

With the teaser rates appearing less frequently banks had to come up with a new wrinkle to entice borrowers with low interest rates without it costing them an ARM and a leg. And so the *graduated payments mortgage* came into existence. This mortgage is a fixed rate mortgage with much of the appeal of the teaser-rate ARM with less of the risk.

What is the appeal of the graduated payments mortgage? For one thing, it offers a low rate in the early years like the teaser-rate ARM. The lender calculates what the current rate is for the fixed rate mortgages at the time and sets the interest at that rate. The first few years are at a below-market rate, though the mortgage is amortized over a fifteen year period. In that way you pay a lower payment in the early years than in the later years, though it is calculated at a fixed rate over the term of the mortgage. For illustration purposes only, assume that the current rate for a fixed rate mortgage is 11%. The bank decides to set the rate for the first year at 6%. The rate will rise in each succeeding year so that in year fifteen, you might be paying 12% or 14%, though the interest rate over the full fifteen years will have been the fixed rate at which it was set.

The Benefits of the GPM

The GPM offers advantages to both lender and borrower. For the lender, there is no worry about being locked into a below-market rate when interest rates rise, forcing the lender to pay high rates to borrow money. The lender has prearranged the payments for the upcoming fifteen year period. For you the borrower, you have eliminated a great deal of the apprehension over long-term interest rates. You know what you will be paying in principal and interest for the term of the mortgage regardless of what happens to interest rates. You have signed for a fixed rate, but you have done better. Though on paper you are paying a fixed rate, you are able to start the mortgage at a low rate and save money initially. With all the unforeseen expenses of an investment in the first year, a low initial rate is welcomed. Furthermore, with an expected increase in your income in future years, you will be better equipped to pay a higher interest rate than in the early years of a mortgage.

THE INTEREST RATE CAP

With the GPM, your worry about sharply increasing interest rates is a thing of the past, since you know in advance of forthcoming increases. However, with ARM mortgages that knowledge is available. From a risk point of view, the ARM mortgages are high in risk. Borrowers are often unsuspecting. Many borrowers are enticed by the low first year rates and pay little attention to the margins or interest rate caps. The mortgage representative, out of obligation, says that the rates could jump by as much as two percent per year, but fails to divulge that they will rise by that much the first few years, if the initial rate is below the market. Due to close regulation by the states, banks usually set a two percent annual interest cap on the mortgage, so that rates cannot rise or fall by more than two percent in any one year. When was the last time you saw banks lower mortgage rates by two percent? Even if the ARM is set at the current interest rate and the interest rate does not rise for the entire year, the mortgage rate will still rise. As you recall, lenders tack on the margin onto the index. So one way or the other, they will manage to tattoo your ARM rate.

   With yearly interest caps being reached more and more frequently, investors need to consider whether ARMs are suitable investments. For an investor who doesn't plan to hold onto the property for more than a few years, an ARM is usually preferable. If the ARM has a low first year rate, it might be worth considering. The rule of thumb is that there should be a rate difference of at least two and preferably three percent for the ARM to make financial sense. If the ARM is three percent less than the fixed, the ARM will be advantageous for the first two years, considering the two percent yearly cap on the ARM. By the third year, you will have paid more for the ARM than for the fixed. The fixed will stay at that rate, while the ARM is likely to keep rising.

Shopping for a mortgage loan can be a costly experience if lenders are not upfront with you. There is an assortment of upfront charges and mysterious terms with which to become familiar. By being well-informed, you can take FUL advantage of ARM investments.

THE FUL ADVANTAGE (First year, upward adjustments, long-term)

First year savings is a primary concern of an investor considering an ARM. Is there much of a difference between the interest rates of the ARM and the fixed? Compare the actual payment you would be making for each. Consider that Slippery Springs Savings & Loan is offering an ARM adjusted annually with a first-year rate of 9%. On a $100,000 ARM mortgage, the monthly mortgage for the first year without taxes is $750. By the end of the first year, the payments would total $9000. The bank down the block, Bumpy National Bank, offers an 11% fixed rate mortgage for the $100,000 you are seeking. The monthly mortgage payment will be $917, or $167 per month than the ARM. At the end of the first year, you will have paid $11,000, or a full $2000 more than the ARM. At least for the first year, the ARM offered substantial savings over the fixed rate mortgage.

Let's look at what happens in the second year. The ARM rate is raised by the two percent annual cap. That puts the ARM rate at 11%, the same as the fixed rate. So for the second year, each pays $917 per month, for a total of $11,000 for the year. For the first two years, the ARM payments would be $20,000. For the same period the fixed rate payments would be $22,000. In the third year, ARM payments would be raised by the annual cap again to 13%, making the yearly payments $13,000. The fixed mortgage would still remain at $11,000 for the year. The three-year total payments for the ARM and the fixed rate would be $33,000. The disparity in the payments would begin with the fourth year. For that reason the standard advice is not take the ARM for a long-term investment.

Upward adjustments are a critical part of any ARM. Don't be persuaded by the low first-year rate because it won't last. Inquire about the following years and ask how likely it is that the rate will rise to the annual cap? If the mortgage representative is honest, he or she will say that it probably will rise in the second year. If the representative states that it probably will not rise, walk the other way, and don't do business with that person.

Long-term is a more important consideration than the first-year rate. What are the payments going to be in three years or in five years? Most ARMs have lifetime caps that put a limit on how high the interest rate can rise over the life of the mortgage. Usually the lifetime cap is five to six points over the first year rate. If the first year rate is 9% and the lifetime cap is 6 points, the maximum mortgage rate can be 15%.

COMPARING THE ARMS

Since large numbers of borrowers took out ARMs, let's see how they stack up against one another over a five-year period.

The ARM Twister

Annual % and Monthly Payment—$100,000

Arm Type—	1	2	3	4	5	Total
1 Year	9%	11%	13%	13.5%	14%	
At 9%	750	917	1083	1125	1167	60500
3 Year	10%	10%	10%	12%	12%	
At 10%	834	834	834	1000	1000	54000
5 Year	11%	11%	11%	11%	11%	
At 11%	917	917	917	917	917	55000

A careful examination of the ARM Twister reveals some surprising data. Over the course of this five year period a 1-year ARM was more costly than either a 3-year ARM or 5-year ARM. The 1-year ARM started at 9%, but was adjusted to its annual cap in the second and third years to bring it in line with the market. By the third year, the 1-year ARM had a higher percentage rate than either the 3-year or 5-year, despite its attractive first year rate. The 3-year ARM did not get raised until the fourth year, when the interest rate was raised, the 2% cap rose from 10% to 12%, and the payments increased from $834 to $1000. Because the interest rate was kept constant during the first three years, the total payments of $54,000 were the lowest of the three.

Serious thinking must enter into real estate decisions. How long you intend to hold the property determines many of the decisions that will be made. If you are holding the property as an investment and will sell as soon as the right offer comes along, any of the varieties of ARMs are preferable to a fixed-rate mortgage. If there is less than a three percent difference between fixed and adjustable, you should choose the fixed. We are living in unstable times and the more things you can keep under control, the better it will be for you. How stable your interest rate will be depends on the index to which it is keyed. To find out the stability of your index, check the Index Watch.

THE INDEX WATCH

One-year Treasury Index

- somewhat stable
- average yield of all outstanding treasury securities with one year left to maturity

11th District Cost of Funds

- very stable
- average of interest rates paid on deposits at savings institutions in the 11th District of the Federal Home Loan Bank Board

Six-Month Treasury Bills

- very unstable

Three-Year Treasury Notes

- more stable than other treasury indices

A popular ARM is the *One-Year Treasury Index*, which is tied to the weekly index of yields on one-year treasury securities. The rate changes weekly, with the index for the week released the next Monday by the Federal Reserve Bank. Though this index does not vary a great deal from month-to-month, it could vary by two or three percentage points from one year to the next.

Another popular ARM is the *11th District Cost of Funds Index*, called COFI. The 11th District of the Federal Home Loan Bank Board consists of Arizona, California, and Nevada. In recent years, one of every five ARMs throughout the country uses the COFI. In California, the COFI is the standard ARM, if there is anything you would call standard. Like any index, the COFI offers pluses and minuses. One advantage is that the interest rate increases slowly even as rates rise. In a recent year, the one-year ARM rose by a full two percent, while the COFI rose only by 0.70 percent in the same period.

Interested in knowing the reason for the discrepancy? The explanation is that the 11th District Cost of Funds Index reflects what the district paid for deposits in the previous month. If the date is May 27 and the index is released, the index will reflect April numbers, despite the fact that it will be the index for the month of June, as far as setting the COFI. It is not difficult to see that the index is not an accurate interest rate barometer. Because of the long lag in the rates, it is not unusual for the COFI to rise for six to nine months once interest rates begin to rise. It is not a pleasant experience to observe your payments or mortgage balance rising and rising each month, even though your rates are lower than investors with ARMs. Of course, when interest rates fall, the opposite happens. You might become frustrated as interest rates take many months to fall substantially, or find yourself still paying the high rates while you read about the low ARM rates everyone else is paying. As the late Gilda Radner used to say, "It's always something."

When you hear the loan representative explain about the COFI, it seems too good to be true. You see the stability of the index and the fact that it did not experience the interest rate roller coaster of the early 1980s. You can easily be enticed by the low interest rates offered. The one-year ARM has a 2% cap preventing the rate from rising or falling by more than two percent in any year, regardless of what happens to interest rates. The COFI fails to offer that protection. The index has a monthly cap, which prevents your payments from being raised by more than a certain percent, such as $7^1/2\%$ in any particular month. The problem arises when the payments are capped and the interest rates might not be. If the monthly cap limit prevents your payments from being raised further and interest rates still rise, you will discover that your monthly payment is not covering the total interest and principal due. The shortfall is added to the balance of your loan. The condition where your loan balance is not totally covering the interest and principal is known as *negative amortization*. Negative amortization can be deadly—so avoid it at all costs.

STANDARD EQUIPMENT

When you are at the car dealer pricing the newest luxury import, you learn that the car has standard equipment, as well as optional equipment. The standard equipment comes with all the cars. The optional equipment varies depending on what you choose. The same is true for ARM mortgages. Some things they all have, while other things, some have and the others don't.

Standard

☞ Index
☞ Margin added to index
☞ Adjustment time period
☞ Initial interest rate

Optional

☞ Lifetime cap on interest
☞ Yearly or monthly interest cap
☞ Convertibility to fixed-rate

THE PREPAYMENT PENALTY

Always read the fine print and have it checked by an attorney. Is there a prepayment penalty in the mortgage document? A *prepayment penalty* is a fee charged by the lender if you pay all or part of your loan before it is due. The lender spends large sums of money in paperwork and is not happy to have to recalculate mortgage payments. However, if the mortgage note does not include a prepayment penalty, you can send in optional payments to pay off your mortgage earlier. Naturally if you plan on holding the property only until you find the right buyer, prepaying the mortgage is not a sensible alternative.

There are investors who buy and hold properties and don't sell. For them, prepaying a mortgage makes sense. If you have a thirty-year mortgage, you can shorten it substantially by making additional payments along with the monthly mortgage payment. Regardless of whether the bank reduces your minimum monthly payment through the year, continue paying the amount in the coupon book and write a check for the optional payment. Make sure that you indicate on the face of the check, on the line for memos, that the payment is to be applied to the principal. You will find over time that prepayments shorten the life of your mortgage substantially and save you many thousands of dollars.

To see how prepaying a mortgage can save you money we will assume that you have a $70,000 fixed-rate mortgage at 10%. Your monthly payment for principal and interest is $614. Every month, you send in a check for $614, which is your regular payment, and a check for $100, which is your extra payment. If you start on day one of your mortgage and make both payments each month, your thirty-year mortgage will be paid off in 20 years and 4 months. If instead of $100 each month, you send extra payments of $200 each month, your mortgage will be paid off in 15 years and 6 months, cutting the length of your mortgage almost in half. If you send along an additional check for $300 each month, your mortgage will be paid off in only 10 years and 3 months. If you are an investor who buys rental properties and holds them indefinitely, it definitely pays to consider prepayments. Time is money.

THE ASSUMABLE MORTGAGE

Whenever possible get an *assumable mortgage*. An *assumable mortgage* can be taken over by a purchaser who continues making payments to the lender. A buyer can save thousands of dollars in closing costs by assuming a mortgage instead of taking out a new one, as well as possibly being given a lower interest rate. Buyer and seller gain by not having months for the time-consuming mortgage application process to be completed. Nowadays many assumable mortgages stipulate that the interest rate upon sale will be at prevailing rates, but it still is an improvement over starting from scratch. Furthermore, having an assumable mortgage will make selling the property that much easier when you decide to sell.

WINNING ON POINTS

When you shop for a mortgage, it can be costly to miss the point. A *point* is a percentage of the mortgage that the lender has you pay upfront. Almost every new mortgage has points, though you often can't tell from the newspaper ads. Points are a way for the lender to earn additional money without waiting for monthly payments. Is a mortgage with the most points always the most expensive mortgage? Not necessarily. There is a way to determine the true cost of a mortgage while comparing points.

Consider how long you plan to keep the property. Then divide the amount of money paid for points over the length of time you plan to hold the property. You will then have an annual expense to add onto your mortgage interest to calculate your true percentage rate. If you have a $100,000 mortgage and you are paying points, the 2 points are really 2% of $100,000 or $2000. Over the course of thirty years, the $2000 amounts to less than $6 per month over thirty years and increases the interest rate by less than one tenth of one percent per year over thirty years.

Review the point spread evaluation. There are three fixed-rate mortgages being compared over a three-year, five-year, ten-year and thirty-year period. By comparing the interest rate and points, you can learn to evaluate the variables of a mortgage and judge which is the best mortgage.

The 11% mortgage with 3 points will cost $12,000 per year over the first three years, or $1000 per month without taxes. Over the first five years, the same mortgage will cost $11,600 or $967 per month without taxes. Over the first ten years, the mortgage will be $11,300 or $942 per month without taxes. And over the entire thirty years, the mortgage will be $11,100 or $925 per month without taxes. Clearly when considered over a thirty-year period the cost of points is negligible. The cost of points is a big factor when the mortgage with three points is held for three years or less. If this property is held for three years, the true annual percentage rate is 12%, for five years 11.6%, for ten years 11.3%, and for thirty years 11.1%. As you can see, over the thirty-year life of the mortgage, the points expense on the 11% mortgage accounts for only $100 per year or slightly more than $8 per month. On the 12% mortgage, the expense is even less, with an added cost for a full year of $33.33 or less than $3 per month additional, over a thirty-year period. Summing up the impact of points, the points expense is really only a factor if you are holding a mortgage less than ten years.

With the information in hand to compare the expense of mortgages, you are ready to begin the mortgage application process. The process is a time-consuming one, as you bite your fingernails and await approval. You are never informed of the numerous steps in the mortgage process, but here they are.

STEPS TO A MORTGAGE

1. Application is completed.
2. Lender begins to process the application.
3. Lender orders an appraisal, credit report, and employment verification.
4. Lender sends you a booklet with a good-faith estimate of closing costs.
5. You receive the Truth-in-Lending statement and closing cost estimates.
6. The lender approves the loan.
7. You sign the closing documents and make payments at closing.
8. Lender gives funds to the closing agent and seller is paid. You receive title.
9. Documents are recorded at the county clerk's office.

The Application

A mortgage application is lengthy and requires detailed information, such as employment history, assets and liabilities, and other information considered pertinent. Sometimes it seems it takes as long to get the mortgage approved as it does to build the house. There are many tedious and unnecessary steps along the way, from the appraisal to the umpteenth time the lender doesn't return your call for an update. Is there something you can do to expedite the process? Yes, there is.

The No-Income Check Mortgage

The secret to speeding up the application process lies in the *no-documentation mortgage*, also known as the *no-income check mortgage*. With this type of mortgage, you can obtain a loan without proving you have the income to keep up payments or repay the loan. The fact that you don't have to document your income and assets does not suggest to anyone you are any less trustworthy than the next borrower. You might be a responsible, credit-worthy investor who manages your investments wisely but might not qualify for a loan according to the lender's unrealistic standards. You know that you will meet your financial responsibilities even if the lender doesn't think so. Or maybe you just feel that your financial records are private, and you don't want them scrutinized. In any case, you can secure a no-income check loan. In return for this benefit, usually you are required to make a higher down payment than otherwise. Often twenty to twenty-five percent of the purchase price is required at closing.

Why Borrowers Prefer No-Income Check Loans

☞ You don't have to submit your 1040 tax return to the lender for scrutiny.

☞ You can receive loans or gifts from friends or relatives without having to account for them.

☞ You might have an all-cash business and be unable or unwilling to substantiate all the income.

☞ You might not have sufficient income to qualify but have cash for the down payment.

☞ You might need a quicker decision.

☞ You could be self-employed and not have a W-2 to submit.

The Federal Home Loan Bank Board contends that no-income verification loans are risky. Nothing can be further from the truth. First of all, a borrower has put down between twenty and thirty percent of the purchase price in cash, as a down payment. A full documentation borrower might have put down as little as ten percent. Certainly a person who has paid thirty percent of the purchase price in cash is not willing to lose the investment by defaulting. The person who has paid ten percent down is a more likely candidate to walk away from the loan. Consequently, for the investor who wants a problem-free, quick loan and for the lender in search of a lower-risk borrower, the no-income verification loan is best.

A popular song once said "everything old is new again." It certainly is in the financing business. Years ago, there was the second mortgage. Today, there is the home equity loan. Somehow the home equity loan sounds less onerous and less risky than the second mortgage, but they both put a lien against your property. In both cases, your property will be foreclosed and seized if you fail to make payments. The second mortgage is a loan drawn against the property in one lump sum, while the home equity loan is frequently an open-ended line of credit. With the home equity loan, you are given a credit limit and are able to write checks against the loan up to the limit.

Who takes out a home equity loan? The Consumer Banking Association conducted a study to find out. These were the findings. The typical borrower is:

☞ married and between the ages of thirty-five and forty-nine with two children

☞ the owner of the current home for nine years and ten months

☞ approved for a maximum of under $37,000 for the loan

☞ carrying a mortgage with a balance of almost $25,000

☞ carrying other outstanding debts in addition to the first mortgage and the home equity loan

With the tremendous advertising blitz of recent years, home equity loans have become as popular as Mom and apple pie. Read any newspaper or magazine and you see it. "If you do not have a home equity loan you are not taking advantage of the substantial equity in your home.'' Most people who invested in major cities on the east and west coasts in the late 1970s and early 1980s have enjoyed substantial appreciation.

As the name implies, the home equity loan is backed by the equity you have built in your home. A lender usually lends up to eighty percent of the home's value, after subtracting the amount of the mortgage you have outstanding. You are issued a line of credit of which any or all can be used up until the maximum allowed. It can be repaid and borrowed again and again over the term of the loan. It is very convenient, since you can use as much or as little of the loan you want as long as you don't exceed the limit. But keep in mind that you are paying for the convenience. A lender usually charges two to three percent above the prime rate for a home equity loan. A first mortgage is almost always issued below the prime rate. The *prime rate* is the rate at which banks lend their most credit-worthy customers. IBM could be expected to borrow at the prime rate, but not XYZ Shoe Repair.

The Home Equity Nestegg

When you examine the total picture, home equity loans to a financially prudent investor, can be a great asset. Investors, such as ourselves, use it as an ever-available credit line for investment opportunities. Though it is readily available, you do not pay interest until you actually take possession of the funds. If you need fifteen or twenty thousand dollars to purchase a foreclosed property or a property from a motivated seller, you have the funds available. To further sweeten the pot, the home equity loan on your primary residence up to $100,000 is fully deductible, whereas credit card debt is not. On the downside, the cost of setting up a home equity loan can often exceed $2000. If you should fail to make the payments on the home equity loan, you risk losing your financial interest in the property.

The Five-Year Retirement Plan

If you are the type of person willing to live with the conditions of the home equity loan and can meet your financial obligations, then a home equity loan can pave the way to financial freedom. It can be done through the Five-Year Retirement Plan. The idea is to have your money work for you so that you don't forever have to work for your money. The Five-Year Plan consists of purchasing one property below-market each year for five years. Each property must be at least 15-20% below comparable properties in the area. Consequently at the end of five years, you own five properties. Having been bought substantially below the market, they can be expected to increase in value until they approximate the comparable properties, which will likely be increasing.

The Sixth Year and Beyond

In the five years, you have laid the groundwork for your financial future. Now it is time to have the money start working for you. In the sixth year, you borrow against the equity that has been built up in the first property you bought. You pull out some of the appreciation from the property and use it for your living expenses. In the seventh year, you borrow against the appreciated assets in property two for your living expenses for that year. In the eighth year, you borrow against the assets in property three, etc. etc. By the end of the tenth year, you have borrowed against all five properties, as they have appreciated in value. You have been able to retire and live off the appreciated values of your real estate.

No one knows with certainty how quickly real estate prices will rise over a number of years, though they are likely to appreciate and a new set of real estate millionaires will emerge. Depending on how quickly they appreciate, you can borrow on your equity build-up. A good part of becoming wealthy in real estate is remaining flexible. If things don't work out exactly as planned and you still believe in your decisions, hold on and wait. No one knows how long a market will stay soft or strong, but nothing lasts forever. Should another period of rapid price appreciation appear, you might be able to borrow from your equity before the sixth year. Optimistically, you will be able to retire in the sixth year.

The Road to Retirement

Assuming that real estate cycles continue as they have over the decades, real estate prices will continue to outpace inflation and rise as they always have. If you're considering the Five-Year Plan with borrowing against the equity buildup, you have one unanswered question. What do you do after year ten? The answer is borrow all over again. Therefore in year eleven, borrow against property one, in year twelve against property two, etc., etc.

What happens if you don't want to borrow against a property or can't because a particular property hasn't appreciated sufficiently? So don't borrow. Remember, it is only a plan. There can always be a change in plans. You can customize the Five-Year Plan to fit your individual needs. If you purchase more than five properties in the five year period and prices have appreciated rapidly, you can choose to borrow against all five before the five years have elapsed. If the market is soft and prices haven't risen much, hold off implementing the plan. Acting more or less aggressively is your prerogative. The key to successful real estate investing is flexibility. Nothing is written in stone and can't be changed. If you can't raise the water, lower the bridge.

OBTAINING THE FINANCING

Five letters prevent you and others from getting started with the plan. They are M-O-N-E-Y. Real estate seminars often tell you to apply for a home equity loan, and you'll have your money with a snap of your finger. That would be nice, but the real world doesn't work that way. Lenders have requirements and one of them is usually that the property be owner-occupied. There is nothing you can do with banks that are as inflexible as that. You must turn to other sources.

For the last several years the real estate market has been money-driven instead of market-driven. There has been plenty of money around for loans from sources other than banks. There are mortgage brokers, private investors, finance companies, mortgage companies, and other sources.

PREPARING THE PROPOSAL

If there is money to be made with a controlled risk, there will always be people or firms to lend you money. The lender must be assured that the deal is sound, you are a professional, and that if the deal goes sour, he can recover his invest-ment. There is a way to convey a professional appearance. That is to be pre-pared and thorough in your presentation. Begin your presentation by having an appraisal done of each of your properties by an appraiser who has a designation from one of the professional appraisal organizations. Take the individual apprais-als to your CPA. Instruct your CPA to prepare a proposal showing your current positive cash flow and profit and loss projections for the next few years. Of course you furnish concise, accurate data to your CPA to make the most credible presentation. You want your CPA to consider your properties as a package so that you are perceived as a professional real estate investor and will be granted consideration as such. Based upon the substantial equity in your portfolio, you will be considered for a home equity loan in the form of a line of credit. You will be issued the line of credit with a credit limit. You will be able to borrow up to the credit limit. Over the years, as you demonstrate your creditworthiness, you might apply to have the line increased.

THE MORTGAGE BROKER CONNECTION

Should you not want to incur the expenses and time used in preparing a pro-posal, you might decide to engage a mortgage broker. Mortgage brokers are licensed by each state to obtain loans from lenders. There is more money than there are deals, so that the mortgage broker has a variety of sources to approach to obtain the funds you are seeking. Mortgage brokers make their living by being apprised of the money market, so they can advise you of the possibilities that suit your needs. A mortgage broker, without any fee to you, will match your needs to a lender's. Should a deal result, it is the lender, and not you, who pays the fee to the mortgage broker.

When Bad Things Happen to Good Borrowers

What happens when the lender gives you the R word? Rejection. You certainly don't jump for joy when the letter begins with "Please be advised that your recent application for a loan has been denied." You feel personally insulted that the lender doesn't feel you can be trusted. And well, you should. But remember that the rejection doesn't have to be the final word. Often lenders are willing to negotiate. If you can substantiate your creditworthiness, you have a chance.

Why Loans Are Rejected

Lenders estimate that about ten percent of all mortgage applications are turned down. In your part of the country, the actual figures might be higher or lower. A variety of reasons are cited, but the Big Four reasons are:

1. Poor or no credit history.
2. Frequent job changes.
3. Insufficient assets.
4. Insufficient down payment.

How to Get an Application Reconsidered

Knowing the reasons for your rejection does not remedy the situation. What you need to know are steps to follow to get your application reconsidered.

To get off the starting block, do not call up the lender. The lender is required by law to send along a written rejection letter. A form letter is acceptable, according to the legal disclosure laws, even though it does not provide a reason for the rejection. If you call, you might or might not be able to reach the decision maker. Your attempts to reach the party after not having your calls returned, could in fact harm any chances of reconsideration you had. No one likes to be harassed by a caller.

The Well-Written Letter

A better approach to getting your application reconsidered is to send a well-written letter to the specific person who signed the letter. If the letter is unsigned, call the company anonymously and ask for the name of the person who makes the mortgage decisions. The letter should be to the point and explain why your application should be reconsidered. Along with the letter you can supply documentation to strengthen your case and encourage the lender to give you reconsideration. You could enclose such items as a payoff notice on a car loan or another item that shows you pay your obligations promptly. A written correspondence gets more serious consideration than a phone call. A phone call conversation is forgotten by the lender as soon as the phone conversation is concluded while a well-written, succinct letter is a physical reminder that a problem remains unresolved. Although there are no guarantees that an application will be reconsidered, there is a better chance than if you do nothing.

Your Rights as a Borrower

Loan application denials are arbitrary. Often there is not a valid reason for the rejection. Lenders base their decision on the credit report. Often you don't know that there is inaccurate information in the credit report. By law the credit reporting agency must furnish you with a free copy of your credit report upon request, if you have been rejected for credit. You have the right to read through it and notify the agency in writing of the inaccuracies. If your allegations are correct, the inaccuracies must be corrected and all the firms that rejected you must be notified of the inaccuracies.

Are the lender decisions sound? Sometimes they are and sometimes they are not. Frequently they turn down your loan application because of the number of other loans you have outstanding, despite the fact that all loans are current, and you have never been late with payments. You could have assets of one million dollars and loans totalling one hundred thousand dollars. Yet your friendly bank will turn you down by informing you that you have excessive obligations. A down-to-earth mortgage company or mortgage broker will easily be able to overcome these objections and get you a loan if you have a clean payment record. Merely selling one property will realize enough capital to pay off the loan. The lender knows it has a minimal risk.

SUMMARY

When purchasing real estate, due diligence must be given to the type of investment and terms of the mortgage you are seeking. Though you can make a much sweeter deal by purchasing for cash, you frequently don't have the capital to make it possible. The result is that you have to seek financing.

To ARM yourself or not is a choice to be made. Mortgage types and rates seem to change as often as the weather forecast. Adjustable Rate Mortgages, known as ARMs, have become very popular in recent years. With low first-year teaser rates, the ARMs attracted hordes of borrowers. Borrowers had been able to obtain ARMs at two or even three percent less than the fixed-rate mortgage.

Lenders began to find they could no longer afford to offer below-market first year rates, and so borrowers began to balk at ARMs.

More recently borrowers have been returning to fixed-rate mortgages. With ARMs no longer at artificially low rates, borrowers find the rates of the fixed and ARMs to be closer than before. They prefer the certainty of a fixed interest rate to an ARM that could skyrocket in a few years.

There is no definitive answer about whether one type of mortgage is better than another. That depends on the borrower's circumstances and needs. How long you plan to hold the mortgage, how many points you are charged, the yearly and lifetime caps, as well as the index to which the rates are tied determines the attractiveness of the mortgage.

Applying for a mortgage is usually a tedious, time-consuming process. But through the no-income verification mortgage, the process is made simpler. With such loans, consideration is given to the value of the property and your creditworthiness, instead of solely relying upon your income. Borrowers have a myriad of reasons for not applying for a full-verification loan. Among the reasons are insufficient income or down payment, an income off the books, or other personal reason.

Buying property at least twenty percent below market value will set your direction for a five-year retirement loan plan. The home equity loan is another financing vehicle for the real estate investor. It enables the investor to borrow against the equity that has built up in the property. Such loans are fully tax-deductible up to $100,000 and can provide a cushion or nest egg for future investment opportunities. Among the best features is the fact that you have access to the money, but do not pay interest on it until you actually use it.

Loans are often rejected for what seems like insufficient reason. Don't accept a rejection without a fight. Furnish substantiation in a letter addressed to the lender. If you are still turned down, try a mortgage company that offers to be more accommodating. One thing to remember is that nothing comes easy in real estate. Success comes from hard work and perseverance.

9

Shrewd Negotiating

WHETHER YOU ARE BUYING A CARPET, AN ANTIQUE CAR, OR A STRIP SHOPPING center, the thing to remember is that everything is negotiable. Every price can be reduced by the seller if the seller really wants to make the deal. The price you ultimately pay for real estate depends on how effectively you negotiate and how much information power you have on hand. You must enter the real estate game with the same perspective as you would a card game. First examine your own hand, then pick up as many clues as to your opponent's holdings and needs. Try to evaluate the remainder of the deck, and how you should play your cards. The more cards that are on the table or the more information you know about a property the more power you hold to effectively negotiate the best deal. For example, if you know that the seller has bought a commercial property two blocks down and needs the proceeds from this sale to close on his purchase, your negotiating leverage is improved.

THE NEGOTIATOR FORMULA

In essence, the seller needs your cards and will be more likely to make concessions than otherwise. To win the game, you must negotiate or plan the better strategy. Using the negotiator formula will give you the information power that is necessary to plan your strategy. Major questions must be answered by the seller or the realtor for you to strike an effective bargaining position.

There are nine major questions that should be answered by a seller or a seller's real estate agent before you can expect to negotiate the best deal. It is called the NEGOTIATOR formula.

Number of years the property has been owned.
Equity in the property.
Going to make repairs.
Offers that have been received.
Time property has been on the market.
Income evaluating.
Arriving at the price.
Time needed to close.
Offer down payment for terms.
Reasons for selling.

Number of Years the Property Has Been Owned

If the seller has owned the property for many years, it is likely the person has a substantial profit. What does that mean for the buyer? It means that the seller can reduce the selling price and still make a considerable profit. This seller is a good candidate for negotiations. If the seller has only had the property a short time, is it for sale because the property is not making the profit that was expected of it?

Equity in the Property

If you are playing Blackjack, it is not enough to know which cards are in your hand. And just because you know how much makes 21 is still not the advantage you need. You have to figure out which cards are in the dealer's hand and in the deck. You try to gain as much information as possible by observing the cards that are face up. In real estate investing, it is advantageous to observe as much as possible so that you have the upper edge when negotiating. In the property, does it seem that everything is original and hasn't been replaced?

One thing you need to know is how much is owed on all mortgages. Who owns the first mortgage? Is there a second mortgage? Ask about the mortgages outstanding. How much is owed on each one? With whom is each mortgage? Do you know the mortgage account numbers?

With the initial information in hand, you can verify the amounts of the mortgage and its terms. Call up each lender or visit with a list of prepared questions. How much of the mortgage is outstanding? Is it assumable? On what terms is it assumable? Are the payments current? With all the facts in hand, you can negotiate better terms, as well as to calculate if the deal makes sense to you. If the mortgage is assumable at a low rate of interest, and you have enough cash to take it over, you can save thousands of dollars in closing costs as well as having a lower monthly payment.

Offers that Have Been Received

Ask if any other offers have been received. If the person has received dozens of offers and turned them down, it is helpful to know. Maybe the person doesn't really want to sell. If there have been a substantial number of bids and there has been no deal, maybe the property is overpriced. Ask why the offers have not been accepted. Your question might initiate some soul-searching as to why the property hasn't sold.

Wait for the response to the question about why the house hasn't sold. Don't speak. You can gain more from this response than any other. If the seller seems totally inflexible or thinks she is sitting on a gold mine, you have at least learned that the seller is not likely to negotiate with you either. Better yet, the seller might finally realize that her inflexibility or overpricing is the reason the property hasn't sold. There is nothing to lose except a good opportunity.

Time Property Has Been on the Market

Have you ever purchased a sweater you couldn't live without? You couldn't wait to get it home and wear it. The first few times you wore it, you felt that you had a certain radiance. Then after wearing it a few dozen times, it became relegated to the bottom of the drawer. You were tired of looking at it.

To a real estate agent, the property becomes the old sweater. The first few times the agent marvels over the modern entrance, ceramic tiles, or track lighting. After many return visits, it loses some of its lustre. In the agent's eyes the property soon takes on an unexciting look. The agent lacks enthusiasm for the property and would prefer to show a newer listing, a more exciting property to prospective purchasers.

The time a property has been on the market is an important consideration. It makes a big difference whether a property has been on the market for ten days or ten months. If the property has only been on the market for a week or so, the seller might have expectations of selling at the asking price and be unwilling to negotiate. However, if the seller has been on the market for ten months, it might be advantageous to convey the idea to the real estate agent that you like the house but feel it is overpriced when compared to comparable properties you have seen. You could explain that you would be interested if the seller were more flexible with the price or terms. Make it known that you are willing to wait until the property falls into a more realistic price range. If the seller or agent wants to make a deal, time is on your side.

With a property that has remained on the market for a long time there is usually more room for negotiations. Try to gain concessions by helping the seller. You could offer increased financial security with a bigger down payment, and earlier closing date or a closing as late as the seller wants if there is a delay in the other deal. Concessions often cost you nothing and are very appreciated. If, for example, you paid the full asking price, you could ask the seller to accept a smaller down payment in return. After all, the seller doesn't gain possession of the down payment until after closing. In return for full price, you might request that the seller hold the mortgage. This could save you thousands of dollars in closing costs. When the timing is right it could be a win-win situation for the seller as well.

Income Evaluation

Unless you are purchasing the property to sell or to occupy, property is bought to produce income. If the current owner is renting the premises, you must obtain a copy of the lease. How much are the tenants paying? Are the amounts realistic to the going prices for the area in the advertisements? If all of the apartments or stores are not legal ones, do not count them as income. Despite what the owner tells you, a violation from the local government will end your illegal rental income, even if the current landlord has never had any problems. Only legal incomes are considered in calculating total rental income. The amount must be enough to meet your expenses and generate a positive cash flow.

Add up the monthly income and multiply it by 12. This gives you the yearly income. Ten times the yearly income is the absolute top price you should consider paying. Eight times the income would be a bargain property price. For example, consider a mixed-use property that rents for a total of $1600 per month, producing a yearly income of $19,200 (1600 × 12). Ten times yearly income values the property at a maximum of $192,000. Priced at eight times yearly income values it at $153,600. At that price the property would be a bargain. How much you'd be willing to pay depends on your monthly expenses. Keep in mind that this guide is only to establish a general bargain buying price. Remember your own monthly mortgage payments, taxes, insurance, repairs, and general expenses would be deducted from the monthly income. As a smart negotiator, you must negotiate the selling price.

Arriving at the Price

Have you ever asked a seller how the selling price was arrived at. You're probably thinking you would never do that. It's being too pushy. But pushy can save you thousands of dollars. It is possible that the seller never really thought about how she arrived at the price. Even if she did, maybe some of the factors changed. Now there could be three comparable properties for sale at lower prices, it is winter, and there is a reduced demand for swimming and boating, making the property less desirable for now. Many other tangible and nontangible factors might have caused a need for a property's price to be readjusted. A full discussion with the seller could result in the realization of the true situation, that the property is priced too high to sell in the current market and needs to be reduced to make a sale. You could diplomatically point out advantages that competing properties hold. For example, one property could be vinyl sided, while another's exterior needs painting. Be sure to point out the improvements and costs you'll need to make their property livable for you—livable not luxurious. Windows, insulation, proper venting, new appliances, upgrading electric or plumbing to standards are appropriate to secure a lower purchase price.

Time Needed to Close

Benjamin Franklin said it, ''time is money.'' He was right. Time is a very valuable commodity. Ten thousand dollars in your hand now is preferable to the possibility of having fifteen thousand dollars in six months. The sure thing now is better than something that might or might not happen later. Whether the reasons for selling are financial or emotional, the sooner the seller unloads the property the sooner she can get on with her life. It's a good deal for the seller and you.

A seller's time problem can be your time bonanza. The need to close quickly often offers numerous opportunities. The urgency might open a window of opportunity. Perhaps you can make a minimum down payment. If you are like we are, you use OPM (other people's money) to purchase real estate. Of course you don't lose sight that the money has to be repaid with interest over time. But if you aren't required to put a large amount of your own money into a deal, you have money or credit available for the next deal. Arrangements for a line of credit from a home equity loan or credit card are handy resources and allow you to move on deals that you would otherwise have to pass.

Time can also be used as a sweetener. In the spirit of good will offer the time sweetener. It is used to uncomplicate the seller's world. Like sugar, the sweetener can be fattening, but it only fattens your bank account. Offer to pay all cash for a deal and close immediately, and you might be able to chop thousands of dollars from the selling price. You can always refinance later on better terms. Offer to close within a week, if the selling price or down payment can be reduced substantially or if the seller will give back financing, in the form of a first mortgage. Cutting off closing costs and chopping down the purchase price were great solutions for sellers with time problems.

Offer Down Payment for Terms

Every once in a while you find yourself with a great deal but without money. It happens to everyone, even Donald Trump. So what do you do when you do not have ready funds or credit?

It won't work every time, but it is worth a try. Sometimes a seller might agree to forego the down payment in exchange for a higher selling price. If not the entire down payment, then maybe the seller might accept one or two thousand dollars down, just to demonstrate that you are serious. Assume that the seller has agreed to accept $150,000 with a $7,500 down payment. Since you don't have or would rather not pay $7,500 in cash, offer to pay $160,000 instead of $150,000. If the seller wants to make the deal, as well as a higher profit, she will accept the offer.

Such a deal is beneficial to everybody. The seller gets more for the property than originally agreed. You don't have to raise funds you don't have readily available. The seller might balk at your offer, saying that you have nothing to lose from walking away, but you could counter by showing that even with a substantial down payment you could use your contract escape clauses if you felt the need. Since you don't have to raise the money, that same bargain at a few thousand dollars more does not materially change the attractiveness of the deal.

Reason for Selling

Anyone who wants to save money on a purchase should inquire about the seller's intentions. A seller's reason for selling is not always classified information. Sometimes the reasons are quite public. The real estate agent and the seller make no secret about an impending move to Florida. In that case, the cards are on the table. You can offer something to the seller to sweeten the deal. Being several thousand miles away from his investment, the seller would like nothing better than to be freed from the financial obligation, the sooner the better. Being aware of the seller's urgency you can tailor a solution to the particular circumstances. If the person cannot make payments, you can offer to assume payments in return for a lower selling price, lower down payment or second mortgage. If the seller doesn't need the money but really wants to be freed of the obligations of the property request that the seller give you a mortgage. He'll get monthly payments from you. If the seller needs your money to close on his new property then you must offer the time sweetener in exchange for price cutting. Of course, any agreement must be in writing and approved by your attorney. A person in a predicament is likely to be willing to negotiate. And that could mean a good deal for you.

NIWIN PRINCIPLE

Before becoming involved in any negotiations you need to learn the *NIWIN principle*. The *NIWIN principle* states that if a statement is not in writing it's nothing. Without prudent use of the NIWIN principle, you leave yourself open to No-Win negotiations. A real estate agent, lender, attorney, or seller can promise you anything and often will. Later on when you remind the person, you are told it was never said. If you don't have the promise written down on the document, the promise doesn't exist. "Trust me" doesn't count in court. In any negotiation, if the statement is worth saying it is worth putting in writing. Anything else is just hot air. Remember the NIWIN principle, and you will never have to trust your memory or someone else's. Everything will be in writing. If you get the realtor to cut the commission or pay for a repair, and you didn't get it in writing, then you just imagined the concession. Don't count on it. When you hear "don't you trust me?," tell them yes, but that your accountant (or the professional of your choice) needs it for his records. If you forget to get it in writing, you can forget it.

THE CAT AND MOUSE COMPROMISE

Being well-informed is vital in negotiating the best deal. The NEGOTIATOR formula avoids costly mistakes. Without knowing the vital facts you are vulnerable to paying too much for a property. Don't assume that the asking price is the price actually expected by the seller. A shrewd seller gets a ballpark estimate from the real estate agent or a professional appraisal with credentials from the ASA, MAI, or SREA. Then the seller adds ten or twenty percent to the estimate, expecting that the buyer will make a lower offer. No intelligent investor ever pays the full asking price. The negotiating process is a cat and mouse game. The thing to remember is that you must always be the cat.

Deep down few sellers realistically expect the full asking price. Sure, they would like to get it, but they know it is improbable. If the market is soft, it becomes even more unlikely. Think about it, if you made a first offer and it was accepted, you would justifiedly be suspicious. You would wonder if you could have bought at much lower prices.

How does the bidding begin? Usually you make a low offer, which you expect to be turned down. It establishes a price floor. In a buyer's market, where there are large numbers of properties for sale, a seller will usually come back with a counteroffer, which serves as a price ceiling. The counteroffer will attempt to bridge the gap between what the seller has asked and what you have offered. For example, a property is listed for $200,000. You offer $130,000. Realistically you don't expect the offer to be accepted. You feel the property is worth about $180,000. The negotiating continues with the seller reducing the price by 10% to $180,000, which you feel is fair, but the retail price. Since you only buy wholesale, you raise your offer by 15% to $150,000. Now there remains a gap of $30,000 between your offer and the asking price.

While the gap is not mind-boggling, it is still wide enough to drive a truck through. You have made your $150,000 offer and await a response. The seller, if she wants to make a deal, will reduce her asking price by another 10% to between $160,000 and $162,000. If that happens there will only be a gap of about $10,000. Either you will raise your offer or the seller will reduce hers. Maybe you will split the difference. Often a real estate agent will cut the sales commission to complete a deal. When there is a meeting of the minds and a signed agreement, there is a deal. When neither party is really happy, that is a good compromise.

It all sounds good. In fact, it sounds a little too perfect. It does work out this way frequently, but a savvy investor is prepared for the times it doesn't. If the seller is asking $200,000 and you offer $130,000, you often get menacing looks. Words like ''you must be bleeping crazy'' or ''get out of my face'' often go along with the looks. The negotiations are at a standstill, and the person doesn't want to talk to you anymore. Or maybe the seller will blurt out ''I'll take $180,000 and not a penny less.''

There seems to be no room for negotiation with the sellers who feel they are dealing the cards. In many major urban areas, such as the Northeast, there was a protracted price appreciation lasting many years. Property owners mistakenly believed that prices could only go in one direction and consequently became unwilling to negotiate. Now as the markets normalize, sellers once again must must engage in the negotiating process or properties will not sell. Negotiation does not involve confrontation. A good negotiator makes sure the other person feels he got a fair deal. Each side should win some points. Your job is to seek out a compromise that will make the deal work. Nice guys do make good negotiators.

Negotiating Secrets

There is a basic rule of successful real estate. The rule is never to buy retail—always buy below the market. If a seller won't negotiate or compromise the price or terms, *walk away*. Go after another property. A motivated seller will negotiate, some more than others. Your ingenuity gives the seller reasons to consider your offer which is substantially less than the asking price. If the market is soft, why not mention the large number of vacant and unsold properties, the fact that comparable properties sold for less in the last thirty days, or that the property is not in the best location. Local newspaper advertisements serve as excellent instant visual substantiation of your feelings.

CONCESSIONS LEAD TO DEALS

A trained eye gets you onto the right track. Walk around with a pad or make mental notes. Observe the obvious drawbacks and use them to your advantage. If the drawbacks are legitimate, they will have to be handled. Either the repairs will have to be made for you or for the next potential purchaser. It might as well be you. Therefore, it is in your best interest to gain the concession from the seller and offer your own concession to reach a deal.

Concessions in time often promote favorable deals. If you know when a seller would prefer to vacate a property and you agree to close on the property one month sooner or one month later to suit his needs, it might be well worth his while to move at this convenient time. In return for your flexibility on a closing date, a seller might negotiate the price or terms in your favor. Just make sure you can live with the arrangements.

GIVING BACK FOR LARGER GAINS

Sometimes through tough negotiations you might gain concessions you sought, but upon using hindsight would prefer to trade one concession for another. For instance, if you had worked out a deal to have all the cracked windows replaced. Such a repair would be inconvenient and costly. Instead of having the seller replace the windows, perhaps the person would agree to take $500 or $1000 off the purchase price. Another possibility is to purchase the seller's carpeting, built-in furniture, fixtures, or window treatments. Developing a good working relationship, you might be able to negotiate better terms to suit your individual needs.

Negotiating can be thought of as the See-Saw theory. When both people on the see-saw apply equal pressure there is a stand-off, and the see-saw is balanced. When one person applies less pressure, that person loses control of the see-saw, and the see-saw becomes unbalanced. You and the seller are the people on the see-saw. You have the capability to lessen the pressure so you rise above the seller. By purchasing the seller's personal property or changing thorny issues of the original agreement, you are attempting to defuse the situation and alleviate the pressure. Agreeing not to have the windows repaired or the driveway resurfaced might put the seller into a more conciliatory mood, granting you a lower selling price, some owner-financing or other concessions. Realistically, hairline cracks in windows don't have to be repaired or replaced immediately. With attractive window treatments covering the windows, they are not very noticeable. But if not demanding that they be replaced leads to more cordial negotiating and a better deal, it will be a pane you can endure.

TYING UP PROPERTIES

Since you were a youngster you were told that you can't have your cake and eat it too. Fortunately in real estate you can have both. Shopping for real estate involves finding the bargain before the next investor. If you're buying a sweater you can assess the quality and judge the value in relation to comparable sweaters. In real estate, the comparisons are not so simple. There is no way for you to know what is inside an interior wall. You don't know with certainty if the property is zoned for something other than it is being used. There are dozens of things you don't know at the time you sign on the dotted line. Still you want the property, so what do you do?

Sign the document with subject-to clauses for your protection. On the face of the binder or document, write Subject To clauses, which are described in more detail in the chapter Good Buy or Good Bye. The agreement could be subject to your attorney's approval, a home inspection, termite report, etc. Without escape clauses, you could be asking for financial problems.

ASSIGNING A CONTRACT

When you structure a deal, think of the future. If you sign a contract today and tomorrow are offered $20,000 more, what are your options? Must you close on the property and pay all the closing costs and possibly even lose the buyer in the extended time span? If you structured the deal correctly, all you had to do was to be allowed the right to assign the contract.

When you *assign the contract*, you are being given the right in writing to make a deal to sell the property to another person before actually closing on the property. You are assigning all the obligations of the contract to another person, so that you are relieved of the terms of the contract. Whatever financial deal between you and another person is only between the two parties, but the terms of the original contract remain intact.

You should only assign the contract with the aid of an attorney. Your attorney will insert the words *or their assigns* alongside your name as the Buyer on the contract. As a result the contract will read—Buyer—John Smith and Jane Smith or Their Assigns. Those last three words can mean many thousands of dollars to you as it allows you to assign the contract to another buyer should you choose to before closing. Make sure you allow yourself enough time to find a buyer if you decide to flip your property before closing. If you don't find a buyer, of course you are obligated to live up to the terms of the contract, which is to purchase the property.

CONTRACT OF SALE made as of the 31st day of January, 1994

PARTIES
Between: JIM DANDY
Address: 13 Almond Drive, Nutley, New Jersey
Herein called SELLER who agrees to sell:
And Lester Orr and Gail Orr, his wife OR THEIR ASSIGNS
Address: 2470 Park Drive, Wantagh, New York

Herein called PURCHASER, who agrees to buy the above property under the terms below.

PREMISES
Street Address: 1 Pecan Place, Shelby, New York
Tax Map Designation: Section 53 Block 214 Lots 390-392

Doing Your Assignment

Assume you are purchasing a property for $130,000. You are familiar with the market because you have done your homework. You estimate that the property has a market value of $145,000. After taking into account the debts and expenses you determine that you have an equity of between $10,000 and $15,000. Should you assign the contract, you will make a tidy sum for just locating the property, finding a buyer and putting together a deal. Once the buyer signs the contract with you he assumes your responsibility. You walk away with a profit and can begin searching for a new profit-making opportunity. As long as you can continue to find buyers willing to pay you more than you agreed in the contract that you are assigning, you can't lose.

Clearly the idea of buying and assigning contracts to properties is not for everyone. Some people don't like the pressure of having to find a buyer for their contract within a certain time period. There is risk involved. Remember if you don't find a buyer for your contract, it is your obligation to close the deal.

Negotiation Action Line

There are so many ingredients that make a real estate deal. Among them are the buyer, seller, their attorneys, real estate agent, lender, and title company. How you handle yourself with other parties helps determine what kind of deal you ultimately make. Careful negotiations between you and the other parties can save your assets. No one is as concerned with your protection as you must be. Your attorney is being paid by you but is first concerned with covering his own tail— you come second. The real estate broker represents the seller and not you, since you are the buyer. The expression "eat or be eaten" was never more applicable. Below are many of the dangers present in the negotiations process and what you should do.

Problem—Seller asks for release of the down payment at contract signing.
Solution—Refuse to release any of the down payment. It protects you from the seller reneging on the deal.

Problem—Seller refuses to close because there is no C.O.
Solution—Your attorney should set aside an amount of money in escrow until the C.O. is obtained.

Problem—Seller has tenants living in the house who you wish to vacate.
Solution—Your attorney should put in writing that tenants must vacate before closing or pay a per day money penalty for each day beyond closing.

Problem—Seller hasn't signed the binder that the agent presented.
Solution—Remember the NIWIN principle. Give a deadline for the binder to be signed or you walk away.

Problem—You don't have an attorney and the real estate agent offers to get you one.
Solution—Hire your own attorney because this attorney must have some allegiance to the real estate firm that recommends him.

Problem—You can't tell if there is anything wrong with the house. You don't want the house if there is.
Solution—Your attorney should put in the agreement ''Buyer has ten days to have the house inspected. If the buyer is not satisfied with the inspection report, he shall have the right to cancel the contract and have the down payment returned.

Problem—The real estate agent says that she can have the house inspected for you.
Solution—Hire your own inspector. The inspection company recommended by a real estate firm might owe some allegiance to the real estate agent to push through a deal.

Problem—The real estate agent or seller suggests you don't need an attorney.
Solution—Make sure you have an attorney to at least read over the documents. Don't buy real estate without a real estate attorney.

Problem—You want interest on your down payment.
Solution—Open up a joint account with the seller's attorney. If the attorney refuses, offer the seller to split the interest in a joint interest-bearing account.

Problem—You don't want to lose your down payment if you can't obtain a mortgage.
Solution—Your attorney will include in the contract that unless you are able to secure a mortgage at an agreed-upon rate for thirty years, the contract will be declared null and void and the buyer shall receive back his down payment.

Problem—The seller tells you that everything stays with the house when she signs the binder. You want to be sure it does.
Solution—Have the specific items you want written into the contract.

Problem—You are concerned that the property will deteriorate from the date of contract to the time of closing.
Solution—Have your attorney include a clause that states ''Seller assumes all liability for fire and other damage prior to closing.''

Problem—Because of other arrangements you need to move in by a specific date.

Solution—Write a specific date for closing to take place in the contract and specify that "time is of the essence." Put financial penalties for each day the seller is late in vacating. If a substantial amount isn't set, a seller might find it more convenient to remain a month than relocate to a hotel.

Problem—You must move into a newly constructed house by a specific date.

Solution—Have the builder write into the contract that he will pay the hotel and storage costs if the house isn't finished by the time specified in the contract. Include the "time is of the essence" clause.

Problem—You want to be certain that you have marketable title. Simply put, you want to make sure that you and you alone can sell the property.

Solution—Have your attorney write the clause "The seller shall give and the buyer accept a title that any reputable title company will approve and insure."

Problem—Before closing be sure the plumbing, heating, roof, and appliances are in working order.

Solution—Call up the sellers and make an appointment the day before closing to visit and make sure everything works.

Problem—You have plans to rent the property. You don't want to lose a month's rent by waiting until after you close to start showing the house to prospective tenants.

Solutions—Have your attorney insert a clause "Buyer shall have the right to show property to prospective tenants during the contingency period."

THE UNINFORMED SELLER

In the Negotiation Action Line, there were many practical negotiating secrets that are overlooked during negotiations and cost the buyer in time and the pocketbook. So many of these situations come up and the buyer finds himself unprotected when dealing with an experienced seller. If you have a choice, one of the best negotiating secrets is, if possible, deal with an uninformed seller. That does not mean that the seller is unintelligent, but rather uninformed about the particular situation. The seller might not know how much the house is worth and price it unrealistically.

Sellers are uninformed for any number of reasons. A parent might have relocated or died, leaving the property to be sold. A seller might be the heir to an estate, looking to sell the property to pay taxes. Seller A might have lived in the house for twenty years and learned that the person on the next block sold her house for $400,000. Seller B remembers that she only paid $30,000 for the house when she bought it and has everything original. Seller A would probably expect too high a price, while Seller B would likely expect too low a price.

What do you do if a seller is out of touch with reality in pricing a property? Do you lecture the person? Not if you want any chance of making a deal. If the asking price is in the stratosphere suggest that the seller call down three local real estate agents to give informal estimates. If the seller doesn't have the time, ask if you can call the real estate people. Once you have three estimates, average them and you have a starting point for negotiations. It is then that you can start to implement some of the previously mentioned negotiating secrets.

When negotiating with an uninformed seller, you might occasionally find that despite logic and persuasion, the seller won't agree to your offer. What do you do? You could walk away or instead pay what you consider to be an inflated price. What if there were another alternative? What if you could pay the full asking price without closing for several years? It is possible to do with the lease with option to purchase.

LEASE WITH OPTION TO PURCHASE

You are impressed with the property and its potential but don't like the price. What can you do to have your cake and eat it too? Agree to a lease with option to purchase or to have a lease option agreement as an alternative to an outright purchase of a property.

The lease with option to purchase holds two important advantages over an outright purchase.

1. It allows you to purchase a property at today's prices with tomorrow's dollars. Inflation is not going to go away. The prices of everything will be higher than they are today. No one's salary goes down. That means the cost of manufacturing and selling goods will rise with wages. Similarly, it will take more dollars each year to buy the property you can buy today. A lease option serves as an insurance policy against inflationary pressures.

2. It ties up the property for a definite time period so that the seller is not legally permitted to sell the property to anyone else. If you don't have the down payment to qualify for a mortgage, but still want to purchase the property, a lease with option to purchase makes it possible. For a fee of a few hundred to a thousand dollars, you can enter a lease option agreement.

There is one distinct disadvantage to a lease option agreement, from the viewpoint of the purchaser. The monthly payment for rent is set by the owner at an above-market rate. Though the agreement stipulates that a certain percentage of the rent shall be used towards the ultimate purchase, all moneys are forfeited if the option is not exercised within the time period set forth in the agreement.

Teresa and Osvaldo were a family with two young children. He owned a limousine company, and she was a bookkeeper with an import company. His limousine company required large outlays of money as part of a cooperative of owners. Teresa and Osvaldo wanted to purchase a home but had no cash for a down payment. We signed with them a lease with option to purchase agreement.

In the agreement it was specified that the price of the house would be set at $130,000. The option would be for two years and the rent would be set at $800. At the end of two years, if the option were not exercised, a new purchase price would be set. There was no charge for the option in exchange for none of the rent being applied to the purchase price, but two month's security was held just like any rental house or apartment lease. At the end of the two-year period, Teresa and Osvaldo exercised their option and purchased the house. The two month's security that we held was credited to their down payment.

Most lease with option to purchase agreements differ from the one we entered with Teresa and Osvaldo. Most include the payment of a percentage of the purchase price or a flat fee for the option. Two or three percent of the purchase price would be an appropriate option price. Then anything from two hundred dollars to the full rent would be applied to the purchase price. If the option is exercised, all the rent as well as the option fee are credited towards the down payment.

A lease option agreement for buyer and seller is a win-win situation. For the buyer, you recapture a portion of the rent paid. In effect you live rent-free for the year. If you don't exercise the option, and decide not to purchase, your only extraordinary expense is the option fee. If the option fee is worded properly, you could have it assigned to another party and recover your option fee.

THE LEASE OR BUY COMPARISON

Cost. With a lease-option you lock in the property at today's price and won't have to pay until tomorrow, the time you exercise the option. All or most lease expenses are recoverable at the time you exercise the option. If you try to buy the property a few years later, you might discover that the price is out of your price range.

Cash. With a lease-option your only outlay is the option expense and the monthly payments. In short, the money you are spending for rent is substantially less than the twenty percent or more down payment or a monthly mortgage payment.

Monthly Expenses. More than likely, the monthly rent will be lower than the combined total of mortgage payments, taxes and insurance paid by the seller. In many cases the seller offers a lease-option because he has been unable to sell or rent. The lease-option serves as a sweetener to rent more easily.

Location. Many people seeking to own property cannot afford it. The intentions are there but the required down payment is not. With the lease-option the person who otherwise could not afford the property might be able to ultimately purchase it.

Maintenance and Upkeep. When you are the property owner any repairs are your responsibility. As a person leasing a property, your responsibility is as a tenant, unless something different is specified in your agreement. Many leases specify that the appliances are provided as a service and that the tenant is responsible for any and all repairs. If you are not responsible for repairs, your costs will be kept lower.

A sample lease with option form is provided. Consult with an attorney to make sure that the terms are legal in your state.

LEASE WITH OPTION TO PURCHASE

RECEIVED FROM _____

the sum of _____

herein referred to as the BUYER,

evidenced by cashier's check payable to _____,

OWNER as financial consideration which will be deposited upon acceptance by BUYER and SELLER.

The deposit shall be credited to the purchase price of _____.

The BUYER agrees to lease from the OWNER the premises situated in _____, County of _____, State of _____ at the following address: _____

Term—The term shall begin on _____, 19_____ and continue for a period of twelve months ending on _____, 19_____.

Rent—Rent shall be _____ per month, with the first and last month's rent to be paid in advance. Payments shall be paid on the first day of each month directly to the OWNER. A late charge of $25 will be incurred if the rent is not paid by the seventh day of the month.

Security—The security deposit shall be applied directly to the purchase of the premises. Any balance remaining on termination of the agreement shall be returned to the BUYER.

Maintenance—BUYER will keep the property clean and in good repair during the option period. Any repairs including termite service necessary to obtain a loan will be paid for by the tenant.

Default—If the BUYER fails to pay the rent when due, after ten days the OWNER shall give written notice of default and the OWNER, at his option, may terminate the agreement. At that point the OWNER may elect to continue the lease and attempt to collect the rent or terminate all the BUYER'S rights and legally seek to recover the premises.

Deposit—Should the BUYER not exercise the option within the twelve month period, all payments will be considered rent and no compensation will be paid by the OWNER.

Extension—Any extension after the expiration period, with the OWNER'S consent, shall be construed as a month-to-month tenancy.

Option—For as long as the BUYER is not in default of the terms of the lease, the BUYER shall have the option to purchase the property at a price of _____, with the following terms and conditions:

1. The price of the option shall be _____.
2. _____ of the monthly rent shall be applied to the down payment.
3. BUYER when exercising the option shall make a payment equal to ten percent of the purchase price.

Closing—BUYER shall close within thirty days from the exercise of the option.

Expiration of option—The option may be exercised at any time after _____ and shall expire at midnight _____, unless it is exercised earlier. Upon expiration, all obligations of OWNER and BUYER shall cease.

Exercise of option—The option shall be exercised by mailing written notice to the OWNER before the expiration of this option and by a payment of the balance of the ten percent down payment.

OWNER and BUYER acknowledge receipt of a copy of this page.
        Dated _____

_____   _____
      OWNER   BUYER

_____   _____
      OWNER   BUYER

SUMMARY

Negotiating is vitally important in any real estate transaction. It is through negotiating a good purchase price that you make money in real estate. Buying property at wholesale prices and on favorable terms makes every deal ultimately
profitable, even in a soft market. Remember what Donald Trump did when he
purchased the Eastern Shuttle. First he submitted a low bid for the shuttle.
When Eastern Airlines went on strike, Trump claimed that the value of the shuttle had been reduced by the strike. Then he returned to the bargaining table
some time later agreeing to honor the original offer if seven more planes were
included. A deal was struck at the original price with sweetened terms.

You cannot expect to make deals like Trump, but you can utilize negotiating
tactics to make every deal more profitable. With the NEGOTIATOR formula,
you can ferret out relevant information to uncover a seller's vulnerabilities and
needs to maximize your opportunities. Our negotiating secrets further simplify
the process as you and the seller attempt to reach an understanding with which
you can both live.

The negotiating process is often time-consuming and difficult. However you,
as the buyer, do not want to lose a deal because of loose ends that remain untied.
You learn to tie up the property so it cannot be sold to anyone while you negotiate the best deal possible. Having the option to assign your contract responsibilities allows you to flip for an immediate profit. The best deals are reached when
some of the seller's needs are met as well as your own.

Occasionally opportunity knocks and your checkbook isn't home.

Everyone temporarily lacks resources from time to time. But the shortfall
does not have to prevent you from tying up the property. If you can't buy it
because you lack the down payment, lease it. With a lease-option agreement,
you pay for the option and the monthly rent. All or most of the payments go
toward the purchase of the property if you exercise the option and purchase the
property within the specified time period. A lease-option agreement might be
the only way some people can purchase a property. Its advantages are locking in
a price for a time period and not having to raise the large down payment.

Whether negotiating a lease with option to buy agreement or a contract to
purchase, there are many potential dangers to avoid. Care in negotiating and representation by an attorney can help avoid problems. Agreeing to release any part
of the down payment to the seller, failing to include escape clauses, and not using
precise wording on the closing date can all prove to be costly mistakes. Avoiding
real estate booby traps and engaging in careful negotiations can lead to the highest profit possible.

10

Working with Attorneys

THERE ARE MANY MISCONCEPTIONS ABOUT ATTORNEYS. ONE OF THE MAIN misconceptions is that they only work on a time basis, by the hour. That simply is not true. Attorneys do work on a flat fee basis, though they prefer not to. They would much prefer being paid on an hourly basis. They can earn much more money by the hour. Quite often a person has a problem and asks the attorney for the projected fee. Frequent responses are "It won't be much," "Don't worry about it," or "What are you worried for." All responses are aimed to disarm you and get you to forget that you want to put a cap on your expenses. Don't have the attorney begin work until you have a firm price for the work. You want to be certain that the attorney doesn't mean "I'm not really sure how to handle it. Until I try a couple of different ways at your expense, I won't be sure.

Most attorneys who are experienced in a field and have confidence in their abilities will not hesitate to accept a flat fee and put it in writing. Of course, there are exceptions. Some highly competent attorneys suffer from delusions of grandeur and feel it is beneath them to negotiate price with a client. If one with whom you consult won't work for a flat fee, thank him for his time and move on.

Below is a true story. The names of the parties are fictitious, though the events did take place.

Bruce and Rose Miles were active real estate investors, having owned a number of residential properties. They had become interested in a foreclosure property and had an inside track on successfully obtaining it. The owners of the property had admittedly missed several payments and received a Notice of Default from the bank's attorneys. The property owners approached Bruce and Rose immediately, since Bruce and Rose held a junior lien, a second mortgage on the property. Bruce and Rose asked their attorney from the law firm of Cheetham and Howe if he would handle the case and what his fee would be. The attorney couldn't give an exact fee but said "It wouldn't be much."

The following day, after meeting with Bruce and Rose and the property owners, the attorney faxed an authorization by the property owners to request permission for Bruce and Rose to assume the existing mortgage and purchase the house. Bruce and Rose called the attorney once a week for the next few weeks to learn if the bank's attorneys had responded. Each time, the attorney informed them that he had just called the bank's attorneys, and the attorneys had not reached a decision.

Two months later, after a few dozen phone calls, the bank granted permission for Bruce and Rose to purchase the house, as long as they closed within six weeks. Their attorney had insisted that he could not get an answer from the bank's attorneys, claiming that they would not return his phone calls. Rose took the initiative, called the bank's attorney and insisted to speak with the person who was handling the purchase of the property. The bank attorney read the figures over the phone to Rose, as Rose recorded the specifics, and Rose asked that a copy of the closing figures be sent to their attorney at Cheetham and Howe.

Several days later their attorney called to inform them that he had the figures, as if to say that he had obtained them. Rose informed him that she had called to get them, to keep down her legal expenses. The amount they would have to pay, according to the papers was $5500 for missed mortgage payments plus $1300 for bank attorney fees. Bruce and Rose began to pool their resources and tap their credit lines to meet the obligations. Every once in a while their attorney would call for bits of information for the couple to furnish or documents to sign. One week before the deadline given by the bank to close, the attorney called Bruce to pick up a release form for the current owners to sign and return. Bruce immediately visited the owners, had them sign the documents, and returned them to their attorney the next day. Once again Bruce asked "Do you have an idea what the fee is going to be?" The attorney calmly responded, "Don't worry about it. It shouldn't be much."

The next morning the attorney was on the phone. The forms they had returned to him were unacceptable. They were xerox copies for demonstration purposes. He needed original documents. Once again the sellers were asked to sign the documents, and Bruce hand-delivered them to the attorney. With days before the imposed closing deadline, Bruce and Rose asked the attorney for the exact closing figures, so that they could immediately send along a check. As usual, he said that he would get back to them.

Having not received a response from their attorney, Rose called up to speak with him. He had bad news and explained. The bank's attorney decreed that there could not be a closing by mail. It had to be a face-to-face closing. He exclaimed to the flabbergasted couple that the bank's attorneys were a big law firm, and they wouldn't return his phone calls. He would try again to reach them.

Not satisfied with the timid attorney's behavior, Rose decided to visit the bank attorney's offices and resolve the situation face-to-face. Rose had no forewarning of the news she was about to hear. The closing figures were now up to $12,500 plus the $1300 in bank attorney fees. A mail closing was non-negotiable, so Rose set up a closing date.

Upon returning home from the bank attorney, Rose and Bruce called up their attorney and informed him that the closing date was set. Under ordinary circumstances attorneys would set up a closing date, but this was no ordinary situation and no ordinary attorney. The little attorney had difficulty dealing with the big law firm. In the conversation Bruce conveyed his dismay that the closing figures had risen from $5500 to $12,500. The attorney's response was, "So what's another $7,000." After scraping himself off the ceiling, Bruce again asked for the attorney's fee. This time the response was "whatever is in the machine." When asked for more specifics the attorney just shrugged his shoulders and smiled.

Seeing that they were getting nowhere by having their attorney make arrangements, Bruce and Rose decided to write a strongly worded letter to the president of the bank's law firm about what they perceived as overcharges, as well as detailing the unresponsiveness of their attorneys. Playing hardball with Bruce and Rose and making several veiled threats, the president agreed to drop $220 in late fees from the total bill.

At closing the next day, Rose and Bruce informed their attorney that they had convinced the bank attorneys to drop $220 from the closing costs. Their attorney's response was "I could have done that." If he could have why didn't he, instead of telling them that the closing costs could not be negotiated. The closing began as their attorney looked over the documents and nodded his head in approval. Bruce immediately called his attorney's attention to the fact that the mortgage rate was set at 13%, instead of the 11% in the agreement. The correction was made, all the papers were signed, and the closing was concluded. At least that was what Bruce and Rose thought.

Bruce and Rose were invited back to their attorney's office to settle the financial arrangements. They were handed the bill. It was a good thing they were sitting because there wasn't far to fall. The bill presented to them was an astronomical $2100. In a state of shock, Bruce asked where the figure arose. Their previous house closing with Cheetham and Howe was for $750. The attorney presented them a computerized tear-off and remarked that his expenses accrued at the rate of $150 per hour. Every phone call to the bank's attorney where his call was not returned was billed for $37.50. Rose observed that he had included eight phone calls to her, totaling two hours or $300. He also charged two hours or $300 for the closing.

There was dead silence in the room as the attorney waited for a response. Bruce and Rose were too shocked to speak. When asked directly for a response, Bruce and Rose expressed their disappointment and feeling of betrayal. They reiterated their constant queries throughout the case about the cost and their attorney's evasive responses. Finally the attorney agreed to deduct for the calls to Rose and the closing, bringing the total cost down to a still-astounding $1500. Reluctantly, Rose and Bruce accepted the compromise and wrote three checks to be cashed on an installment basis. For Bruce and Rose it was a mixed blessing. They had paid considerably more than they expected as their attorney received a course in Bank Attorney Law 101. But on the positive side, they had learned never to agree to hire an attorney unless it is on a flat fee basis.

What can you as a real estate investor learn from Rose and Bruce's experience? For one thing, the reason that attorneys such as theirs charge by the hour is that they often lack the expertise or experience to handle the matter. They haven't done it before, are reluctant to admit it, and are going to charge you for their education. If the attorney had done the procedure many times prior, he would have had a good idea of the amount of time required. In Bruce and Rose's predicament, they financed their attorney's education in the purchase of foreclosures. He was not knowledgeable on the subject and needed the $1500 in-service course paid for by Bruce and Rose. The next time clients approach the attorney about buying a foreclosure he will say, "Sure, I know all about foreclosures. I just bought one for my clients Bruce and Rose." The next time he might agree to work for a flat fee or not accrue enormous billing hours. An attorney like the one in this story might be working in your city. Don't hire him. If you are told not to worry about the price, start to worry. When it comes to hiring attorneys, "Flat is where it's at. And if it's not in writing, you're not biting."

FINDING AN ATTORNEY

At a mortgage company closing room there sat three people. There was a high-priced attorney for the seller, a low-priced attorney for the buyer, and a tooth fairy. An attache' case filled with thousand-dollar bills totaling the cost of the house—one million dollars was on the table. Suddenly the lights went out, and there was total darkness. When the lights came on again, the attache' case was open, and the money was gone. The police were called. They immediately knew who had taken the money. Who do you think took the money, the high-priced attorney, the low-priced attorney, or the tooth fairy? It had to be the high-priced attorney. The other two are figments of your imagination.

Attorneys are not always admired or well liked. They are frequently criticized for their over-billing and other deceptive practices. Yet, like them or not, attorneys are indispensable in any real estate transaction. When you take into account the amount of money you are investing in a real estate transaction, you definitely need legal representation. One omission or misrepresentation by another party could cost you many times the legal fee charged by the attorney.

It is a commonly used axiom that a person who serves as his own attorney has a fool for a client. Without a doubt anyone who is involved in a real estate should have an attorney for representation, even if it is only to read over the papers. In many states, real estate transactions are done without an attorney, but a few hundred dollars is a small price to pay for your financial protection. So much of what is written is in legal gobblygook. Agreements and contracts are often made vague to allow parties to interpret them their way. The law is written in such a way that one word or expression omitted or included in a contract could cost or save you thousands of dollars. Knowledgeable investors do not enter into any binding agreements without consulting an attorney.

An attorney representing you is no guarantee that everything will work to perfection. Even with a competent attorney a real estate investor could be seriously damaged. Any attorney is not appropriate to handle your real estate transaction. You have to hire a real estate attorney to handle your real estate. You wouldn't hire an oral surgeon to do a quadruple bypass, and they are both doctors. Similarly, you don't hire a corporate attorney to handle your real estate closing.

If you read the attorney's shingle and see that he or she handles everything from divorces, wills, real estate, bankruptcies, traffic violations and accident cases, you have a distinct possibility of becoming his next victim. If an attorney is competent and successful why would he or she have to handle so many diverse areas of the law? A successful attorney would not have to dabble in so many fields to make a living. Does your auto mechanic also fix storm windows and install vinyl siding?

Can any attorney handle a real estate closing? Yes. Should you hire any attorney to handle your closing? No. Any attorney can read and understand the legal jargon of a contract and closing, but there are so many protective clauses that a competent real estate attorney should put in a contract to protect the client, whether buyer or seller. When things go smoothly any attorney can handle the contract and closing, but all too often experienced legal representation is required.

How do you select an attorney to handle your real estate? Do you hire your nephew Jackie who is working for a big law firm? Do you hire the neighbor across the street with a shingle on his front lawn because he always drives late-model cars? Do you hire the attorney who won you a four-figure settlement in your accident case? The answer to all three questions is an unequivocal, maybe. Any of the three attorneys under consideration could be right to handle your transaction. You don't have enough information to base a decision.

A wise real estate investor calls up an attorney on the phone. The person asks for an appointment and states that he or she is looking to hire an attorney for representation in a real estate transaction. Ask if there will be any charge for the meeting. There should not be a charge if the meeting lasts less than fifteen minutes. If there is, ask how much and decide if you want to pursue the matter. If you are reluctant to pay for the initial meeting, say that most attorneys do not charge for the initial meeting and that you prefer one that does not charge. Thank the attorney for his or her time.

When you are seeking an attorney, avoid shingle shock. Don't select an attorney to interview until after you have pursued other avenues. There are a number of worthwhile sources to finding competent and responsible attorneys. Read through Keys to Choosing an Attorney.

KEYS TO CHOOSING AN ATTORNEY

Contact:
☞ Friends involved in real estate
☞ Local bar association
☞ Lawyer's referral service
☞ Local real estate investment club
☞ Martindale and Hubbell Law Directory

QUESTIONS TO ASK AN ATTORNEY

☞ Is your practice devoted mainly to real estate?
☞ How long have you been handling real estate?
☞ Will you be doing all the work or will you be giving it to a paralegal or secretary?
☞ Will you be charging a flat fee instead of an hourly fee?
☞ What are some of the escape clauses you use in your contracts?
☞ Have you handled foreclosures, 1031 exchanges, or equity participation?
☞ What will your fee be?

After receiving responses from several attorneys, collect the data, and evaluate the information. Remember that you will be paying the attorney. You have the right to know what you are paying for. Certain of these areas should be non-negotiable, while others deserve consideration. It is then up to you to compare the price. Don't worry about being shy. We're talking about spending your hard-earned money. If necessary, you have to force yourself to get tough. Hiring the wrong attorney is like not getting oil changes for your car. You are going to pay sooner or later.

Question an attorney about his use of escape clauses in the contract. If the attorney attempts to disarm you by asking what you mean, explain that you mean the clauses with subject to. Representing you as a buyer, the attorney should mention subject to obtaining a mortgage, being able to sell before closing, a house being free of termites and radon, a professional inspection, etc., etc. If the attorney is unable or unwilling to supply you with several escape clauses, it is a signal to you to escape from the attorney with your assets intact. Any experienced real estate attorney will be very familiar with the use of escape clauses, having used them dozens of times. Don't accept an attorney's stock answer to questions he or she is unwilling to face, "Just leave it up to me. Don't worry about a thing." You might have plenty to worry about.

A flat is a terrible inconvenience, except when it is the attorney's fee. You want it spelled out and agreed to in certain terms before work begins. You don't want to pay by the hour unless you want to discover first-hand that "time is money." You will be charged for every phone call, ten-minute meeting, and personal appearance the attorney makes on your behalf. Even if the attorney never picks up the phone and has his secretary speaking with a clerk in another office, you will be billed for it. The attorney calls it billing hours, but you will call it highway robbery. Don't accept "It won't be much" or "Don't worry about the fee." Insist that you are informed how much the charge will be. Make sure that there will be no other fees or costs. If you don't receive specific answers, consider whether you want to hire an attorney who will not be open and responsive.

A specialization in real estate is a must in selecting an attorney, whether the shingle reads "practice limited to real estate" or not. Any attorney can sit across from another attorney and write a contract for sale. A nonaggressive attorney just agrees to let the other attorney write the contract. An aggressive attorney takes charge. With the use of word processors, the drawing of a contract is not the time-consuming ordeal it had been. The problem facing your attorney is what protection is being offered and how familiar is the attorney with the various options you could choose in the contract and the purchase. With a problemfree contract and closing, you might not detect any lack of experience or expertise in the attorney. However, without sufficient protection you could be seriously damaged by an inexperienced attorney in real estate. An inexpensive attorney could be the most costly attorney you could ever imagine.

DO'S AND DON'TS FOR DEALING WITH ATTORNEYS

☞ Don't leave important deadlines up to your attorney. Keep track of dates.
☞ Don't accept oral promises. Get everything in writing, including binder signatures.
☞ Don't be afraid to ask the attorney anything you don't fully understand.
☞ Do ask for interest on your escrow money if you are a buyer.
☞ Don't accept a lawyer recommended by a real estate agent, unless you check him out.
☞ Do ask for a second opinion if you disagree with your attorney.

☞ Don't let the attorney convince you to release the down payment to the seller.

☞ Don't allow the attorney to refuse to close because necessary papers are missing. Instead suggest that a substantial amount of money be held in escrow.

☞ Do ask your attorney to include escape clauses in all contracts to protect your interests.

☞ Do ask your attorney if he or she has a business relationship with the bank or title company being used. It might be kickback time.

☞ Don't put escrow money into a lawyer's account unless it is stipulated as an escrow account.

☞ Don't allow your attorney to include a closing date without precise vocabulary. Use *on* instead of *on or about* if you are a seller, so the buyer doesn't stall. Use *on or about* instead of *on* if you are a buyer. This way a buyer has more time to make the closing arrangements.

☞ Do ask the attorney to use plain language in the contract.

☞ Do get your understanding of your fee agreement in writing.

While it is true that almost any attorney can handle your contract and closing, you need protection when problems arise. Often an attorney will not admit unfamiliarity with a subject. Rather than saying he or she doesn't know, he answers with what he feels is an acceptable response and hopes you buy it. So it is in your best interest to check into his background, integrity, and knowledge. As a guide, use Questions to Ask an Attorney.

Misconceptions

Everyone has heard the story about the guy who has a heart-to-heart talk with his father before getting married. He says, "Dad, when I was a teenager I didn't think you were too bright. I can't believe how much you've learned these past few years." Like the young man who thought he knew it all as a teenager, we have discovered there was a great deal we had to learn about attorneys. Everyone begins a relationship with an attorney in total awe and trust. Then, after bumps and bruises, you learn that many beliefs and assumptions have been misconceptions. Here are some commonly held misconceptions about attorneys that many unsuspecting people believe. Attorneys are neither more or less honest, intelligent, or trustworthy than any other professional, but a better understanding of a relationship brings about a better result.

1. Attorneys are omniscient and cannot be questioned.
2. Fees are written in stone and cannot be negotiated.
3. Attorneys always watch after your interests and money as you do.

4. An attorney is qualified and suited to handle any legal matter, regardless of the field of expertise.

5. An expensive attorney always will give better representation than a lower-priced attorney.

Screening Attorneys

In the legal profession there are countless outstanding attorneys who will give you excellent representation. The problem is in locating and screening the attorney for individual situation. One excellent source of information about attorneys is a series of reference books known as *The Martindale and Hubbell Directory*. The books are listed by state in alphabetical order. They are as follows:

Volume 1—Alabama – California
Volume 2—Colorado – Georgia
Volume 3—Hawaii – Maryland
Volume 4—Massachusetts – New Mexico
Volume 5—New York – Ohio
Volume 6—Oklahoma – Texas
Volume 7—Utah – Wyoming
Volume 8—Law Digest – Uniform Acts

As you research *Martindale and Hubbell*, you will discover that attorneys are listed by city and state. Within the section encompassing the state, you will find the individual cities, also in alphabetical order. If you were looking through Volume 5, which covers attorneys in New York State, you will find the listing for attorneys in Albany on the pages before you will find the attorneys in Yaphank, which is a town in Suffolk County.

If you were interested in an attorney in Ocala, Florida, you would first find Volume 2—Colorado – Georgia. In this volume, you would find listings for states such as Connecticut, Delaware, and Florida, in addition to Colorado and Georgia. Since Florida is listed between Colorado and Georgia, you would find listings for Florida between those states. Thumb through the Florida section until you locate the subheading Ocala. Below the subheading are many of the attorneys in Ocala. Not all the attorneys in Ocala are listed, but the book offers an excellent starting point in selecting a local attorney to meet your particular needs.

The Martindale and Hubbell Directory is an excellent source of information, but it is not the *Bible*. Listings are based upon the recommendations of attorneys and judges in each local area. It is quite likely that many outstanding attorneys in a locality are not included in the directory. It is possible that an attorney could be omitted for reasons other than legal ability or that persons included are no more competent than the average attorney. In the listings, attorneys are given a rating, based upon the confidential recommendations of judges and attorneys in the area where the attorney practices. With human nature as it is, and the good-old-boy network in full operation, listings should be given consideration, but they should not be the sole reason for hiring an attorney.

Ratings are assigned in recognition of an attorney's legal ability, in addition to the attorney's code of ethics and reliability. For legal ability, the ratings are "a" for very high, "b" for high to very high, or "c" from fair to high. For ethics and reliability, the rating is "v" for very high. Where a rating is given, the ratings are av, bv, or cv. Not every attorney listed has a rating beside the name. The highest rating awarded any attorney is "av." Bear in mind that the rating is based upon the documentation supplied to *Martindale and Hubbell*. Other attorneys and clients might hold different opinions about the ratings of the attorneys, though it remains an excellent resource. We know of many excellent attorneys who are either listed with no rating or who are not listed. Look at the sample listings below. It is not an actual listing, but is merely used to demonstrate how to use the data.

Floral Gardens

Ashe, Bruce '39 '65 C.235 L.516 206 Main Street

Cohen, Abraham '45 '70 av C.102 L.560 1300 Jersey Avenue

Guarino, Fred '41 '68 C.434 L.564 1776 Liberty Avenue

In the sample listing, there are three attorneys. Let's examine first the data on Abraham Cohen. Mr. Cohen was born in 1945 and received his law degree in 1970. He holds the av rating, which means that he holds the highest rating in legal ability and has very high ethical standards. C.102 represents the college he attended. Looking it up in the directory of colleges at the beginning of the book you discover that Mr. Cohen graduated from Brooklyn College. To the right of C.102 is another number and letter. It is L.560, representing the law school from which Mr. Cohen graduated. Looking up L.560 you learn that he graduated from New York Law School. The final entry in the listing is the address of his office—1300 Jersey Avenue.

With the information in hand for the rated attorneys for any city in a given state, you can make a more educated decision on your choice of attorney. To guide your decision there is an inclusion of fields of practice in which the attorney participates. Though many listings omit such biographical information, attorneys affiliated with large law firms usually contain that information. If there is not as much information listed as you would like, call up the attorney and gather your own information.

SUMMARY

When choosing an attorney to handle your real estate, be sure you hire a real estate attorney. Just as you don't hire an oral surgeon to perform an appendectomy, you don't hire a corporate attorney to handle your real estate transaction. Questions you will ask an attorney should elicit if his practice is limited to real estate, if he is charging a flat fee, how long he has been handling real estate, if he is familiar with escape clauses, and if he has experience with foreclosures, 1031 exchanges, and equity participation agreements.

It is important to check out an attorney's background before hiring him. There are a number of useful sources to locate competent and responsible attorneys. The keys to choosing an attorney are:

☞ Friends involved in real estate investing
☞ The local bar association
☞ The lawyer's referral service
☞ The local real estate investment club
☞ Martindale and Hubbell Law Directory

Attorneys are indispensable in any real estate transaction. One omission or misrepresentation without an attorney's advice could cost many times the legal fee charged by the attorney. Any time you enter a real estate deal make sure you are represented by a real estate attorney. Even the most expensive attorney might be the lowest-cost investment you'll ever make, if it means having your rights protected and avoiding costly legal action.

11

Commercial vs. Residential Property —What's Right for You?

COMMERCIAL PROPERTY CAN BE THOUGHT OF AS RETAIL STORES, MOM AND POP convenience stores and delis, strip shopping centers, shopping malls and flea market properties. Commercial property does not appeal to as many investors as residential property. It has many advantageous aspects, as well as drawbacks. One of the primary advantages of a commercial property over a residential property is the number of hours required in the care of it. When a problem arises with residential property, you are on call twenty-four hours a day and seven days a week.

With a commercial property, the retail store has a bedtime. That is when the store closes. If the store has a closing time of five o'clock for six days a week and remains closed on Sunday, the hours in operation are the only time you will be called. With a residential property, you are not as fortunate. A leaky faucet or lack of heat often will produce a phone call any time of day or night from 6 A.M. to 12 midnight, seven days a week. The contention is that if the tenant can't sleep, there is no reason for the landlord to sleep either.

Not only is the commercial property owner not summoned at inconvenient hours, in general, the owner is not called at all. For the most part, commercial properties require a reduced management effort.

The only time you and the tenant usually see one another is to pick up the rent. Otherwise months can pass without contact. The commercial property tenant is operating a business and often does not have time for complaint calls to a landlord. The tenant is too busy trying to earn a living to be bothersome.

COMMERCIAL PLUSES

Commercial properties offer other advantages to the investor. There is less tenant turnover since tenants are running a business with loyal customers and are not likely to relocate. In another location, they might be unable to attract their present customers to the new place of business. Resultingly, commercial tenants tend to stay in one location for many years. The end result is that the landlord has stability, and the tenant has a continuing location for the business.

If you like having a piece of the business, then you have another reason for wanting to own commercial property. In strong retail areas, the landlord and tenant work out profit-sharing agreements. In the lease a percentage rent is arranged so that the rent is based upon a percentage of sales. Once the sales exceed the prearranged levels, the landlord receives added income. In a thriving location, you have a win-win situation. As your tenants prosper, so do you. You receive a share of the proceeds without working the long hours and putting up with difficult customers and daily problems.

COMMERCIAL CONSIDERATIONS

Before you begin to write a check for your first commercial property, pause and reconsider. There is no Utopia. Every investment has challenges. When the market is soft and properties are not selling, you might wait several months before finding a suitable tenant. It is probable that you would lose several months' rent because it is much more difficult to rent a commercial property than a residential. The explanation is simple. A person needs a place in which to live. A person does not necessarily need to open a pizza shop.

Other drawbacks exist with commercial properties. They often carry long-term leases with fixed rents. If taxes and your insurance rise, as they so often do, you have no way to recapture the increases. Your rent is fixed for many years, unless pass-on expense adjustments are written into your lease. A residential lease is usually for one year. If taxes rise, you can incorporate it into the rent increase for the upcoming year.

Would you resent having your local government dictate how much you are permitted to charge for rent? How would you feel about being told that your rent increase is higher than allowed by law? Big brother often gets involved in such regulation under the title of, Rent Control. Rent control laws vary from locality to locality, mostly affecting residential apartments. Commercial properties are seldom affected by rent control. Rental agreements on commercial properties are between landlord and tenant, and they are usually not controlled by outside parties.

Up until now, commercial property investment has been mentioned favorably. It should be remembered that there is a downside as well. You must be concerned about being paid if there is a snowstorm and the store takes in no money, or a competitive store opens across the street. Sure, there is a lease, but if there is no money then there is nothing with which to pay the rent. That situation doesn't arise with a residential property. Your residential tenant knows that the rent is due on the first or fifteenth, regardless of any personal problems. With the commercial property, the tenant's personal problems become yours.

SUMMARY

Commercial and residential properties can each be potentially rewarding investments. Individual situations dictate whether particular investments will be rewarding or not. Both commercial and residential properties offer advantages and drawbacks that must be weighed before making a decision.

Surprisingly, commercial and residential properties each have their own personality. Commercial properties are suited more to the laid-back investor than the residential. Commercial investing requires less management effort and sees a lower tenant turnover. On the whole, commercial investors receive fewer complaints from tenants than the residential tenant who might call any time of day or night. The commercial owner has a piece of the action in the tenant's success. If the tenant prospers, the landlord can raise the rent or work out a percentage lease. If the tenant fails, the landlord is left with a vacant property and a debt of several month's rent.

Commercial properties, it should always be remembered, are more risky than residential properties. Though many have long-term leases to avoid the worry about the tenant turnover and vacancies, the long-term arrangement works to a disadvantage. The rent price lock-in for many years puts a lid on the amount of rent that can be charged since the ink is already dry on the lease. If, for example, there is a ten-year lease, rent cannot be raised regardless of inflation or interest rates for the entire ten year period.

When things run smoothly with a commercial property, there is nothing better. When you have a vacancy, that is when the problems start. It often takes many months to find the right tenant. Empty stores do not pay your mortgage payment. In a healthy market, stores do not remain vacant for long. In a weak market, it is much more difficult to rent commercial space than residential. It takes a certain type of person to be a commercial property investor. The person assumes higher risks for higher rewards. Which is more suited for you?

12

Retail Stores and Shopping Centers as Investments

IF YOU EVER HAVE WANTED TO GO INTO BUSINESS WITHOUT MAKING THE HUGE investment and buying the three-piece suit, then you should consider an invest-ment in commercial property. With commercial property, you can have it all. Certain types of leases allow you to prosper along with your tenants. If that sort of arrangement sounds enticing, then commercial property might be the right investment vehicle for you.

Shopping centers are an excellent source of investment for the aggressive investor. There are many kinds of shopping centers to consider, with types to suit any investor, regardless of the amount of capital to invest. Whether it is fifty dollars or five hundred thousand dollars, there is a shopping center investment within your grasp.

TYPES OF SHOPPING CENTERS

There are at least five distinct types of shopping center investments. They are the super-regional, regional, community, neighborhood center, and convenience center. They vary in size, layout, location, and purpose.

The Super-Regional Center

The super-regional center is the huge shopping mall, usually with two levels or one level containing many strips of stores with interconnecting aisles. Of all the shopping centers, the super-regional is the largest, with some as large as one million square feet. There are currently several super-regional centers in Canada and the United States large enough to contain indoor amusement parks with roller coasters and ferris wheels. In a super-regional center, you could expect to find three or more major department stores, as well as one hundred or more stores. The stores are largely national chain stores, as well as food courts with a variety of international and fast foods. Since the super-regional centers cost tens if not hundreds of millions of dollars, they are often owned by investor syndicates or publicly traded corporations. Some are listed on stock exchanges.

The Regional Center

The regional center is much like the super-regional, but on a smaller scale. Rather than containing one hundred or more stores, it has usually between sixty and eighty stores. Instead of three or more major department stores, the regional center often has one or two. If the center has two stores, there is one on each end of the mall. The growing trend is for regional centers to expand into super-regional centers, as investor groups gain additional financial backers and enlarge. A primary example is the Green Acres mall in the New York metropolitan area. For many years, it had one major department store on each side of the mall, much like bookends. On one side, there was A&S and the other side was Stern's department stores. Between them there was an enclosed promenade with stores on both sides. Then in recent years, stores such as Sears joined the mall as a second floor was added, as well as interconnected aisles of stores. The regional center was transformed into a colossal super-regional center with a glass elevator and breathtaking atrium.

The Community Center

Smaller than the regional center is the community center. A community center has a large variety store or discount store as its major tenant. It can be expected to have about fifty stores along a single strip and cater to shoppers within a ten to twenty minute drive. In a community center, the leading tenant could be a K-Mart, Caldor, Bradlees, Steinberg's, or Wal-Mart, which attracts other retailers to the center as tenants. A large supermarket and drugstore such as CVS, Rite Aid, or Walgreen's is generally located in a community center. A group of investors or individual investor usually owns it.

The Neighborhood Center

The neighborhood center is the shopping center commonly found on main roads throughout the country. Anchoring the neighborhood center is the supermarket, resulting in titles such as The A&P shopping center. The presence of a supermarket attracts the majority of shoppers to the center. Any number between ten and fifteen stores might be part of a neighborhood center. Bakeries, pizza shops,

Chinese take-outs, hardware stores, beauty shops, and pharmacies are usually the stores. The stores in the center fill the daily needs of shoppers. The majority of people travel no more than five to ten minutes, either walking or driving.

The Strip Shopping Center

Familiar to everyone and smaller than the neighborhood center is the strip shopping center. The strip shopping center doesn't contain a major supermarket to attract shoppers, as the neighborhood center does. It relies on its individual stores to generate business on their own without a major attraction. Situated in a strip shopping center is a convenience store such as 7-Eleven. Like the neighborhood center, the strip shopping center enables local people to meet their daily needs. Stores such as a laundromat, video rental store, liquor store, insurance office and stationery store are found in a strip center.

Competition and the Strip

Have you ever noticed that so many strip shopping centers look alike? You get the feeling that you've seen it before even if you've never been in the town prior. That is a potential problem for the investor. Without a major business attraction, a shopper could just as easily shop at your center as they could at the one on the next block. Unless your strip shopping center has a store with a major following, anyone with construction money can build a competing center, after satisfying any zoning or building requirements, in a relatively short period of time and drain customers from your tenants, as well as attract your tenants. The threat of another strip center to siphon away business is a constant which should never be overlooked by an investor.

GUIDE TO SHOPPING CENTERS

Super-Regional Center:
- Many major department stores
- 100-200 stores
- Travel distance up to twenty miles
- Thirty to forty-five minutes driving time

Regional Center:
- No more than two major department stores
- 80-100 stores
- Travel distance up to twenty miles
- Thirty to forty-five minutes driving time

Community Center:
- ☑ Discount department store
- ☑ 40-60 stores
- ☑ Travel distance up to five miles
- ☑ Ten to fifteen minute drive time

Neighborhood Center:
- ☑ Supermarket
- ☑ 10 stores
- ☑ Travel distance up to five miles
- ☑ Five to ten minute drive time

Strip Shopping Center:
- ☑ Convenience store
- ☑ 5-10 stores
- ☑ Travel distance of one to two miles
- ☑ Three to five minute drive time

SHOPPING CENTERS SUCCEED

Investors frequently favor commercial property over residential. The reasons have been discussed in Chapter 11. Shopping centers stand a greater chance of success if certain steps are taken before they begin operation, and prudent management is maintained thereafter. There are numerous reasons why shopping centers have particular appeal to investors. They are:

1. **Fewer management responsibilities**
   When you manage a shopping center you will experience fewer complaints from tenants, unless maybe something is malfunctioning, the property isn't being maintained or the tenant wants you to share in an effort or responsibility.

2. **Better returns on investment**
   When you consider the total amount of square feet you are renting, shopping centers are more profitable than apartments. In many cases, a store in a strip shopping center is the size of one room in an apartment, yet the rent is many times that of the apartment.

3. **Lower building cost**
   A row of retail stores does not require extensive architectural plans or complex instruction. Basically, a strip shopping center is a long cement building divided into sections with cement walls. Plate glass windows with a brick or vinyl-sided front is all that is required in the physical structure. The costs are much lower than other types of construction.

4. **Long-term leases**

When you rent an apartment, the lease is usually for one year. When the lease expires you frequently have to seek another tenant. Experienced residential investors know how agonizing that can be. When vacancies occur a positive cash flow quickly turns negative. Tenant turnover is both time-consuming and costly.

A different predicament exists with commercial leases. A commercial lease frequently extends for ten years or longer. But longer leases are not always advantageous. Inflation quickly turns a healthy rent into an inadequate rent, as costs rise and your rent is agreed-upon for years into the future. Building graduated percentage rent increases into the lease or having a lease based upon a percentage sales helps protect against the ravages of inflation.

5. **Shared expenses**

With a residential lease you collect the monthly rent once and then pay, pay, and pay again. The residential lease most often includes all expenses. The tenant pays the rent and somehow feels entitled to having everything perfect. The end result is calls for repairs and improvements on a regular basis, as well as using the air conditioner twenty-four hours a day in the summer.

The situation differs in a commercial lease. In a commercial lease, the tenant most often pays all the utility costs, as well as any costs for internal improvements and decorations, such as signs and awnings. The internal improvements remain with the store, though the fixtures are usually sold by the tenant when vacating. Some expenses that are not incurred by a residential investor are incurred by the commercial investor. Operating expenses such as garbage removal, snow removal, and upkeep on the parking lot are shared on a negotiable basis, with each tenant of a shopping center.

Selecting a Shopping Center for Investment

Most people when purchasing real estate say the only three factors to consider are location, location, and location. Another factor enters into the picture with commercial property. That factor is competition. You can have the greatest location, but if a shopping center opens up nearby with the same product or service and better prices, you would face a serious problem. So if competition seems to be a formidable challenge, you would be wise to proceed with caution.

WHAT MAKES A GOOD LOCATION?

How many stores that couldn't miss went out of business within a year? They were selling the right product and maybe even at the best price. Still they couldn't draw enough customers to make a living. The problem could have been insufficient parking.

Importance of Parking

If the store has insufficient parking and customers have to park three blocks away, they likely will shop elsewhere. A store or strip-shopping center should have a parking lot. Each store in a strip-shopping center should have at least four spaces. Fewer than four and there could be a problem, as customers might feel frustrated at not having a parking space and refuse to shop at the store. With a shopping district or shopping area along a main street, a corner location is preferable to any other. A corner location offers visibility from two streets, as well as parking possibilities.

The Actual Location

Before anyone plans a shopping center, he needs to carefully analyze the needs and characteristics of the population it serves. Is the location in a heavily traveled area or a sparsely populated area? The volume of traffic and density of the population will help determine the success or failure of the shopping center. Many shopping centers are built to service the everyday needs of a housing development's residents. Bakeries, grocery stores, laundromats, banks, and stationery stores that are walking distance to a housing complex stand to become highly successful, since local residents frequent them daily. If these same businesses are not near a housing complex but are in a radius of two miles of heavily populated areas, they too can be expected to enjoy success.

Closeness to Competition

Everyone develops hunger pangs after several hours on a car trip. What do you do? You pull off the parkway at the next exit in search of fast food. Dotted on the strip are a dozen different fast food eateries. Why? Because it works. Where you see a McDonald's, you see a Burger King and Wendy's. That is because of the spillover traffic from competing businesses. The same applies to strip shopping centers. If people don't find an item they seek in one shopping center, they are willing to drive one block or two to the next center. The proximity of two shopping centers often motivates shoppers to visit an area and perhaps shop at both.

The Super-Regional Center Connection

Ordinarily an investor would think that opening a shopping center across from a mall is financial suicide. But that is not the case at all. Actually, proximity to a super-regional center can give a boost to business. Malls, in general, have specialty shops that cater to a person's nonimmediate needs. You can buy a pair of designer shoes, a three-piece suit or a set of golf clubs. Most probably, you would not find a supermarket, drugstore, or hardware store in a mall. The person in need of a prescription, an emery board, or a box of spaghetti would most probably need to make another stop before heading home. As a result, the super-regional center shopper would welcome a strip shopping center near the mall. Another potential consumer would be the person living a relatively short distance from the strip shopping center.

UNDERSTANDING COMMERCIAL LEASES

The three common types of commercial leases are the fixed lease, the percentage lease, and the minimum percentage plus.

The Fixed Lease

The fixed lease is the lease most favored by the commercial tenant when it is a long-term lease. It binds the landlord to the same rent, regardless of what happens to the size of the business or your operating costs. If the business volume doubles with a fixed lease, you as the owner don't share in the prosperity. And if you receive increases in insurance, utilities, mortgage payments and taxes, you have no legal right to raise the rent while the contract remains in effect.

Some landlords insert a protective clause into the fixed lease. To guard against inflation, they insert a clause to have the rent rise along with the C.P.I., the Consumer Price Index. In that manner, as your costs rise, at least the rent adjustment will help defray part of the increase.

The Percentage Lease

In a perfect world, a percentage lease would be the ideal lease for both landlord and tenant. The landlord would have an incentive to encourage the business to expand and would likely even help with the advertising expenses since he would be receiving an increased rent. The tenant would willingly offer a percentage of the increased profits to the landlord. A percentage lease is structured so that the rent is based upon a percentage of sales within a particular time period. Theoretically, when sales are strong, the rent is higher than in a period when the business revenues are weak. The cash register receipts and books would substantiate the sales of the business for the time period. Unfortunately with human nature as it is, tenants often don't subscribe to the "make it and pay it" philosophy and resent giving back a percentage of their sales. They, in turn, seek ways to circumvent the agreement. By making sales for cash and not putting proceeds in the register, as well as keeping two sets of books, they seek ways to avoid showing income. The smaller the sales shown, the smaller the rent will be under the straight percentage lease.

Still another factor to consider with the straight percentage lease is the lower end of the percentage. If sales are very low, does that mean that your rent will cover the principal, interest, taxes, and insurance? You have expenses to pay and need the assurance that a substantial amount of money will be paid every month. What happens if a store with a straight percentage lease does little or no business, resulting in no payment to you? How will you pay your expenses? A straight percentage lease is not a viable lease for the investor in need of assurances of monthly income.

Minimum Percentage Plus

If you fear the fixed lease because of the lack of protection against inflation and the straight percentage lease because of your difficulty in monitoring income, what do you do? You choose the minimum percentage plus lease, of course. As the name implies, an agreement is reached for a minimum rent to be paid regardless of business results. The figure is based upon a percentage of the sales, but with a minimum rent. In that way, the investor knows the least rent he can expect for a given month. Most leases for shopping center tenants are minimum-percentage-plus leases. They are preferred by landlord and tenant because they are win-win situations for both parties. The tenant pays his fair share and both parties have a piece of the action and profit when the business is successful.

FINANCING THE PURCHASE

Numbers of real estate investors avoid commercial property. Financing is the problem. Financing is not usually available from the neighborhood bank. Non-commercial banks such as savings banks and S&L's offer primarily residential mortgages. If you don't have a business relationship with a commercial bank, you can't expect their serious consideration of your needs. Investors seeking financing must find other sources of financing.

Owner Financing

Owner financing is always the easiest and most efficient way to complete a commercial property purchase. You put up a percentage of the purchase price, and the seller takes back a mortgage for the remainder. There are no closing costs to pay or lengthy applications to complete. There are no time-consuming delays in the approval process. If the seller is highly motivated, the deal becomes even more interesting. The seller might offer more favorable terms. Among them might be a principal payment, without interest for the first six months, or even no payments at all for the first six months or year. Whether or not a particular seller will agree is unknown, but there is nothing lost in asking.

Reit Purchases

For the person with little money to invest, as well as the more substantial investor, the Real Estate Investment Trust, (REIT), is an excellent investment vehicle for commercial properties. They are publicly traded companies composed of investors who have pooled their money to purchase real estate. Investors who purchase REITs enjoy advantages not present in other types of real estate investment. You can buy a REIT on Monday and sell it the same day or whenever you choose. All it takes is a call to a stockbroker to buy or sell. Prices of shares are listed in newspapers every day. You can check on the past performance of the REIT, as well as uncover the individual real estate holdings by writing to the company or reading any of the many research reports published by investment advisory services.

REITs have drawbacks, as well. After all, there is no perfect investment. A REIT cannot be considered a tax shelter. With outright ownership of property, you can deduct property taxes, mortgage interest, and take depreciation, but such deductions are not permissible on your REIT investment.

Real estate securities analyst Robert Frank calls REITs ''push-button real estate investing'' because of the ease with which you can purchase, sell, receive price quotes, and diversify your investment dollars. With your investment dollars, you can get experienced real estate managers with enviable track records to select and manage properties throughout the country. With the continuing S&L problems and the creation of the Resolution Trust Corporation, REITs are positioned to purchase portfolios of properties at reasonable levels.

TYPES OF REITS

There are three different types of REITs. There is the *equity* type, which invests in shopping centers, office buildings, hospitals, nursing homes, hotels, and motels. There is the *mortgage* type, which invests by making construction and mortgage loans. There is the *hybrid*, which is a combination of the first two and purchases properties, as well as issues construction and mortgage loans.

Before You Buy a REIT

1. **Check the management.**

   Make sure that the current management has been in place for at least the last five years and that the management has no job other than to manage the REIT. A conflict of interest can be very costly to the REIT and you.

2. **Study its markets**.

Investigate to see where the REIT is planning new investments. If the properties are in rapidly growing areas or areas coming off rock-bottom, it is a healthy situation. Such properties are likely to be the fastest to rise. Within these areas, shopping centers located in built-up neighborhoods offer solid investment potential, since competition cannot easily arise.

3. **The numbers count.**

Though you might not have an accounting background, before investing you must examine the balance sheet of any REIT or have someone do it for you. You might write the company for a copy of its most recent annual report. To find the mailing address of a REIT, visit the reference section of the public library and request the *Value Line Investment Survey*. *Value Line* publishes in-depth analyses of thousands of publicly traded companies, including REITs. In addition to comments on each REIT's outlook, it offers a financial history of the REIT, as well as the name of the chief executive officer and mailing address.

While examining the balance sheet, be sure to check that the debt is not more than fifty percent of the company's equity. Too high a percentage of debt compared to equity could present a liquidity problem eventually. If the REIT has problem properties with high vacancies or worse, the REIT might have difficulty meeting its debts as interest payments begin to rise.

INSURANCE COMPANY FINANCING

Have you ever wondered how the insurance companies make money? It's not from poor payouts on claims. They earn their substantial profits through investing those dollars. Insurance companies are heavy hitters in real estate with billions of dollars to invest. If you are looking for a fifty-thousand dollar loan, the insurance company is not your source of investment funds. But if you and a group of investors are planning a multimillion dollar investment, an insurance company might be interested. That interest might be substantial, especially if you can provide written commitments from several major tenants.

How to Buy a Shopping Center

With the information on hand about the types of shopping centers, the differences and investment alternatives, you are still missing the most important step.

That is how to actually buy a shopping center. Certain sequential steps should be followed:

1. Read newspapers and visit real estate offices specializing in commercial properties. Study the individual shopping centers and make comparisons.

2. Hire a professional appraiser to do comparables and determine if the shopping center represents good value.

3. Hire a certified public accountant to examine the books and verify the figures including income and expenses.

4. Make an offer fifteen to twenty percent below the asking price, as the first step in negotiations. Be prepared to negotiate back and forth, but do not agree to pay more than eight to ten times the yearly rental as the purchase price.

5. At contract, include subject-to clauses that allow you to back out of a deal if unexpected developments occur. Have the deal subject to an inspection, attorney's approval, mortgage approval, etc., etc.

6. Examine the leases to make sure there are percentage leases with minimums instead of fixed percentage leases. After you acquire the property, continue whatever leases are in effect without change. Be certain there are operating cost escalators to enable you to pass along expense increases. Be sure the majority of the leases are not scheduled for renewal as soon as you expect to close on the deal.

SUMMARY

Investing in commercial properties can be very rewarding. The field is not for the uninformed and requires extensive preparation and flexibility to be successful.

There are many types of shopping centers available for investment. The super-regional is the largest. It is the mammoth shopping mall with many major department stores and in excess of one hundred shops. The regional center has one or two major department stores and between sixty and seventy stores. The community center, still smaller, has one variety-type store and about fifty stores, to serve local residents. The neighborhood center is the shopping center along a main street with about ten to fifteen stores, including a supermarket. The strip shopping center is the small center with individual stores and no supermarket. Usually, there is a convenience store such as a 7-Eleven. Depending upon your capital and preference for investment, there is a shopping center for your price range.

Why should you invest in shopping centers? There are a number of reasons. There are fewer management responsibilities. The tenant takes care of most of them by himself. There are better returns on investment than on residential properties. You get paid a higher rent per square foot for a commercial than for a residential. There is a lower construction cost. With a strip shopping center being primarily cement blocks, it is less costly than a residential property with plywood. Leases are longer for commercial, offering the investor stability and less tenant turnover. Expenses are shared by landlord and tenant for such things as snow removal, parking lot maintenance, and garbage removal. Paying one half of the operating expenses is considerably better than paying all.

A number of factors make one shopping center location better than another. The availability of sufficient parking spaces is one. Closeness to traffic and a population center also are helpful. Being in close proximity to competition causes a spillover of business. If a shopping center is in the path of a super-regional or regional center, shoppers will likely stop at the shopping center for their daily needs.

When you have purchased a shopping center or have had one built, you need to be concerned with the leases you sign. A fixed lease ties you up for a long time at a fixed rent. A percentage lease bases the rent solely on a percentage of whatever business the tenant does. Preferable is the minimum percentage plus lease, which sets a minimum rent, that will be paid regardless of business results.

Financing a shopping center can be tricky and time-consuming. The best way to go is owner-financing. It cuts down on time and eliminates closing costs. Insurance companies are primarily involved in the multimillion dollar transactions.

An investor interested in shopping center investments with a minimal investment and management responsibilities might consider the REIT. The REIT is publicly traded, with share prices published in newspapers after every business day, and can be bought and sold through a stockholder with just a phone call. Through shares in an REIT, you are able to diversify, so that if one investment in the portfolio goes sour, your entire investment does not. Other investments in the portfolio can offset an unsatisfactory one.

When purchasing shopping centers, care must be taken. Properties must be inspected and appraised by professionals, as with residential properties. Leases must be reviewed and carefully structured to avoid unprofitable or untimely situations. Facts and figures must be examined by a CPA to verify that what is claimed is accurate.

Shopping center investments of all types can be profitable vehicles for investors who have made careful preparations. More expertise is needed for individual shopping center investments than for a residential property. With proper planning, shopping centers can offer you a brighter financial picture.

13

Office Buildings
as Investments

It has been said that office buildings are the most risky form of real estate investment. Whether you agree or not, one thing is certain—office building investing is not for everyone.

The first thing you need in any large commercial investment is an attorney knowledgeable and experienced with commercial properties in general, and office buildings in particular. The attorney makes certain that all pertinent information is contained in the purchase agreement.

THE STANDARD CONTRACT

If the seller hands you a contract containing the words, *standard contract*, don't believe it. There is no such thing. Despite the word, *standard* there could be a number of potentially damaging requirements and restrictions that could be hazardous to your wealth. Therefore, any contract must be examined by your attorney. Though the following information deals with commercial contracts, many aspects also have relevance to a residential contract.

The Option

With so many details to check out, you would be wise to get an option-to-buy instead of an outright purchase. The option allows you, for the payment of a few hundred dollars, to purchase the office building at an agreed-on price for a limited period of time. If the inspection, CPA, or financing do not turn up the expected results, you can walk away from the deal. All you have lost is the cost of the option.

FIXED AND PERSONAL PROPERTY

When an office building owner sells or the tenants vacate, fixtures and personal property seem to disappear. Sellers frequently remove air conditioners and shelf systems. If an item is attached to the wall or ceiling, it is considered a fixture. All fixtures and personal property you want to stay with the building should be written into the purchase agreement.

DELIVERY OF THE PREMISES

When you are purchasing an office building, your tenants are dependent upon you. It is urgent that you take possession on the date you promise the tenants. To avoid delivery problems, have your attorney specify "time is of the essence" clause. Simply, it forces the seller to close on that date. In addition to "time is of the essence," have your attorney include a substantial daily penalty for each day the premises are not vacated. The threat of late charges will discourage the seller from delaying closing and not vacating on time. If the seller does close late, at least you will be well compensated for the inconvenience.

RESTRICTIONS OF USE

When you are purchasing an office building or other commercial property, the last thing you need is a directive that you can't operate it as you intended. If there are local ordinances that put restrictions on the type of businesses that can be run, you want to be able to check out of the deal without penalty. Check this out while you have an option on the property. Otherwise be sure there is a weasel clause about restricted use added to your contract.

WARRANTIES OF CONDITION OF PREMISES

An office building in turnkey condition would be an ideal situation. It would allow you to get down to the business of managing instead of renovating. One step in that direction is to have all warranties committed to writing. If the seller claims that the air conditioning system is in working condition and puts it in writing, you can be assured that such will be the case. If not, you have no legal recourse. Of course, you check out the working condition of everything before closing. If renovations are needed, get written bids from contractors on the amount each will cost. You can present the bids at contract to possibly gain added concessions. You also have a better idea of your expenses when you choose to make renovations.

LOCATING AN OFFICE BUILDING

Your primary concern after getting a good buy on an office building is earning a profit. Before agreeing to purchase any office building, make sure it is examined by a professional. A professional engineer, architect, or professional inspector can all help determine the feasibility of a purchase. Studies can be conducted to first determine if a building is structurally sound. Then, additional examinations can be made to determine if the building's use can be modified to make more prudent use of the space.

If the building's use can be modified or the interior space can be better utilized, an office building can become considerably more profitable. For example, if one large office can be split into two smaller units by adding a door and some walls, will the two units pay a higher combined rent than the larger unit? On an immediate level, the more rental units you have, the larger your rent roll will be. Moreover, the value of your property will be increased. Since a property is valued at a multiple, which is a certain factor times the rent, an increase in the rent increases the value of the building. Usually the factor used is seven to ten times the yearly rent.

FEATURES TO CHECK FOR IN A BUILDING

With modern superstructures emerging in major cities, it is apparent that there is a world of difference among office buildings. Yet certain features are common to all office buildings.

The Walls Have Ears

Many years ago the walls of office buildings were thick and there was little problem with acoustics. With today's construction costs, walls are considerably thinner and walls are not as well insulated. Frequently, you can hear conversations with neighboring tenants. Elevator music becomes a necessity.

If you have an office building constructed or you are purchasing one, make sure that the walls are sufficiently thick. Visit the building at a busy time of the work day and listen.

Ventilation

While windows in modern office buildings are smaller than years ago, most buildings still have them. Some even open. There has been a trend to construct windows that do not open. This results in sterile air circulating throughout a building, increasing the risk of respiratory diseases, as well as uneven temperatures. If possible, avoid an office building with windows that do not open.

Modern structures are featuring HVAC, which is highly sophisticated Heating, Ventilating, and Air Conditioning. The HVAC helps both tenant and owner to reduce costs, as well as to better utilize the increased office space.

Elevators

Do you remember when elevators in skyscrapers had uniformed elevator operators? An operator was needed to run the elevator. Most very old office buildings still have the operators. Today's office buildings have automated elevators where the passenger controls it manually. Rather than one large elevator, today's buildings usually have several smaller ones as a courtesy. Elevators are inspected periodically for safety. Inspection certificates should be posted inside.

Lobbies and Hallways

Enter any office building and you form a first and lasting impression as does the potential tenant. The appearance of the entrance, lobby, and hallways is a critical factor in your decision to purchase because it will be just as important to tenants and visitors. A shabby and run-down appearance will make it very difficult to attract quality tenants. Lobbies, hallways, and entranceways must be attractive. As a potential purchaser, you need to cognizant of the costs of rehabbing. Frequently, replacing the lighting and repainting is all that is needed to restore an aging building to an acceptable appearance. As with any repair that could prove costly, get estimates from several contractors on the cost of renovation. Based upon several estimates from contractors, you can make a determination if the building will be an alligator that will swallow your profits or turn into a cash flow.

The Employee Factor and Location

Any time you consider the purchase of a commercial building, you must consider its employees. To attract employees and the general public, the building should be close to public transportation or situated on a heavily traveled street. Customers or clients should be able to reach the building easily by bus, train, or car. Furthermore, the employees desire to be near services and retailers for visits during lunch, as well as before and after work. Employees welcome restaurants, dry cleaners, take-out food stores, and anything else that makes the job more pleasant. Parking must also be considered, for employees and customers. For each office there should be between five and eight spaces.

Importance of the Ground-Floor Tenant

The ground-floor tenant is a must consideration for a number of reasons. First of all, it is the initial impression the public and tenants get of the building. As a potential purchaser, consider the importance of the ground-floor tenant. Carefully investigate the tenant, the terms of the tenancy, including the length of the lease. Research the firm in the *Dun and Bradstreet Million Dollar Directory*, available in many public libraries. Listed in the directory would be the company name, address, and phone number of the firm, as well as the company sales, and the names of the principals of the company. While the information does not offer any guarantees, knowing the sales numbers and decision makers does give you some insight into the stabiilty of the company.

CONSIDERATION OF CURRENT FINANCING

Don't overlook a building's financing when purchasing it. The amount of financing is often an indication of its value. Since office buildings carry high price tags, it is not unreasonable to assume that the current owner is financed for the maximum allowable. The rule of thumb is four times the gross rental for older buildings and six times the gross rental for newer buildings. Lenders contend that a newer building is a sounder investment from a risk standpoint so they are more willing to extend loans. You can more easily obtain financing on a newer building than an older one.

THE OFFICE BUILDING STRUCTURE

Any time you consider the purchase of an office building, consider the tenants. Since it is the tenants who pay the rent and sign the lease, you are wise to consider what tenants deem to be desirable qualities. Look at the building as a whole. Is it functional as-is to meet their needs or is renovation required just to attract tenants? Don't let your emotions become involved in your decision. If the interior is narrow and without lighting, requiring extensive electrical work, be aware that it will be costly to implement and then recover the expenses through higher rents. Tenants will be reluctant to pay the higher rents and without them you don't earn a profit. To justify acquiring an office building in need of repairs, the repairs must be minor and cosmetic, rather than major and required.

GOOD MAINTENANCE KEEPS GOOD TENANTS

When tenants are paying market rate, they expect and appreciate landlords who offer quality maintenance and are responsive on a day-to-day basis, as well as emergency situations. Tenants are likely to be silent when things run smoothly and very vocal when the expected services aren't provided. A tenant must know that you will respond to his or her needs promptly and efficiently. The seeds you sow early will bear fruit for many years because the costly and inconvenient tenant turnovers will be kept at a minimum.

THE CHANGING OFFICE BUILDING MARKET

Investors not familiar with office building markets might believe that the market is an easy one in which to prosper. It is actually quite difficult because of the overbuilding of the last few years. Major cities have large amounts of unoccupied office space. Tenants seeking high-quality space with the latest features relocate from older undesirable quarters when leases expire.

Times have changed in office building construction. Historically, supply and demand would control the amount of construction. It used to be that building would continue until the demand for offices was met. Then, it would stop. Today's office market is different from other eras. There has been a ready supply of funds for construction. The availability of capital rather than the demand factor has been the driving force behind the building boom. The steady stream of money is continuing construction even beyond common sense, as tenants hopscotch from office building to newer office building with added amenities. Tenants have no loyalty to an office building.

In years to come, it is not expected that demand will keep up with the supply of unoccupied office space coming onstream. That is not to suggest that all new construction is doomed to failure. High-quality office space will always be preferable to an average or aging office space. As an investor, you should be careful before investing in any office space that is not high quality. Businesses trying to maintain a prestigious image will shun anything but the highest quality. Investing in anything but the highest could leave you with vacancies, unable to earn a positive cash flow.

AVOIDING OFFICE BUILDING ALLIGATORS

What could be worse than owning an office building and having several floors of vacant offices? It can be avoided with an ounce of prevention. Prudent investors and lenders make certain that a new project is at least fifty percent preleased before construction begins. In fact, many bankers insist on a building being preleased to a large degree before granting financing and require prelease agreements. The feeling is that preleasing, as well as partnership agreements, spread around the risk and for investors, avoids financial difficulty.

SUMMARY

Investing in office buildings can be a rewarding, yet risky investment. So much depends on the condition of the premises and the needs of the tenants. More than with a residential contract, it is vital that all promises be put in writing, that everything is suited to the needs of the tenants and in working order at the time of closing.

Office buildings are not at all alike. Walls can be thick or paper thin. There might be old-fashioned fans or state-of-the-art HVAC. Lobbies can be modern with contemporary architecture and lighting or narrow and shabby. The presence or lack of up-to-date facilities is crucial in the decision whether or not to purchase a property. Cosmetic improvements to make a building suitable are fine, but extensive renovations do not usually make sense for an investor. It is better to look elsewhere.

Location, location, location are said to be important in real estate. For an office building it is important for another reason. Employees want and need to be near conveniences to keep up their morale. The location of a ground-floor tenant is also important. A prestigious tenant brings prestige to the building and other tenants. It is necessary to check out any potential ground-floor tenant.

An office building investor must be responsive to the needs of tenants, both before and after renting. Before purchasing, you need to ascertain what tenants deem to be desirable qualities in a building and whether or not those qualities are present. After purchasing, tenants' needs cannot be overlooked. When things run smoothly, no accolades are given. But when things are overlooked, watch out. A wise investor is a hands-on manager who makes certain services flow smoothly or hires management and then actively oversees the performance.

Over the last few years the office building market has changed. It has become money-driven. New construction continues, and tenants jump to newer and more modern offices. Investors considering low-quality office buildings need to take precautions before putting up their capital. Precautions, such as preleasing before construction begins, can pay substantial rewards and avoid monumental headaches.

14

Industrial Properties as Investments

INDUSTRIAL PROPERTY DOES NOT RANK HIGH ON THE HIT PARADE AMONG A large number of real estate investors. Because of the degree of risk it remains a very specialized investment area. It seems to be much less complicated to purchase a one-family split level or even a stationery store than a factory that manufactures zippers. And yet to the informed investor, industrial properties can be a profitable avenue of investment.

What is industrial property? It is property zoned for industrial use by a local planning commission or zoning board. Simply, it is real estate intended to be used for industry, sometimes for the manufacture of products and other times for warehousing. Is all industrial property a good buy if it is at a low price? Not necessarily. Is all industrial property then to be avoided if the price seems high? Again, not necessarily. What you need to have is information. You need to know the purpose for which the property is currently intended, whether or not tenants can easily be secured for the property, the amount of capital needed to customize it for a tenant, whether the property is a sound value, and whether or not you can at least cover your expenses every month.

INDUSTRIAL PROPERTY VARIABLES

When you invest in any real estate, you should be concerned with the factors that will build or enhance the value. Among industrial properties there are a number of factors that enhance the value of the property:

☞ Unique plant design
☞ Rapid obsolescence

☞ Location of plant
☞ Tenant stability
☞ Limited market for rentals
☞ Difficulty in re-renting
☞ Lender indecision

Unique Plant Design

With a store in a strip shopping center, one store is basically the same way as any other store. If a flower shop tenant moves out, a tennis clothing shop or movie rental store can easily move in without any structural changes. That situation does not exist with industrial properties. Since industrial properties are designed for such diverse activities as manufacturing automobiles, building computers, constructing gas turbines, or refining petroleum, it is apparent that the same plant design cannot be used for manufacturing automobiles as refining petroleum. Different functions require different plant designs.

Considerable sums of money are expended in customizing an industrial plant for a tenant. Once the plant is completed, it is suited to the particular tenant and no one else. The problem arises when the tenant decides to relocate. The owner finds himself with a property no one else wants in its present form. Large sums of money must be spent to make it suitable for another tenant.

Rapid Obsolescence

Technology is changing rapidly. If you don't believe that look at the personal computer market. Companies that are on the cutting edge discover themselves selling obsolete products just a few years later. That isn't only the problem of the company. It becomes your problem. If the company can't remain in business, you have an empty industrial property. A company that can't compete cannot pay its rent, leaving you with an empty industrial plant and no income to pay your mortgage.

With today's changing technology, it is not unusual for an industrial plant to find its products obsolete within five years. As the owner of that property, you have to be aware of this fact of life before investing in an industrial property. For many potential investors, the rapid obsolescence factor is enough to dissuade investments in industrial properties.

Location of Plant

An industrial plant is priceless if the location is convenient, yet it becomes worthless if it is not conducive to business. When the investor thinks of convenience or inconvenience, he considers the availability of employees, nearby modes of transportation, low cost of utilities, the availability of recreation, and the proximity to colleges and universities.

The primary concern of a company seeking to locate is its potential employees. In the area are there large numbers of people with the necessary skills to be hired? If the people possess the necessary skills, would they be willing to work for the wages the company is willing to pay? If a computer hardware or software company plans to relocate, would it want to open its facility in an area known for its high-tech market, where there are large numbers of engineers and other university-trained personnel? It would be unlikely to open such a facility in an agricultural area such as Vero Beach, Florida. The high-tech areas more likely would be the Long Island area of New York, the Boston area, and the Silicon Valley area of California.

Nearby modes of transportation must be considered before agreeing to purchase an industrial property. Even if you select the most reliable tenant available, it will not work out if the property is not well situated. There must be reliable transportation available to move the merchandise efficiently after it has been manufactured. The property should be accessible to major highways and airports since super highways make the movement of goods an efficient method of transportation. The growth of the air freight industry and industry competitiveness make air transportation another cost-effective method.

When selecting a site for an industrial plant, serious consideration should be given to the utilities servicing the area. The gas and electric company's rates are an important factor that can spell success or failure to a business. States such as New York have had the highest electric rate in the nation for many years. Factor the high rates into the total picture before reaching an investment decision. If the utilities costs are too high a percentage of the operating costs, it will discourage tenants from leasing your property.

The United States has become a leisure-oriented society. We spend a large percentage of our time and money pursuing leisure activities, from attending sports events and live concerts to chartering a fishing boat. Though it might seem to have no relation to the job or industrial plant, indirectly it does. Workers prefer to live in a city/town that has a major league sports team within driving distance. They also appreciate a night life with top performers in concert. When these kinds of leisure activities are present in a locality, it becomes a more interesting area to work and employees will want to relocate there. It offers you a larger employee base.

For the manufacturer of snack foods, it doesn't matter whether there are higher education facilities since no one receives a master's degree in potato chip technology, but for a scientific-oriented company it makes a substantial difference. Careers requiring technical knowledge involve keeping up with the latest technological changes. Being situated near a university is considered desirable to an employee at a high-tech firm. Such an employee can attend workshops, seminars, and enroll in courses at a university to keep abreast of the latest developments. A well-situated facility near a university might attract many employees.

Tenant Stability

If you must customize an industrial plant, you need assurances that the tenant will be responsible and remain for many years. It is the only way your expenditure is justified. Therefore, you have to conduct an extensive credit check to make certain that the tenant has a favorable credit history. How much in loans does the tenant have outstanding? Have his payment been made on time or have they been delinquent? If there are outstanding loans, are they likely to interfere with the payment of your rent?

Why is it so important about the credit history if you have a long-term lease? Won't the long-term lease protect you no matter what? Long-term leases in actuality will not help you if the tenant becomes insolvent. You can sue until the moon turns green, and you still won't collect. If the person has no assets there is nothing you can collect. A word to the wise is to thoroughly screen the tenant carefully before signing a lease so you don't suffer the consequences later. Regardless of how thorough or well written the lease might be, it is only as good as the person who signs it.

Limited Market for Rentals

At the time you purchase an industrial property, you would be wise to have a written agreement with a tenant. You shouldn't make improvements on an industrial property until after the signing of a lease. Customizing a property is very costly. It serves no purpose to make improvements without input from the tenant who will be paying the rent. Another less expensive alternative for you would be to lower the rent in return for the tenant paying for his own renovations. A tenant who is willing to supervise and pay for needed renovations is a serious one.

Difficulty in Re-Renting

If you are the owner of IAN Envelope Company and the machinery becomes obsolete, your company either modernizes or closes up. If it can't raise the capital or stem its losses, it closes up. You, as the owner, find yourself with a building suited only for envelope manufacturing. A plastic plate or shoe manufacturer cannot use the facilities in their present form. Thus a vacant industrial property can stay that way for a considerable time period, sometimes as long as a year.

Lender Indecision

With the banking crisis of the last few years and collapse of real estate prices in many parts of the country, lenders hesitate before granting loans for commercial activities. Lenders are aware that industrial plants and products become obsolete rapidly and don't lend money with the intention of not having it returned. You have to convince a lender, with written documents, that the tenant not only will sign a long-term lease, but also has a sound financial background and represents a good risk. As with every transaction with a banker, you have to present a strong case for your loan. A well-established tenant with an excellent reputation improves your chances.

SUMMARY

Industrial property is affordable and offers profit potential to the investor who seeks the necessary knowledge and proceeds after taking precautions. Any time you invest, be aware of the factors that will affect the value of your investment. With industrial property seven variables can have an effect on the value of your property:

1. Unique plant design
2. Rapid obsolescence
3. Limited market for rentals
4. Difficulty in re-renting
5. Location of factory
6. Tenant stability
7. Lender indecision

Industrial properties can prove highly profitable if you keep in mind the seven property value variables. Once you secure a solid long-term tenant with financial stability and a well-received product and sign him to a long-term lease at a substantial rent, you are in an enviable position. With little active management necessary, you will be able to enjoy the profits of your industrial property investment.

15

When It's Time to Sell

IT HAS BEEN SAID THAT YOU MAKE MONEY WHEN YOU BUY AND NOT WHEN YOU sell. And that is true. The bargain-hunting techniques used in buying set the stage for making profits in real estate when you sell. Selling is merely the culminating activity in the money-making process.

GETTING READY TO SELL

Though your secret to making money in real estate lies in locating the right property and buying at the right price and on the right terms, you should not lose sight of one point; real estate is purchased to eventually be sold. You marry a man or woman, not real estate. Nearly every investor will sooner or later sell the property, so an organized approach should be put into place to help maximize profits.

Regardless of whether or not you plan to sell privately or through a real estate agent, the chances are that an agent will ultimately have a piece of the action. In fact, statistically more than eighty percent of properties sold are sold through a real estate agent. Many people begin to sell privately before turning the listing over to a broker. Others initially list with a broker, avoiding the enormous expenditure of time and money.

WHY SELL THROUGH A REAL ESTATE BROKER?

Nobody likes to pay sales commissions just as no one wants to pay taxes. Obviously everyone would prefer to put the maximum amount of money into his pocket. Research shows, however, that you will maximize your profits if a professional handles the deal. Sellers often tend to let their emotions get in the way, both in pricing the property and accepting a deal. Sellers are frequently out of touch with the market, either pricing too high or too low. When offers are made, the seller turns down a deal because of external factors, not having to do with the property. It could be a bad day at work or an argument with a spouse or co-worker that results in poor judgment decisions. The real estate agent, on the other hand, is not emotionally attached to the property and can usually act more rationally.

JUDGING THE MARKET

When you decide to sell, you must have knowledge of the real estate market in your area. Whether it is a buyer's market or seller's market will have a bearing on the price you will realize when selling, as well as ease with which you sell.

A buyer's market is the opposite condition of a seller's market. In a buyer's market, sellers are having difficulty selling properties because of the overabundance of properties for sale. Large numbers of "for sale" signs are evident. Prices are weak, and sellers need to reduce their prices to make a sale. To make a deal, sellers frequently have to offer givebacks such as offering owner financing.

In a seller's market, everything appears rosy. There are few properties for sale and large numbers of buyers. The imbalance produces intense bidding and higher selling prices. Properties are often tied up within hours of reaching the market, as buyers sometimes bid up the price in excess of the asking price.

Should you care which market is in effect? Of course, you should. As an investor you love a buyer's market because you can pick up bargains, often with OPM (other people's money). To make a deal, a seller might react favorably to the idea of giving back a mortgage. You don't welcome a buyer's market when you are a seller. There are just too many properties competing with yours for investment dollars, causing you to re-evaluate the asking price and likely to reduce it in order to make a deal.

On the other hand, as a seller you love a seller's market. With so many buyers making offers, you can be selective about which to accept. Rather than tying up the property and missing out on a better deal, you can take the stance that no binders will be accepted, only signed contracts. The first to go to contract purchases the property.

SHOULD YOU SELL?

If you have ever considered selling without a broker, you are not alone. More than 500,000 owners each year sell without a broker. The transaction is known as *FSBO* (pronounced Fizzbo), a property *For Sale By Owner*.

With many properties selling for $200,000 or more, a real estate agent being paid a six percent commission receives a nice piece of change, to the tune of $12,000 or more. With that amount being sliced from the selling pie, it is easy to understand why many sellers are reluctant to sell through a broker. The feeling is "Why pay a broker all that money if you can do the same thing?"

STARTING TO SELL A PROPERTY

Price It Realistically

Just because the person across the street or around the corner sold a property for $300,000 does not mean your property is worth that amount. Yours might be worth more or less, but you don't know until you have it checked out by a professional. Hire a professional appraiser with credentials from either SREA, MAI, or ASA. Expect to pay less than three hundred dollars for an accurate barometer of the approximate value of your property, give or take a margin of five percent.

Take the Temperature

There are a number of ways to judge how hot or cold the market is in your area. Notice how long properties in the neighborhood stay up for sale by observing the length of time you see the "for sale" signs. Call up several real estate agents with whom you are acquainted and get a guesstimate of your property's value in the current market. Phone the local office of the Multiple Listing Service or the Board of Realtors, and pick their brains. Ask how many properties are for sale in the area and the average number of days a property stays on the market. If you are told thirty days, it is a fairly hot market. If it is ninety days, expect a long wait.

Learn the Market

You never know how the marketplace will react to your property. A property has a personality, which might have much or little appeal to a purchaser. To learn the market for your property, become a good listener. Keep your ears attuned to the comments of potential buyers. Let the visitors do most of the talking. See if you get the same reaction from many people.

Sellers often learn surprising things about their properties. Frequently they discover that the property is priced too low. You will know this if the first potential buyer makes a full price or near-full price offer. Wait about a week before accepting a full price offer. Keep a clipboard or list in the foyer to record each visitor's name, phone number, and bid. Explain that you will accept the highest offer. If your property is genuinely priced below the market, you will generate a substantial interest in the property.

Make Cosmetic Improvements

Perhaps you can't judge a book by its cover, but people seem to judge real estate by its exterior. If a property's exterior is not physically appealing, buyers are immediately turned off. Paint the exterior, install shutters, a new door, and anything else to add "curb appeal" while keeping costs under control. If it's a house that you're selling, make certain that the kitchen and bathrooms are pleasant to the eyes and to the scent. An old trick is to boil vanilla to provide the kitchen with a refreshing fragrance. A cake baking in the oven also provides a warm feeling and positive scent.

Pay to Advertise

If your choice is not to list with a broker, you must advertise. One effective way is with a professionally made sign. Don't buy a store-bought sign of the seventy-nine cent variety to sell a $250 thousand-dollar property. On the sign, list your phone number and ask interested parties to phone for an appointment. In this way, you discourage strangers from knocking on your door.

In addition to a professionally made sign, take out classified ads. The local Pennysaver or free newspaper delivered with the supermarket flyers is less expensive than the daily newspaper and often brings better results. For help with your wording, read ads that appeal to you and adopt the format. Visit or call a large local employer and speak with the personnel director. Ask if any executives are in need of housing or will be relocating to the area.

Create a Prospectus

Prepare an information sheet, also known as a *fact sheet*, with vital statistics about the property. List the dimensions, the taxes, heating, and electricity expenses, etc. List the appliances, fixtures and other equipment that will be part of any deal.

Check Out Buyers

If you are not selling through a broker, it is incumbent upon you to check out the background of prospective buyers. If you know a retail store owner, you can pay a nominal amount to have a credit check run. Immediately you will have in your fingertips a financial profile of the person. You will know if the person is loaded with loans or is a good credit risk.

As a condition of the purchase, request that the buyer make a twenty percent downpayment as a show of good faith. The person with a twenty percent downpayment will more easily qualify for a mortgage, and also will be unlikely to back out of a deal.

Though we are not attorneys, we always insist that our attorney include a protective clause in our contract when we are selling. It reads as follows, "If there are any material misstatements or misrepresentations about the buyer's financial condition and the buyer can't obtain a mortgage, he forfeits his deposit for keeping the property off the market."

Help with Financial Advice

The burden of obtaining a mortgage is the buyer's, but it pays for you to be involved. Study the mortgage market and know the current rates. In that way, you can advise the buyer in obtaining a mortgage, if there is any difficulty. You might want to expedite the process by referring him to your mortgage company. If rates aren't reasonable you might choose to offer owner financing.

Have a Binder and Contract for Sale

What would you do if a buyer appeared at your doorstep tomorrow? Would you be ready? You should have a binder available with blanks to fill in. In that way, you can tie up a buyer until you go to contract. You should also have a "contract for sale" incorporating the clauses you need for protection. It should be prepared or at least reviewed by an attorney. The contract form only has to be prepared once and can be xeroxed for future transactions. All you do is fill in the blanks.

Become a Shrewd Negotiator

Anyone who has ever tried to sell a property by himself knows it is difficult because your money is involved. Decisions are so much easier when it isn't your money at stake. That is one major reason why brokers are employed to sell your property.

If you handle the selling attempt yourself, you need to learn how to put a deal together. When an interested party calls on the phone, be sure not to negotiate right then. Suggest that you meet over a cup of coffee, preferably in a non-threatening atmosphere such as a local diner or coffee shop. If the person balks at meeting you over a cup of coffee, you have a good indication that the person is not sincerely interested or has something to hide.

What do you discuss at the meeting? Basically you do public relations in which you accentuate the positive while justifying your asking price. You might decide to present bills for major repairs and improvements completed. In documenting the expenditures, you are solidifying your bargaining position.

If after discussing the pluses of your property, the buyer still appears interested, try to get the person out of the starting block. Ask in a casual way, "I don't want to put pressure on you, but if you have an interest, I would like to know'' or ''I guess I told you all there is to know. Are we ready to make a deal?''

Hopefully you have taken the person by surprise. Quickly get quiet. The first one to speak loses. The moment's silence will seem like an hour to the buyer. You gave the person rope and are waiting for him to trip. Your deliberate silence might prompt action in the form of a commitment or offer. Watch what happens while you wait for a reaction.

Close the Deal

Once you have a meeting of the minds on a deal, get it in writing as soon as possible. Arrange for your attorney to call the buyer's attorney the next morning to set up a mutually agreeable time for a contract signing. The contract signing customarily is held in the office of the seller's attorney. The closing usually is held in the bank attorney's office. Get every agreement you reached orally into written form. Don't accept oral promises. Justify getting the promises in writing by quoting the well-known real estate expert and talk-show host Sonny Bloch, ''If it is worth saying, it is worth putting into writing.''

SELLING THROUGH A BROKER

Despite every effort sometimes, a property won't sell. Out of necessity, you call in a professional. It's always easy to find another good investment, but how do you finance it if your capital is locked up in another property you can't sell? A broker is expensive, especially when you think about the commission in real dollars. Realistically though, the five or six percent commission is not exorbitant when you realize it might be the only way for the property to be sold. Keep in mind that ninety five percent of something is much better than one hundred percent of nothing. If the property doesn't sell, you don't free any of your equity.

Making a Deal with a Broker

Despite what many real estate brokers lead you to believe, all real estate commissions are negotiable. There is give and take in any deal to make the sale. After agreeing on a percentage commission with the broker, a smart broker might make further concessions at contract or closing to cement the transaction. At one closing, when unforeseen expenses appeared at closing, our broker agreed to let us pay part of the commission over six months on an interest-free basis.

Through the entire transaction, the NIWIN principle keeps appearing. As you recall, If It's Not In Writing, It's Nothing. Get in writing anything that the broker promises, in case at some future time you hear ''I never said that.''

Certain things must be insisted upon for the broker to do. For each serious buyer, you want the broker to screen the person carefully, including obtaining a credit report before going to contract. The broker is representing you the seller, not the buyer. Therefore, she must try to obtain the highest selling price, as well as the best terms. Every offer must be presented to you, even if it is below what you have specified. In that way, you have a choice to assess the reaction you are receiving.

The Listing Agreement

Most frequently you have a discussion with a real estate agent and are handed an agreement to sign. The agreement is known as the *Exclusive Right to Sell*. Under it, unless other conditions are noted, you are obligated to pay a sales commission to the broker if the property is sold, even if you sell it yourself. The agreement protects the real estate agent and often motivates the agent to try to sell your property. Usually the agent will advertise your property in return for the exclusive agreement. Try not to sign an agreement extending more than sixty days. Even if you are told 90 or 120 days is the standard, negotiate the time period. Nothing is standard unless you agree to it.

When Problems Arise

What happens if the real estate broker doesn't live up to the terms of the agreement? Perhaps the real estate agent isn't advertising to the extent promised, not holding open houses, or not showing your property. The first thing to do is discuss the matters with the broker who took your listing. Wait a short time for signs that the situation is being improved. If after two weeks, you still don't note any improvement, it is time to discuss the matter with the office manager. A week or so later, if you are not receiving the action you are seeking, it is time to change brokers.

How Do You Change Brokers?

Send a certified letter with a return receipt to the broker. In the letter mention what your expectations were and the fact that the real estate broker did not live up to the terms of the agreement and did not put forth the promised effort. Mention the dates and people with whom you met to discuss your dissatisfaction. Notify the real estate agent in the letter that because of the reasons mentioned you are instructing the real estate office to cease showing your property and terminate the agreement.

ALTERNATIVES TO SELLING

While turning over your property to a real estate professional certainly enhances the probability of a sale, there can be no assurances. Your property might not be sold despite large expenditures for advertising and a full effort. What then?

The Partial Sale

Since your property could not be sold, you might want to consider a *partial sale*. A *partial sale* consists of selling a part of your ownership of an investment. It is usually accomplished by setting up a partnership. Set up by your attorney, a partnership allows you to keep a percentage of your investment while raising investment capital. An attorney specializing in real estate partnerships can structure the deal and apprise you of ways to attract investors, as well as to divide up the property. Shares can be sold to investors and certificates issued as part of the partnership process.

Selling Part of the Property

In addition to a partial sale, there is another selling alternative. That is *selling a part of the property*. If differs from a partial sale in that you are selling either the land or the store/business instead of a part-ownership of your total holdings. Frequently your tenant or tenants would like to purchase the store or office building they are renting, but lack the total purchase price. You can still work out a deal even without owner financing.

Through an attorney, you can reach an agreement to sell either the land or the building and keep the other. If the tenant wants to purchase the building and not the land, he can save taxes by taking the depreciation deduction on his taxes. On the other hand, if he wants to purchase only the land, you can sell him the land and lease it back from him. It is a win-win situation for both buyer and seller. You get a sum of money from the sale of the land. The purchaser gets a monthly rent from you, providing him with a monthly income.

SUMMARY

Even though money is made from the prudent purchase of properties and not the sale, you don't have the check in your hand to re-invest until you make the sale. Selling a property is an important skill to master.

Though you might own the most desirable property in town, a property will not always sell easily. Market factors help determine the salability. There are buyer's markets and seller's markets. A *buyer's market* is a market where it is difficult to sell a property because of an overabundance of sellers and an absence of buyers. A *seller's market* is a market where properties sell quickly because of a shortage of sellers and large number of buyers. When looking to sell, you hope for a seller's market, so that your property doesn't remain on the market for long, and you can bring top dollar for your property.

Before you place a property on the market, you must decide whether you will sell the property yourself or through a real estate agent. Should you decide to sell a property by yourself, careful preparations must be taken to make sure that it sells quickly and a price reflective of the market. Certain steps need to be taken:

1. Price it realistically
2. Take the temperature
3. Learn the market
4. Make cosmetic improvements
5. Pay to advertise
6. Create a prospectus
7. Let the property sell itself
8. Check out buyers
9. Help with financial advice
10. Have a binder and contract for sale
11. Become a shrewd negotiator
12. Close the deal

Sometimes despite the good intentions and diligent care, you find that you are unable to sell a property. It is then that you are wise to consider handing over the property to a real estate broker. A real estate broker can do a credible job for you but you must set down the rules. Care must be taken to find a broker who will screen potential buyers. Get the broker's commitment to advertise and make sure that the broker represents your interest in securing the maximum selling price. Hiring a broker removes much of the emotional turmoil involved in selling, such as making appointments, showing the property, and negotiating.

Though the likelihood of selling your property is enhanced by being represented by a real estate broker, there is still no guarantee of sale. Difficult decisions must be reached. If you're unsuccessful in selling with or without a broker, consider other alternatives.

One such alternative is forming a partnership through a real estate attorney and having the property proportionately sold as shares. In that way you can keep a controlling interest of voting shares, should you choose, while raising funds from the sale of shares. In the "have your cake and eat it too" category, you are able to retain partial ownership of the property while raising cash through the sale of shares. Selling a property, in part or or totally, through a real estate broker or on your own can be a rewarding experience. The reward can be deposited into your bank account or used to purchase another property. The choice is yours.

16

Street-Smart Tips for Successful Real Estate Investing

THERE IS NOT A DAY THAT PASSES WITHOUT A REAL ESTATE DECISION THAT could hit you deep in your pockets. The right decision can save you a bundle. The wrong one can leave you with too much week at the end of your money. For that reason we have compiled *The Street-Smart Guide*.

The Street-Smart Guide is not a listing of theories or an alphabetical compilation of definitions. It is a practical guide that we have developed from our many years in real estate to save every investor time and money. We know the hints work because we and investors like us use them all the time. The 54 hints in the guide will make your real estate work for you, instead of you always working for your real estate.

1. **Abandoned Property**

   Frequently you see an interesting property that is boarded up. If only you could find the owner, you would buy it. One way to find the identity of the owner is to visit the tax assessor's office with the address of the property and ask for assistance. Another way is to visit the title company with whom you have done business. Ask to find the identity of the owner. If there is reluctance, ask how much they charge for the service.

2. **Absentee Ownership**

   Frequently when your property is not owner occupied, you will be resented by the neighbors no matter how hard you try to be neighborly. Call it jealousy or whatever, but neighbors object to the fact that you can afford to rent a property while they can barely make ends meet. If a dog barks or a trash can overturns, your property will be blamed. Try to befriend a next-door neighbor so that at least you know who your opposition is on the block. If you can overcome neighbor objections to the fact you are renting, fine. If you can't, just chalk it up to the envy factor.

3. Attorney Fees

Attorney fees are negotiable. Ask your attorney what the fee will be. Don't accept generalities. Request an exact figure and a letter for your file with the details. Get everything in writing.

4. Attorneys as Tenants

Don't ever rent to an attorney if you can help it. It might seem like an unfair practice, but experience has taught us that renting to one is asking for trouble. From their complaints to their threats to sue, if you don't make a repair fast enough, attorneys are trouble. If you must rent to an attorney, make the lease and allow no changes. Renting to police officers is not much better.

5. Avoiding Points

Points are really another way for banks to charge higher interest. Taxwise, the expense for points has to be spread out over the length of the mortgage. If you are going to hold the property it doesn't matter, but if you are only going to hold for two or three years you resent paying $2000 or $3000 up front. Why not negotiate a higher percent interest on your mortgage in return for fewer or no points?

6. Balloon Payments

Be very careful before agreeing to accept a loan with balloon payments where the balloon is paid off within ten years. Since no one can predict the future, it is best to avoid the risk.

7. Bids from Contractors

When accepting bids from contractors, get everything in writing. Check with the local consumer affairs office to see if the person is licensed or has a history of not completing jobs. Ask to see work done in the area that is comparable to what you are considering. Get at least three written estimates before signing. Consult a professional organization such as NARI to inquire about specifics such as thickness of sheathing and workmanship standards.

8. Bill Paying

If you find that tenants are late with rent even after imposing a late charge, work out a weekly rent payment agreement. Have the tenant pay every week. Call a day before as a reminder.

9. Building and Zoning Codes

Don't take someone's word that a structure complies with building or zoning codes. Visit the building or zoning department in person with the particulars and verify the information.

10. Building Permits

When you contract to have work done, it is the contractor's responsibility to make any and all applications for building permits. The contractor has the right to charge you for them, but it is he who has the responsibility to apply.

11. Cash Flow Increasing

Collect the utility money from the tenants and pay the utility yourself. In that way, you collect the money on the first and don't have to pay the utility until the following month. You have the extra cash on hand as an interest-free loan.

12. Checking Out Tenants

If you have bad vibrations about a tenant, pass on him. If a person seems like a problem during the application, imagine what he is going to be like in your place. Ask the person to fill out an application and then collect it. You might pretend that you can't read some of the handwriting. Ask questions and see if there are contradictions. If it is a couple, have them fill out applications separately and watch for inconsistencies.

13. Collecting Past-due Rents

Real estate professionals often advise you to quickly evict nonpayers. If the tenant doesn't pay by the seventh day of the month, he is out. In theory it works, but not in reality. It takes many months to evict, and tenants know ways to stall an eviction. And in the interim, you will not be getting any money whatsoever. Ask what the problem is and how you can help. Have the tenant give you a written schedule for planned catch-up payments. Insist that he adhere to it.

14. Complaints

Tenants have a way of demanding things from you that you don't even do for yourself. If an outlet burns out in your personal residence, you will use another outlet. But if an outlet burns out in your commercial or residential property, the tenant is on the phone immediately. Be a good listener and promise to have someone look at it.

15. Cost Overruns

One of the biggest problems in rehabbing properties is controlling the cost. You purchase a property and estimate that it will cost

$10,000 to renovate. As the work progresses, you discover that the $10,000 is turning into $30,000 to complete the job. You either have to sell the property, take in a partner, or leave it unfinished until you have the funds. In the meantime no money is coming in.

The workable solution is to contract for work to be done in turn-key condition. Have the contractor stipulate a total price and have that price include everything. The property when finished will be in rentable or move-in condition.

16. Discouraging Tenant Repairs

If you have a tenant who is wearing out your phone wire with calls for repairs, here is a way to discourage the calls. Ask the tenant to call down the repairperson and get an estimate. Before the work begins you must give your approval. The work will begin after your approval. Have the tenant pay the repairperson, and you will deduct the amount from the rent. Many tenants expect you to wait for the repairperson but refuse to themselves. Rather than wait for half a day or pay money, a tenant will frequently decide that he can tolerate the inconvenience and not have the repair done.

17. Eviction

Don't try to evict a tenant unless all else has failed. If a tenant has not paid the rent, send along a friendly reminder in the mail or call in a touching-base approach. Informally ask if everything is all right. Listen to the response and see if a solution can be arranged. If the person is antagonistic and refuses to discuss matters, of course you have no choice but to evict.

18. Fighting Inflation

Everyone thinks about retirement. In order to retire you need to accumulate a nestegg of at least several hundred thousand dollars. On paper it appears easy. You want to save $200,000, just put aside $10,000 per year for twenty years. The problem is that not many of us have that self-discipline.

Unfortunately even if you manage to save the sum of $200,000, it will be worth a fraction of that amount, due to inflation. If inflation averages five percent per year, after twenty years your saved dollar is worth only 38.5 cents. The value of your $200,000 has been reduced to $77,000. Read the chart below and see what different rates of inflation do to each thousand dollars you've saved over the years.

How Inflation Destroys Your Savings

Years	4%	5%	6%	7%	8%
5	820	785	750	715	680
10	680	620	560	510	460
15	560	490	420	370	320
20	460	385	310	260	210
25	380	305	230	190	150

Since it is apparent that you can't keep up with inflation by saving money or putting it in the bank, you need real estate. Real estate does keep with and even surpass inflation.

19. Free College Education

Would you like a free college education for your children? It can be done. If your child goes away to college, assess that local real estate market. Purchase a house below the market in the vicinity of the college. Have your son or daughter move into the house and rent out rooms to other trustworthy students. Your son or daughter is responsible for collecting the rent, the share of utilities expenses, and maintenance of the property. At the end of four years or after graduation, sell the property. Over the years, the rental income has more than paid the housing costs, your son or daughter has lived rentfree, and now you can sell the house for a profit. By purchasing below-market value, it should not be difficult to earn a tidy profit. In many college towns, small homes can be purchased for far less than one hundred thousand dollars.

To make the transaction taxfree as well, there is another thing you can do. By law, you are permitted to give $10,000 to your child taxfree each year. That means you and your spouse can each give $10,000, for a total of 20,000 per year combined. At the end of four years, you have given the total of $80,000. That means that when the house is sold, your tax liability is virtually eliminated, since you have given the entire house to your child.

20. Getting Action from Immobile Forces

When you are dealing with a bureaucrat or obstinate professional, work into the conversation, ''I don't want to start getting my attorneys involved.''

21. Getting Paid Debts Legally but Street-Style

Attend any real estate seminar and the lecturer tells you how easy it is to evict a tenant. "Just issue a Three Day Pay or Quit and the tenant is history," they say. Unfortunately that is not the case in big cities with street-smart tenants. In cities such as New York tenants seem to have unlimited rights and landlords are guilty until proven innocent. It seems virtually impossible to evict a tenant.

Whether or not you live in a big city, it doesn't hurt to know the street-smart defense. Let's take the case of Al, a real estate investor who gave up his full-time job to manage his own properties and make the repairs. Al had one tenant with whom he had an excellent rapport. The rapport was so good that Al didn't raise the tenant's rent in eighteen months. Then one month the tenant simply stopped paying rent. Al discussed with him the need for the rent but was ignored. Not only didn't the tenant pay the rent, he turned Al into the authorities for building violations and heat violations. The tenant remained month after month without paying a cent. Al could not get an eviction.

Finally, deciding to fight fire with fire, Al decided to undertake some street-smart action of his own. He studied their rent application and other documents the tenants submitted to him, Al knew that they were receiving aid to dependent children (welfare) and unemployment benefits. He also knew that Mr. Tenant had a job and where the job was. Al visited the tenant's place of employment and notified the employer that the tenant wasn't paying his rent. He informed them that not paying your rent is illegal, the same as hiring someone who they knew was receiving unemployment benefits and aid to dependent children while working. Al informed the company that if he notified the authorities, Mr. Tenant would be brought up on fraud charges, lose his job, and the company would have explaining to do about their involvement. Shortly thereafter, the company ordered Mr. Tenant to pay his back rent if he wanted to continue working at the company. He did. Al had found a street-smart way to get justice.

22. Judgment Collection Strategy

Any time you rent an apartment be sure to obtain the social security number of both tenants, the maiden name of both mothers, and addresses of the banks they use. Should you take legal action against a tenant and you are awarded a judgment, you will be unable to collect unless you have that information at your fingertips. Delinquent tenants often refuse to pay the judgment that has been awarded, but you can take charge. You can forward that information to the sheriff's office for collection. By furnishing the bank with the last name of the tenant's mother and the tenant's social security number, they will release to the sheriff the money from the tenant's bank account to satisfy the judgment. The sheriff will then release the money to you.

23. Kitchen Renovation

You can do a kitchen renovation for one hundred dollars or for fifty thousand dollars. Why undergo a total rehabilitation of a kitchen when a refacing of cabinets and paint will accelerate a sale in the same way? If you are looking to sell, only do what is necessary to improve your sales prospects.

24. Lease

When offering a lease, great care must be taken in your tenant selection. A problem arises when there is interference from someone other than the tenant. Often the person interfering is the person actually paying the rent, otherwise known as the parent. Whenever a parent or inlaw is involved in the negotiations, terminate the negotiations diplomatically and search for another tenant. You want a tenant who is docile, yet able to function independently without Mom's apron strings. Once Mom or Dad become involved, you are likely to be called whenever Mom and Dad visit, which is frequently. You will be told about a cracked window, peeling paint, or not enough hot water. Togetherness is great, but not on your property.

25. Maintenance

Arrange for any tenant to be responsible for maintaining your personal property or grounds. You only do repairs. In your lease, specify that appliances are provided at the pleasure of the landlord and that the tenant is responsible for the maintenance. Keeping the oven clean so there is not a fire and replacing batteries in a smoke alarm are the kinds of maintenance tenants must do.

26. Mortgage Broker

A mortgage broker is able to cut through red tape and usually doesn't cost you one cent more than dealing directly with a bank. The mortgage broker knows the needs of a particular lender and can assist you in filling out an application to make it acceptable.

Several years ago, we applied to a large New York savings bank to refinance our mortgage. The bank had been advertising a low interest rate widely. When we called to apply, we were told that we were not eligible. We contacted a mortgage broker, who efficiently filled out the application and processed it. Several weeks later we were approved. It turned out that the bank issuing the mortgage was the one we originally contacted and the rate and points were those we couldn't obtain.

Who lost? The bank. The bank had to remit one of the points to the mortgage broker as his commission. Ultimately by working through the mortgage broker we got the best deal.

27. Mortgage Application Fee

When you apply for a mortgage, you don't have to pay an application fee. Sure, most banks charge application fees, but no one says you have to do business with a bank. There are plenty of mortgage companies and mortgage brokers who do not charge a fee. To make the best selection, apply to several companies for a mortgage. That way, when you receive preliminary approval and estimated closing costs, you can compare and decide which offers the best deal. Furthermore, you can play one against the other to gain more concessions.

28. Negative Cash Flow

Negative cash flow is a no-no. It is money coming directly from your pocket. Do not enter a deal where you know there will be a negative cash flow. Unexpected expenses will quickly turn a slightly negative cash flow into a major one.

29. Networking

Networking is one of the keys to successful real estate investing. To be successful, you must have a group of reliable people to meet your needs, from appliance repair to zoning regulation advice. Hardly anyone can succeed without these contacts to solve problems as they arise. When things go wrong, and they do often, you have to have someone to call to get there fast and solve the problem. If you have hands of gold, that's great, but so many of us do not. You need someone reliable and reasonable to solve the problem on the spot. A street-smart investor has a repair person for small repairs, licensed plumbers, electrician, low-cost appliance retailer, painters, wallpaper installers, real estate attorney, CPA, etc.

30. Nothing Down

Don't just buy a property because it is a nothing-down deal. Some times nothing down can mean that something is up. Is the person highly motivated or is he trying to have his alligator devour you the way it devoured him? A nothing-down deal is not attractive if the rest of the deal is not right. Is the property priced below the market? What is the condition of the property? How much money is needed to make it rentable? What is the interest rate you will be paying? Nothing down does not mean it is a good deal.

31. Open Listing

Frequently you prefer one real estate office over another for a rental or sale. You list with a broker by giving an open listing, where your listing is added to their books. Do not give an exclusive listing, unless you get in writing that you can sell the property yourself without owing a commission.

32. Over-renovating

Don't over-renovate, whether it is the patio, dining room, or den. Do what is necessary to correct the problem and promote a sale or rental and nothing more. Know when to say when.

33. Partners

Partners are great if you do comedy, but not if you invest in or manage real estate. The only way a partnership works is if there is a legal agreement drawn up that specifies rights, responsibilities, and decision-making powers. Handshake agreements do not work when money is involved. Frequent disagreements with regard to spending money or maintenance, repairs, and improvements, as well as if or when to sell, arise very often. Without a firm written agreement a partnership is doomed to fail.

34. Painting before Repairing

A coat or two of paint both on the exterior and interior can often save hundreds of dollars in repairs. Why spend for siding on a rental property when paint will accomplish the same thing? If it's for your primary residence, that's one thing, but for a rental property it's unnecessary. Paint and spackle cover up a great deal of physical imperfections.

35. Pets

So many landlords exclude people from consideration as tenants because they have pets. That is a mistake. Most pet owners are caring and considerate. They are more likely to keep your place tidy than a nonpet owner. Furthermore, within a matter of a few months a large percentage of tenants acquire pets anyway. When they have proven themselves responsible tenants you assent to their wishes anyway. Why not consider a pet owner from the outset?

36. Phantom Landlording

Many tenants discover that real estate management works best when tenants do not know that you are the owner. Some investors pose as the landlord's representative. They claim to have no authority to make decisions. They claim to only follow the wishes of the owner.

In that way, they aren't put on the spot for instant decisions and don't have to act as the bad guy.

37. Points

If you are short of cash at closing, and we all have been, request that the points be added to the amount of the mortgage. It is much easier to pay $3000 over 30 years than $3000 over the table at closing. Like chicken soup, it can't hurt.

38. Positive Cash Flow

Positive cash flow is the key word in real estate investing. As long as you keep earning a positive cash flow on each of your investments you can't lose. The trick is to have more money coming in each month than going out. Of course, money has to be set aside for repairs and as a nestegg, in the event there are vacancies.

39. Prepaying a Mortgage

Bar anything in a mortgage agreement that prevents you from prepaying. It can save you an enormous amount of money in interest. If you have a $70,000, thirty-year mortgage at ten percent, your monthly payment for principal and interest will be $614. By adding a check for $300 each month, you will pay off the loan in ten years and three months.

To make a prepayment, you can follow several approaches. One generally accepted way is to send along a check in addition to your regular check. On the bottom of the additional check write the words "principal only." Send the check in whatever denomination you desire. Obtain an amortization schedule from the bank. Calculate which payment in principal and interest you are making on your regular payment. On your additional payment, besides the words "principal only," write the payment number.

40. Pro Forma Statement

Banks are very difficult to deal with when you need money. They constantly say your income is insufficient, your loans are overextended, or your appraisal is too low. There is something you can do to overcome the objections. Have an appraisal done of the property now and what it will appraise for when the renovations you specify are done. Call in a licensed contractor to give an estimate of the cost of the repairs that are needed. Employ your CPA to prepare a pro-forma statement of what the property will be worth when all the work is completed. Submit the two appraisals and pro-forma statement to the loan officer at the bank. Based upon the documentation, he can better assess the value of the property.

41. Property Maintenance

Your objective as a property manager is to have the tenants do as much as possible. To help realize your goals, try to rent to handy people who are not opposed to maintaining or making repairs. Since improvements raise the value of your investment, you can encourage improvements by offering to pay for the materials while they supply the labor.

42. Property Management

Before you hire a property manager consider how you will be able to check up on him. A property manager needs overseeing, that is if you want anything left to oversee. The property manager is entrusted with collecting the rents, making your mortgage payments, assuming repairs, and making the payments. Every street-smart investor makes sure what she thinks she is paying is actually getting paid.

Here is a sad-but-true story of one investor who was a bit too trusting. Andrea owned a property forty-five minutes from her residence and found it inconvenient to manage the property. Andrea hired a property manager, who would collect rents, have repairs made, and rent the property whenever there was a vacancy. Months passed and Andrea found she wasn't making a profit. She could not understand why. Upon questioning her property manger, she learned that her property had been vacant a good portion of the year. Probing further, she discovered that the property had been rented seven times within the span of eighteen months. Her property manager was also a licensed real estate broker and rental agent. Getting the picture yet?

After a thorough investigation she learned that the property manager was renting out the property to undesirables and being paid one month's rent as a commission. When the tenant couldn't or wouldn't make the payment, he was encouraged to leave. Thus the property manger, a.k.a. rental agent, had another property to rent and commission to seek. This went on again and again over the eighteen month period with the property manager lining his pockets, while Andrea had a negative cash flow from having no rental income.

If it sounds as if Andrea were the victim of a scam, she was. But there's more. Not only was she not receiving rent, she was to receive more bad news. She was soon served with a summons. Her property was being foreclosed on for nonpayment of the mortgage. The property manager had been pocketing the mortgage money. Andrea was in an illiquid position, burdened with expenses from her full-time business and unable to raise the funds to avoid foreclosure. At last report, foreclosure was inevitable.

Andrea could have avoided all or most of the problems. Had she checked out the property manager, she could have discovered if any other clients had problems. She could have ascertained earlier why the bank was receiving untimely payments. If she would have contacted the town or bank for statements, she could have learned that payments were not being made. Any of these would have aroused suspicions.

43. Raising Rents

Every year, if the market permits, you should raise rents. You are trying to recover your increased costs for taxes, insurance, and utilities. The tenant thinks you are greedy and are trying to become wealthy at her expense. To alleviate her suspicions, list the increases in each of your costs. The next choice is hers.

44. Rent Collection

Your choice of location for rent collection might determine your success. People value their personal space. When you enter their personal space, they feel uneasy, especially if they owe rent. Even if you are cordial, a tenant owing money feels uncomfortable when the landlord arrives. If a tenant is paying late, arrange to pick up your money in person.

45. Rent Discount

What bigger problem faces a landlord than collecting the rent on time? The tenant feels she can pay the rent late along with the phone and electric bill. You don't feel that way. Give the tenant a reason to pay early. Give a rent discount. In the new lease, increase the rent by an extra twenty-five dollars. Allow a twenty-five dollar discount if she pays in full by the first of the month or whatever day you decide. With a rent discount, you encourage prompt payments.

46. Repair Factor

Any time you purchase a property for rental, be sure you set aside an amount equal to five percent of your rental income for repairs. You never know what could break down. Be prepared.

47. Repair People

Problems frequently arise and you need a repair right away. Your regular repair person is unavailable. Who do you call? You can ask friends and associates for their recommendations or read through the yellow pages or Pennysaver. Only hire people who don't charge for service calls. If your repair turns out to be a fuse, you don't want to pay a $35 service charge in addition to charge for labor and the fuse.

48. Resale of Co-ops or Condos

When purchasing a co-op or condo, be sure to obtain a copy of the prospectus. An owner can promise you anything even if it is strictly prohibited by law in the prospectus. Pets, renting the premises, and barbecuing might not be allowed. You don't know unless you see it in writing before you buy.

49. Screening Tenants

Many landlords get burned when they ask the wrong questions. They ask an applicant for their current landlord. You call up and get glowing recommendations. Can they be trusted? Probably not. Here's why.

Many times a landlord will say anything just to unload the tenant onto another landlord. Therefore, you can't always trust the current landlord. A better idea is to check the two previous landlords. They are not burdened anymore and have nothing to gain by lying.

We didn't become street smart without making mistakes. While trying to rent one apartment we asked for the current landlord. We were given the current address, name, and phone number. This is how the conversation went.

Hello, Mrs. O'Brien, this is Donna Paltrowitz.
I have here your tenant, Mrs. Sayle.
Would you mind answering a few questions?
    No, not at all.
What kind of tenant is Mrs. Sayle?
    She has been an excellent tenant.
Does she pay her rent on time?
    Oh, yes, she always pays on time. In fact she sometimes pays early.
Does she take care of the property?
    Definitely. In fact, her husband just painted the whole apartment. I didn't even ask him.
Thank you very much for your time, Mrs. O'Brien.

After such a recommendation how could you not rent to Mrs. Sayle. We did, and we were sorry. Mrs. O'Brien turned out to be Mrs. Sayle's mother. We weren't really speaking to the landlord at all. From a family of three we found a family of five, with late rent, and wild parties in the garage, which had been turned into a bedroom. The gas dryer was used to heat the garage. The tenant had used her street smarts to gain the apartment. Shortly, thereafter we used ours. We couldn't legally evict her. We told her the house was being sold and that the owner needed occupancy. We offered to return her security and she moved.

50. Security Deposit

Never accept less than a two-month security deposit. With the lengthy process to evict, you need that protection. If the person doesn't have the full two months at lease signing, work out a payment schedule.

51. Small Claims Court

As a landlord, small claims court is a very effective means of recovering unpaid rent. Of course you need to follow court procedures, such as providing proof of having served the summons and bringing to court all evidence. Among the things you bring are a written lease. The tenant must furnish a paid receipt or cancelled check.

52. Split-Rate Loan

For those borrowers who can't choose between a fixed and ARM, there is the *hybrid mortgage*, known as the split-rate loan. It offers a part that is fixed and a part that is adjustable. The fixed part does not change for the life of the loan. The adjustable part is keyed to the London interbank offering rate. International money coming into the U.S. will make obtaining a mortgage easier. The split-rate loan might be worth pursuing.

53. Subject to Sale Clause

When you are selling a property, be sure your attorney puts in a subject-to clause if you need the proceeds from one property to purchase another. If you can't sell, you can back out without a penalty.

54. Two-Phone System

Do you hate to receive tenant calls? Here is a workable solution. Get a second phone line and have that number unlisted. The listed number will be connected to an answering machine. In that way, any tenants who call will be fielded by the answering machine. You can audit calls and answer those you want after hearing the identity of the caller. You also know that any call on that line is unwelcomed, since friends, relatives, and business associates will reach you on the unlisted number.

55. Vacancy Factor

Many investors get into trouble because they don't allow for vacancies. Everyone has them from time to time. Tenants eventually move out. Keep some money aside so you have funds to make your payments. Wise investors figure on a vacancy factor of about eleven percent. Always expect the unexpected, and you'll avoid serious problems.

Index